Computer Communications and Networks

The **Computer Communications and Networks** series is a range of textbooks, monographs and handbooks. It sets out to provide students, researchers, and non-specialists alike with a sure grounding in current knowledge, together with comprehensible access to the latest developments in computer communications and networking.

Emphasis is placed on clear and explanatory styles that support a tutorial approach, so that even the most complex of topics is presented in a lucid and intelligible manner.

More information about this series at http://www.springer.com/series/4198

Jerzy Domżał • Robert Wójcik
Andrzej Jajszczyk

Guide to Flow-Aware Networking

Challenges and Opportunities

Second Edition

Jerzy Domżał
Department of Telecommunications
AGH University of Science and Technology
Krakow, Poland

Robert Wójcik
Department of Telecommunications
AGH University of Science and Technology
Krakow, Poland

Andrzej Jajszczyk
Department of Telecommunications
AGH University of Science and Technology
Krakow, Poland

ISSN 1617-7975 ISSN 2197-8433 (electronic)
Computer Communications and Networks
ISBN 978-3-030-57155-9 ISBN 978-3-030-57153-5 (eBook)
https://doi.org/10.1007/978-3-030-57153-5

This Springer imprint is published by the registered company Springer Nature Switzerland AG
The registered company address is: Gewerbestrasse 11, 6330 Cham, Switzerland

Preface

The Internet is changing. This statement has been true since the first messages were sent between two nodes years ago. "The telephone wire, as we know it, has become too slow and too small to handle Internet traffic. It took 75 years for telephones to be used by 50 million customers, but it took only four years for the Internet to reach that many users."—these words by Lori Valigra emphasize this rapid development of the Internet.

Several milestones have been observed over the past 20 years from the user's point of view. These include the development of websites, which have certainly meant that the Internet has become popular worldwide. The rapid progress in optical networks has enabled faster transmission with higher quality. Peer-to-peer networks have opened the door to sharing resources between users. Finally, as we see currently, streaming transmissions have transformed computers into user-friendly multi-functional machines. Moreover, new devices such as smartphones and tablets have made the Internet present everywhere and for everyone.

Global network traffic constantly grows which is mainly the effect of the increasing number of Internet users and the popularity of Internet streaming services, e.g. video and game streaming. Moreover, in 2020, the pandemic strike forced many people to use the Internet more than ever, degrading the quality of several applications and services. The network should be able to handle high priority traffic without disruptions even under heavy congestion periods. It is a challenge for network operators to ensure proper Quality of Service (QoS) for such traffic without degrading other transmissions in the network. In many cases, the transmission rate is not the key point for these applications. The most important factors are the acceptance delay of the connection, transmission delay, packet loss, and connection reliability. To be up to these requirements, network operators usually add extra bandwidth rather than implement complicated QoS architectures.

Since 1994, when the IETF's Integrated Services (IntServ) appeared, many QoS architectures have emerged. In this book, we present one of the most promising, a relatively new architecture for the future Internet—Flow-Aware Networking (FAN)—which may solve existing problems. It guarantees appropriate quality for transmitted traffic, it is easy to implement, and it is net neutral. FAN eliminates the need for signaling, which has proved unscalable in the past. Despite its simple approach to QoS assurance, service differentiation in FAN works sufficiently well.

The architecture is not flawless; however, some disadvantages are mitigated by several additional traffic management mechanisms proposed within the course of FAN evolution. The most important and promising solutions, mainly proposed and developed by the authors of this guide, are presented and analyzed.

Chapter 1 contains a survey of flow-oriented approaches, which introduces the reader to the world of flow-based networking. This chapter shows the most visible solutions, which are based on the concept of flows.

Chapter 2 presents an extensive description of FAN. Approximate Flow-Aware Networking (AFAN) is analyzed as the latest concept in FAN realization. Chapter 3 presents the scope and evolution of the debate on network neutrality. Moreover, it shows why FAN conforms to the current or future resolutions.

Mechanisms for improving transmission performance of streaming flows under congestion are presented and analyzed in Chap. 4. Seven proposals for congestion control mechanisms, with extensive simulation analysis, are presented. Moreover, we show how problems caused by congestion may be solved in a multi-layer environment. Next, we describe new proposals for enhancing transmission in wired–wireless FAN. At the end of this chapter, we propose a new routing concept to be used in flow-aware networks. This enables maximum utilization of the available resources, reducing the negative aspects of congestion.

In Chap. 5, the aspects of fair transmission in FAN are analyzed. A new method of estimating the values of congestion indication parameters and a new per-user fairness concept are proposed. Algorithms that improve the transmission of streaming flows when a failure occurs are presented and analyzed in Chap. 6. The ideas presented here ensure continuous transmission of streaming flows even when a link in a network fails. Chapter 7 presents FAN's capabilities in relation to service differentiation. We show how much differentiation can be achieved in FAN and at what cost. Also, the problem of transmission waiting time is described. The chapter focuses on delivering a promised level of service in FAN. Unfortunately, the design of FAN's original admission control features some problems. This chapter presents and compares several approaches to solving them.

The implementation aspects of the cross-protect router are described in Chap. 9. We also present the implementation suite, i.e., the Click modular router and the first tests' results of the developed prototype. The implementation process and test results of advanced mechanisms for FAN are discussed in Chap. 10. Some implementation problems are described, and relevant solutions are presented.

This book is addressed to network engineers, students, operators, and everyone interested in the development of the Internet. It can also be a source of valuable information for everyone who wants to better understand the basic principles underlying modern networking technology.

Krakow, Poland Jerzy Domżał

Krakow, Poland Robert Wójcik

Krakow, Poland Andrzej Jajszczyk

Acknowledgement

The research was carried out with the support of the project "Intelligent management of traffic in multi-layer Software-Defined Networks" funded by the Polish National Science Centre under project no. 2017/25/B/ST6/02186.

Contents

Flow-Oriented Approaches 1

Go with the flow

— Latin proverb

The rapid growth and popularization of the Internet has exceeded even the wildest dreams of its founders. In the early days, only simple file transfers were considered and, therefore, the Internet Protocol (IP) with its best effort packet delivery was introduced. The operation of IP is well suited and sufficient for this type of transfer; however, more demanding services have appeared over time. They include interactive communications, multimedia transmissions, and other delay-sensitive applications. Soon, it became clear that IP must be enhanced so that networks are able to fully support various types of services.

1.1 Why Flow-Awareness?

The first significant attempt to introduce quality of service to networks based on IP took place in June 1994 when the Internet Engineering Task Force (IETF) group published RFC 1633 [7], thereby introducing IntServ. This was the first complete approach to differentiating traffic between end-users. Unfortunately, very soon this solution was announced to have severe problems with scalability and complexity [17]. Since then, the development of QoS architectures has taken two directions. One is to retain the flow-based approach of IntServ while improving the scalability. The other, pursued mainly by the IETF itself, focuses on decreasing the granularity of flows (therefore reducing the volume of the required flow state information in routers) and dealing with aggregates rather than single instances. The IETF's second approach is known as Differentiated Services (DiffServ) [4].

This chapter presents the first line of QoS differentiation approaches, which are flow-aware. All the presented architectures try to introduce the differentiation

J. Domżał et al., *Guide to Flow-Aware Networking*, Computer Communications and Networks, https://doi.org/10.1007/978-3-030-57153-5_1

of service for every flow individually. The definition of a 'flow' may be slightly different in each of them; however, they still see a 'flow' as a single 'connection' between end-users. But why is flow-awareness so important? The answer is simple: a 'flow' is the most proper entity on which service differentiation could be imposed. A flow should be seen as a whole, neither as a set of packets that need a preferential treatment, nor as a group of connections classified into one aggregate.

There are numerous studies of Quality of Service assurance techniques based on individual flows. Since the well-known IntServ release of 1994 many new approaches have been presented in the literature. The fact that flow-awareness can be found in technical papers, patents, recommendations, standards, and commercial products proves its viability and importance. In this chapter we present and compare all significant contributions to flow-aware QoS guarantees, assessed either by the originality of the approach or by its common recognition. This chapter is based on the survey [49]. We discuss architectures including Integrated Services, Connectionless approach to QoS guarantees, Dynamic Packet State, Caspian Networks and Anagran, the Feedback and Distribution method, Flow-Based Differentiated Services, Flow-Aware Networking, Flow-State-Aware transport and Flow-Aggregate-Based services.

Technical descriptions of all these solutions are widely accessible, yet comparing them is scarce, to say the least. This survey attempts to compare and contrast the most promising or relevant solutions proposed thus far. Section 1.2 introduces the reader to flow-aware architectures, presenting their common goals, main similarities, development timeframes and a short description of each. Then, instead of presenting each architecture one by one, Sects. 1.4 through 1.7 deal with certain aspects of every proposal. We describe how the flows are defined in each architecture, what the classes of service are, how the admission control and scheduling are implemented and how the signaling problem is resolved. Section 1.8 contains a comparison of all presented approaches, and tries to identify their pros and cons. Finally, Sect. 1.9 concludes the survey, showing authors' opinion and forecast of the future of QoS architectures.

1.2 Background and Development History

This section provides an introduction to flow-aware QoS architectures. Firstly, we define the main goal and common understanding of flow-awareness. Then, the architectures are listed chronologically to help the reader identify their dependencies, relevance and future directions. In Sect. 1.3, we discuss each architecture separately, briefly presenting their backgrounds, main concepts and applied methods. The objective of this section is to provide a general idea on how each architecture works before their specific aspects are compared in Sects. 1.4 through 1.7.

1.2.1 Common Features

Flow-aware QoS architectures, as the name implies, aim at providing guarantees and service differentiation based on transmission of flows. Such architectures recognize that *a flow* is the most appropriate entity to which QoS mechanisms should be applied. In general, *a flow* is associated with a single logical connection, e.g., a single VoIP transmission between any two end-users. Every application can simultaneously create and maintain many flows, and each is subject to separate treatment by QoS mechanisms. Flow-aware architectures refrain from assigning flows to aggregates; however, if it is necessary to aggregate traffic, the QoS differentiation remains on a per-flow basis.

Although all the architectures are flow-aware, the exact definition of *a flow* may differ in each. These differences are described in Sect. 1.4. Nonetheless, the general meaning of *a flow* is maintained.

1.2.2 Development History

The need to introduce Quality of Service was not noticed in the early days of IP networks. Initially, a network was used only for simple file transfers, for which IP was sufficient. The popularization of the Internet, expanding capacities and the emergence of multimedia applications, rendered existing IP protocol unfit. Over time, numerous QoS architectures have been proposed. Figure 1.1 presents the timeline for the flow-aware QoS architectures that are compared in this chapter. The time frames show the development of the particular architectures. Wherever there are ambiguities in determining the exact dates, the time bars are faded into the background while the relevant explanation is in the text.

The QoS issue was first addressed by the IETF in 1994 when the IntServ model was introduced in RFC 1633 [7]. Almost immediately the problem with IntServ's scalability was widely recognized. Nevertheless, numerous papers have been published since, either mitigating some of the disadvantages or providing new functionalities. Especially, since the advent of DiffServ in 1998 [4], several approaches to combining both solutions have been proposed.

The Connectionless Approach to providing QoS was presented in 1998 in [35], although it was based on the automatic quality of service method from 1997 [9]. The Stateless Core architecture (SCORE) (1999, [48]) provided the foundation for the Dynamic Packet State [47]. The results were then discussed in the PhD dissertation of I. Stoica in 2000 [46].

Caspian Networks, Inc. was founded in 1998. In 2000, a patent on micro-flow management was filed with the United States Patent and Trademark Office. Currently, Anagran, Inc. continues the main line of Caspian Networks providing a real commercial product: a flow-aware network router. [27] presents a flow-based QoS architecture for large-scale networks, named the Feedback and Distribution method. To the authors' knowledge, the proposal was not pursued any further,

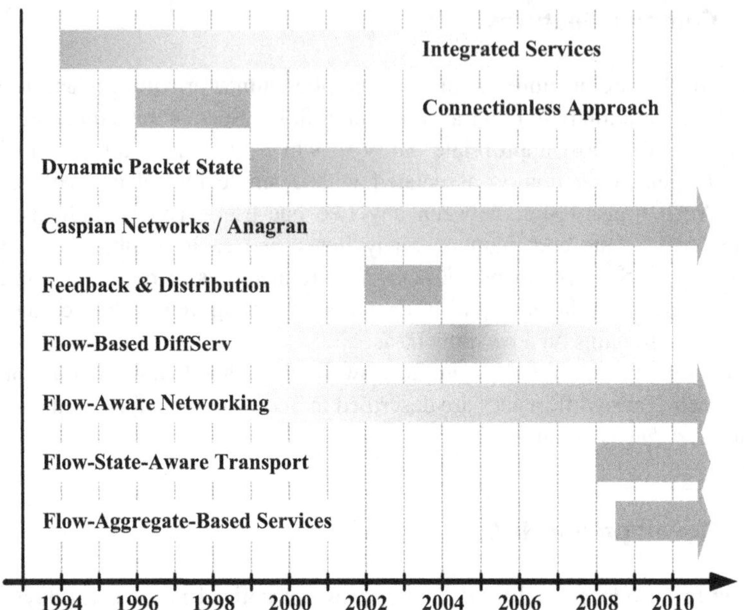

Fig. 1.1 QoS architectures: development history

although it demonstrates an interesting and original approach. The Flow-Based DiffServ architecture is an enhancement of plain DiffServ which introduces flow-awareness. As it is based on DiffServ, the origins of this method date back to 1998; however, the method was presented in 2004 [33]. Since DiffServ is a very popular approach, it is difficult to specify clear boundaries as a flow-aware line of DiffServ may be pursued in the future.

Flow-Aware Networking was initially introduced in 2000 [43], and presented as a complete system in 2004 [30]. Since then many papers have appeared regarding new mechanisms for the architecture improving the perceivability of the solution. Flow-State-Aware Transport was proposed for NGN networks and appeared as an ITU-T recommendation in 2008 [21]. In the same year, the Flow-Aggregate-Based Services architecture based on Flow-State-Aware Transport was proposed [25]. The last three architectures, i.e., FAN, Flow-State-Aware Transport, and Flow-Aggregate-Based Services are currently under further development.

1.3 Flow-Based Architectures at a Glance

Sections 1.4 to 1.7 go through the main aspects of QoS architectures, such as flow definition, provided classes of service, admission control mechanisms, queue management and signaling. However, before such analysis can be presented, the analyzed QoS architectures need to be properly introduced. The following

Table 1.1 Overview of flow-aware QoS architectures

Integrated services	• Obtains user-defined needs dynamically
	• Uses a signaling protocol to reserve resources along the transmission path and manage the connection
Connectionless approach	• Automatically detects the QoS requirements of the incoming flow based on the traffic pattern
	• Applies differentiation mechanisms as proposed in IntServ
Dynamic packet state	• Provides stateless core networks
	• Puts all the flow state information inside the IP packet header
Anagran	• Brings intelligence into the network
	• Automatically classifies flows into classes and treats them accordingly
Feedback and distribution	• Measures traffic in the access system
	• Feeds the inner network with measured information
Flow-based differentiated services	• Divides flows into classes
	• Assigns reservations to each class proportional to the number of active flows in each class
Flow-Aware networking	• Does not need any signaling
	• Introduces measurement-based admission control and priority fair queuing
Flow-State-Aware transport	• Uses aggregations but retains flow-awareness
	• Uses DiffServ mechanisms in the core
Flow-Aggregate-Based services	• QoS architecture based on Flow-State-Aware Transport
	• Introduces inter-domain flow aggregation and endpoint admission control
	• Retains flow-awareness

architectures are presented: Integrated Services, Connectionless approach to QoS guarantees, Dynamic Packet State, Caspian Networks and Anagran, the Feedback and Distribution method, Flow-Based Differentiated Services, Flow-Aware Networking, the Flow-State-Aware transport, and Flow-Aggregate-Based services. Table 1.1 provides general ideas and features of each architecture and explains their main concepts.

1.3.1 Integrated Services

As the demands for a quality of service architecture grew, the IETF proposed in 1994 the first complete model of QoS assurances—the Integrated Services [7]. The authors listed services which are vulnerable to end-to-end packet delay, namely: remote video, multimedia conferencing, visualization and virtual reality, and presented a method of dealing with them. The term Integrated Services represents the Internet service model, which includes best-effort traffic, real-time traffic, and controlled link sharing.

The Integrated Services model's design process was based on certain key assumptions. Since it was a pioneering endeavor, these assumptions were mostly theoretical and not based on previous experiences or simulations. The most important argument concerned the introduction of optical fibers to telecommunication networks, because some researchers believed that bandwidth would be almost infinite, and, therefore, there would be no need for quality of service models. The authors stated, however, that such a prediction is unacceptable, and that there will always be a way of dealing with congestions. The key model assumptions were expressed as follows:

1. a reservation protocol is necessary,
2. simply applying a higher priority to real-time traffic is not sufficient,
3. the Internet should be a common infrastructure for both real-time and elastic traffic,
4. the TCP/IP protocol stack should still be used (without major changes) in the new architecture,
5. the IP robustness should be preserved,
6. there should be a single service model for the whole Internet.

ad. 1) Following [7]: "The essence of real-time service is the requirement for some service guaranties, and we argue that guarantees cannot be achieved without reservations". To allow reservations while not being forced to alter the Internet Protocol, the authors were forced to design a new protocol: Resource Reservation Protocol (RSVP). This protocol is used in IntServ for setting-up and tearing-down connections. Each QoS-enabled connection must be pre-established and maintained by RSVP.

ad. 2) Applying only a single priority would be a simple, easy to implement solution; however, the issue is that as soon as there are too many real-time streams competing to be prioritized, all of them would be degraded. Therefore, IntServ does not limit the number of service classes: each flow can be treated in a different manner.

ad. 3–6) The TCP/IP protocol suite should not be changed, because it would allow current best-effort applications to operate without any implementation changes. Moreover, the simplicity of IP should be preserved, as this is the main advantage of the Internet drives its rapid growth and success. Additionally, the Integrated Services should be the only service model active in the network. If there were different service models in different parts of the Internet, it would be very difficult to see how any end-to-end service quality statements could be made.

1.3.2 Connectionless Approach

Although the complexity and scalability issues of IntServ were quickly recognized, the foundation for QoS architectures were established allowing many researchers to follow the trail. Some tried to go in a different direction and introduce class-based differentiation, such as the IETF in Differentiated Services. The team from Computing Technology Lab in Nortel, however, decided not to abandon flow-awareness and proposed their idea of service differentiation in IP networks, based on IntServ [35]. Their intention was to address scalability issues by removing the need for connection-oriented RSVP. Instead, they proposed an automatic detection of QoS requirements by network devices.

As mentioned, the approach is based on IntServ, but it does not use a signaling protocol, which was the major concern. The architecture of this proposal consists of the traffic conditioner and a connectionless mechanism for ensuring consistent end-to-end delivery of QoS based on application requirements. The traffic conditioner is grounded in the reference implementation framework of IntServ [7]. It contains three elements necessary for managing bandwidth in a router: classifier, admission controller and scheduler. Instead of RSVP, an Automatic Quality of Service mechanism [9] is used to establish the quality requirements on-the-fly and service them accordingly. The detection is based on measuring the traffic pattern of the incoming flow: the transport protocol, the size of the packets and their interarrival times. Unfortunately, the connectionless mechanism for ensuring consistent end-to-end delivery is not addressed. However, the authors express their opinion on the need for such a mechanism, and suggest the option of using the DiffServ marking scheme for the purpose.

Summarizing, distinction of traffic types is based on a simple analysis of packet arrival rates, interarrival times and packet lengths. The characteristics of a flow are measured constantly, as the flows need to be reclassified if they become unfit for the current class. The on-the-fly classification, reclassification and continuous monitoring do not look good for core routers which have to serve thousands of flows simultaneously; however, it does not require a signaling protocol making it is superior to its mother architecture—IntServ.

1.3.3 Dynamic Packet State

Another approach to eliminating the scalability problem of IntServ (and per-flow mechanisms in general) is Dynamic Packet State (DPS). DPS is a technique that does not require per-flow management at core routers, but it can implement service differentiation with levels of flexibility, utilization and assurance similar to those that can be provided with per-flow-mechanisms.

DPS was introduced in 1999 [47] by I. Stoica and H. Zhang from Carnegie Mellon University. In 2000, Stoics finalized his Ph.D. on the Stateless Core

(SCORE[1]) approach [46], which received the ACM Best Dissertation Award in 2001.

In DPS (and SCORE for that matter), only edge routers perform per-flow management while core routers do not. The information that is required for flow-based guarantees is carried in the packet headers. Edge nodes inject the information and each router along the path updates it accordingly. There are, therefore, per-packet regulations in every core node; however, flow-awareness is maintained due to the ingress nodes' proper packet header inclusions. Although core nodes do not see real flows, the information carried in the packet headers enables the packets to be served in a way which provides end-to-end flow-based guarantees. Finally, DPS provides QoS scheduling and admission control without per-flow states in core routers.

1.3.4 Caspian Networks/Anagran

One of the founding fathers of the Internet, Larry Roberts, previously chairman and chief technology officer at Caspian Networks, currently involved in Anagran[2] as its founder and chairman, pursues the notion of intelligent networks. In [40], he presented his opinion about the drawbacks of today's Internet, which include:

1. inefficient TCP flow control based on the slow-start mechanism,
2. lack of QoS support for voice and video,
3. unreliable routing,
4. scalability issues, mainly in hardware,
5. difficult management of large-scale networks.

These drawbacks and issues can be solved, in his opinion, by injecting intelligence into the networks. He criticizes the initial assumptions of the Internet, i.e., 'to stay dumb', which was an adequate approach 10–20 years ago. Now, however, we face more challenges as the network is utilized for many new purposes. Also, QoS-related mechanisms such as DiffServ and MPLS are criticized for remaining dumb and increasing protocol overheads and management. Having realized these issues, L. Roberts and Anagran proposed an optimized flow-based approach to IP traffic management.

One might say that Anagran goes a bit further: along with the proposal of the novel QoS architecture, they also built a device which put their ideas into practice. The device, Anagran FR-1000, is a layer 3 interconnecting device, or simply an

[1]SCORE is sometimes also referred to as 'Scalable Core'.

[2]Caspian Networks, Inc. was founded in 1998 as Packetcom, LLC and changed its name to Caspian Networks, Inc. in 1999. As of September 2006, Caspian Networks, Inc. went out of business. However, Anagran, Inc. was founded in 2004 and is currently located in Redwood City, California. Anagran represents the continuation of Caspian Networks and ideas introduced under the name of Caspian Networks are presented together with those of Anagran.

enhanced IP router. Unfortunately, most of the information about this device and the technology it implements can be obtained from company documents only, which, are marketing oriented. Nevertheless, the idea must be solid and mature enough to have been implemented.

The Anagran approach to QoS in IP networks is based on flow-awareness. FR-1000 uses the *Fast Flow Technology* [2] to maintain constant state information for every active flow. By using flows rather than single packets as the entity on which the traffic management is performed, an insight into traffic dynamics and behavior over time can be gained. Anagran's product automatically sorts the diverse traffic mix into dynamic 'virtual channels'. This allows for the coexistence of various traffic types in the same pipe. The only concern could be the potential difficulty in maintaining the per-flow state for all active connections, as this solution is not considered scalable. However, Anagran defends this concept by stating that:

> Conventional wisdom for the past 40 years had concluded that while potentially enormously powerful, flow technology was too expensive to implement in a commercial product due to the amount of memory required to maintain state information on every flow. However, the steep and rapid decline in memory cost over the past decade has actually made keeping flow state virtually insignificant from a cost standpoint. In fact, flow technology is not just feasible, but is now an extremely cost-effective and efficient way to optimize flows.

1.3.5 Feedback and Distribution

The problem of scalability has been haunting IntServ since its beginnings. Therefore, the team from NTT Access Service Systems Laboratories in Japan proposed an architecture that would be suitable for large-scale networks. Their approach is referred to as the *Feedback and Distribution Method* and is presented in [27]. The method provides per-flow based QoS differentiation for large-scale networks. The operability is based on measuring traffic in the access system, where traffic is divided for each user, and these measurements are fed into the network.

The proposed method is very simple and efficient. The idea is to keep inner-network devices as simple as possible, while performing all the required operations at the edges. This approach is similar to DiffServ; however, Feedback and Distribution retains flow-awareness.

Figure 1.2 schematically shows the basic concepts of this method. Profile meters are put at network boundaries, as close to the end-user as possible—for example at the termination point of every access line. Markers are also put at the network boundaries but on the side of the servers. This distinction may be problematic, as sometimes it is difficult to clearly state which side acts as the server and which as the client. In Internet telephony services or in P2P networks, end-users act as both clients and servers. Therefore, the concept may need to be be adjusted due to the need to provide both profile meter and marker functionalities at all termination lines. Nevertheless, this observation does not affect concept as a whole.

The role of a profile meter is to constantly measure individual user traffic and send the data to the markers. A marker is responsible for setting the priority for

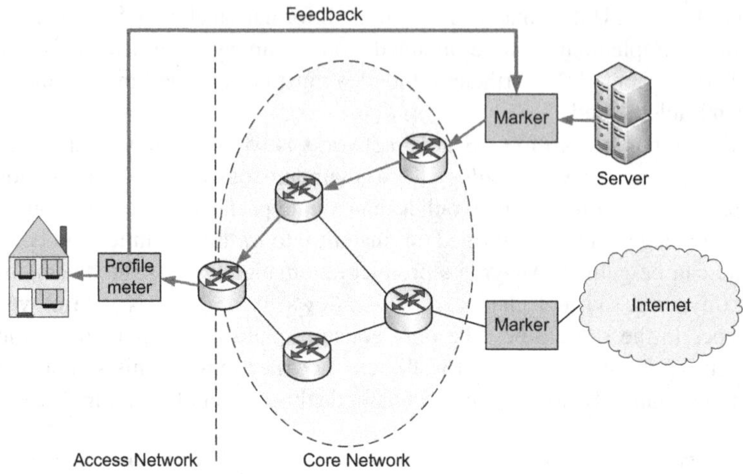

Fig. 1.2 Feedback and Distribution method—concept outline

packets, according to the data obtained from the profile meter. The only role of a network router, which also acts as a dropper, is to forward packets according to their priority: packets are dropped in the priority order when congestion occurs. There are only two possible priority indicators, i.e., high and low. High priority is assigned to packets whose traffic rate is lower than the guaranteed rate, and low priority to the rest. Packets with low priority are more likely to be dropped during congestion. Dropping packets effectively reduces the rate at which the flow transmits, and this reduction process may continue until the measured rate becomes lower than the guaranteed bandwidth, in which case the flow is prioritized again. Therefore, under severe congestion, this mechanism shapes each transmission to the guaranteed rate.

1.3.6 Flow-Based Differentiated Services

Perfectly aware of all the issues related to IntServ, four years later the IETF group introduced another approach to achieving QoS in the IP networks: the DiffServ model [4]. The idea of DiffServ significantly differs from its predecessor, mainly because flow-based differentiation has been replaced by class-based differentiation. Each packet is assigned to one of the previously defined classes and all the packets in the same class are treated as a single transmission entity. Naturally, this approach addresses the complexity and scalability issues of IntServ, as routers need to maintain the number of states proportional to the number of the defined classes rather than the number of active flows. However, considering the perception of the end-users, flow based service differentiation is much more important than class-based.

As this book focuses on flow-aware approaches, DiffServ is outside of its scope as it does not support flow-based differentiation. Still, it is possible to enhance the architecture so that it could provide flow-based proportional differentiated services in the class-based environment. This novel scheme with an estimator for the number of active flows, a dynamic weighted fair queuing scheduler and a queue management mechanism, was proposed by J.-S. Li and C.-S. Mao in [33].

The authors present their approach as a result of the observation that DiffServ does not guarantee that flows classified with a higher priority will really provide a better quality of service than lower priority ones, due to the fact that the distribution of active flows in the classes may be different. In other words, even wider bandwidth allocated to the higher class with a greater number of active flows may not provide better QoS than the lower class with fewer active flows. Therefore, this model proposes a flow-based proportional QoS scheme which always provides better quality for flows with a higher class. In general, supposing that a network provides N classes, the following equation should always be true:

$$\frac{q_i}{q_j} = \frac{\delta_i}{\delta_j} \tag{1.1}$$

where q_i is the service level obtained by class i and δ_i is the fixed differentiation parameter of class i, $i = 1, 2, \ldots, N$. The actual QoS for an individual flow will depend on the number of currently active flows in its class; however, the quality ratio between classes should remain constant. Therefore, the purpose of this model is to ensure the constant proportion between perceived QoS by flows in different classes, regardless of the current class loads.

1.3.7 Flow-Aware Networking

The concept of Flow-Aware Networking (FAN) as an approach to assure quality of service in packet networks was initially introduced in [43], and presented as a complete system in 2004 [30]. The goal of FAN is to enhance the current IP network by improving its performance under heavy congestion. To achieve this, certain traffic management mechanisms to control link sharing are introduced, namely: measurement-based admission control [37] and fair scheduling with priorities [30, 32]. The former is used to keep the flow rates sufficiently high to provide a minimal level of performance for each flow in case of overload. The latter realizes fair sharing of link bandwidth, while ensuring negligible packet latency for flows emitting at lower rates.

The goal of FAN is to enhance the perceivability of the current IP network. In order to do this, FAN introduces a unique router, named the Cross-Protect Router (XP Router). This device alone is responsible for providing admission control and fair queuing. A detailed description of the XP router is presented in Sect. 1.6.

Figure 1.3 presents the operation of FAN. Firstl, all incoming packets are classified into flows. The flow identification process is implicit and its goal is not to

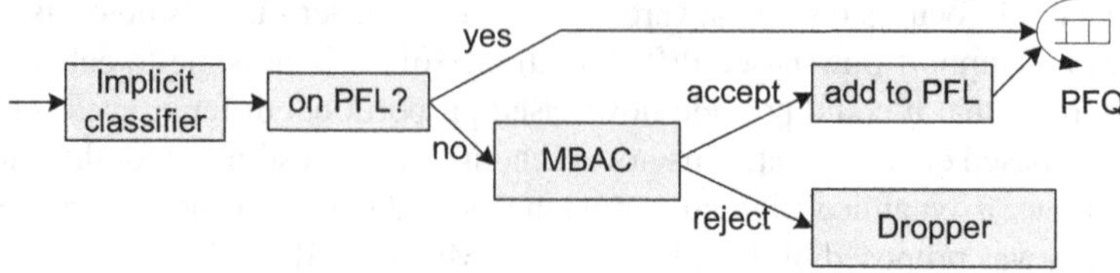

Fig. 1.3 Operation of FAN

divide flows into different classes, but only to create an instance on which the service differentiation will be performed. Then, all the flows that are currently in progress, i.e., are present on the Protected Flow List (PFL), are forwarded unconditionally, whereas all new flows are subject to admission control. The admission control in FAN is measurement based (MBAC) which implies that the accept/reject decisions are based only on the current link congestion status. If a new flow is accepted, it is put onto the PFL list and then all forthcoming packets of this flow are forwarded without checking the status of the outgoing link by MBAC.

1.3.8 Flow-State-Aware Transport

As the concept of Next Generation Networks (NGN) developed, flow-state-aware transport technology (FSA) [21] was presented as a method to introduce Quality of Service in these networks. FSA has been proposed by British Telecom (BT), Anagran and the Electronics and Telecommunications Research Institute (ETRI) in South Korea, and it was approved in the ITU-T Recommendation Y.2121 in January 2008. In general, ITU-T proposes that the target of differentiation should be single flows; however, the QoS architecture, especially at the core, should be based on DiffServ. Therefore, the aggregation of flows is inevitable.

The idea behind the FSA is to provide a robust QoS architecture, with differentiation capabilities matching those of IntServ yet scalable. To achieve scalability, certain flow aggregation was unavoidable, however, the QoS controls operate on a per-flow basis, not on a per-aggregate basis, as in DiffServ. Additionally, the FSA is not to provide strict assurances. ITU-T recommends [21] that:

> ...it is not necessary for FSA nodes to guarantee support under all possible conditions, only that they have high confidence that they can support the resulting request under normal operating conditions.

Such an approach became practically a mainline for all QoS architectures since the IntServ's complete lack of scalability had been claimed.

The FSA QoS controls are designed to be agnostic to the underlying transport technology. This goal is in line with NGN's general trends to separate service functions from transport functions and to be able to provide QoS over various underlying architectures. The last assumption covers interoperability and sharing common network resources among different transport techniques. Any network link may not be dedicated to carrying FSA traffic only. However, when a link is used for transporting a mixture of traffic, the FSA node needs to assume that a certain part of the link capacity is guaranteed to be available solely for the flow-state-aware traffic. There is a set of recommendations in [21] on how to manage and limit the capacity provided for each traffic.

1.3.9 Flow-Aggregate-Based Services

Soon after the official advent of FSA [21], researchers from ETRI proposed their solution to QoS provisioning in packet networks: the flow-aggregate-based services (FAbS) [25]. FAbS originates from FSA and aims at resolving FSA issues, mainly by introducing two novel building blocks: inter-domain flow aggregation and endpoint implicit admission control.

FAbS focuses on three aspects of congestion, i.e., instantaneous congestion, sustainable congestion and congestion avoidance. The distinction between instantaneous and sustainable congestion lies in the observation spectrum. The former refers to packet or burst level congestion (when occasional bursts cause congestion), while the latter refers to flow level congestion (when there are more flows than a network can handle). Instantaneous congestion is mitigated in FSA through proper flow aggregations and packet discards. Sustainable congestion is resolved by admission control, rate limiting and flow discards. Finally, for congestion avoidance, a protection switching mechanism is proposed.

1.4 Flow Definition

All presented architectures perform service differentiation based on individual flows. However, a 'flow' is not understood exactly the same in each instance. The most common identification is the so-called 5-tuple, i.e., source and destination IPv4 addresses, source and destination IPv4 port numbers and the transport protocol used for transmission. In case of IPv6, the 5-tuple changes into a 3-tuple: source and destination IPv6 addresses and the flow-label field. This means, that a 'flow' is considered as a set of packets that have the same values in the mentioned 5-tuple (or 3-tuple in case of IPv6). Next, we elaborate on the differences in flow perception.

In the basic Internet architecture all packets receive the same quality of service; usually they are forwarded in each router according to the First In, First Out (FIFO) queuing discipline. For Integrated Services, every router must implement an appropriate QoS for each flow. The flow is defined as a stream of related datagrams from a single user activity (e.g. a single voice transmission or video stream). Because every flow is related to a single service, all packets within the flow must be treated equally, with the same QoS.

In the Connectionless Approach, a flow is defined as a stream of packets between two applications, in a client and in a server. Flows are uniquely identified by a 5-

tuple. Therefore, the same set of end-users may easily create many flow instances in the network and each of them is treated individually.

The exact definition of a flow does not appear in the available descriptions of the Dynamic Packet State approach. However, the author of [46] states that applications that share a link create separate flows, e.g., a file-transfer application and an audio application create two flows. Hence, the approach is similar to the common understanding of a flow.

Caspian Networks and Anagran adopt the flow recognition by the 5-tuple of IPv4 header fields or the 3-tuple in case of IPv6.

Similarly to DPS, the authors of Feedback and Distribution do not specify exactly what a flow means. From the analysis, however, it can be deduced that a flow is associated with a single transmission. Given that there is a clear distinction between TCP and UDP flows, the standard 5-tuple recognition can be applied to this model.

In Flow-Based Differentiated Services, the distinction between flows is based on the source-and-destination (S-D) pair of IP addresses and a value of the DiffServ field (DS field) [36]. Therefore, all transmissions between the same end-users, and classified to the same class of service, are regarded as a single flow. This approach is not perfect as, for example, an S-D pair may be identical for all connections between two networks hidden under NAT (Network Address Translation), which in extreme cases may even exacerbate the QoS for high priority flows with respect to the original DiffServ. Nonetheless, statistically it enhances the end-user perception of DiffServ.

The definition of a flow in Flow-Aware Networking comes from [37]: "By flow we mean a flight of datagrams, localized in time and space and having the same unique identifier". The datagrams are localized in space, as they are observed at a certain interface, (e.g., on a router) and in time, as they must be spaced by no more than a certain interval, which is usually a few seconds. The space localization means that a typical flow has many instances, one at every interface on its path.

The identifier is obtained from certain IP header fields, including IP addresses and some other fields, e.g. the IPv6 *flow label*. One idea is to allow users to freely define flows, that correspond to a particular instance of some application. The intention is to allow users as much flexibility as possible in defining what the network should consider as a single flow. Such an approach is beneficial for the user; however, it always introduces the possibility of malicious behavior.

A flow label may also be deduced from IPv4 header fields. Typically, it could be a standard 5-tuple. However, this approach limits the flexibility, allowing users no control in defining their flows.

An important contribution of the Flow-State-Aware transport is the elaborate description of flows and their parameters and classes of service to which they may belong. Recommendation [21] defines a flow as: "a unidirectional sequence of packets with the property that, along any given network link, a flow identifier has the same value for every packet". A flow identifier is recommended to be derived from the standard 5-tuple of the IP header as well as the value of the DS field. However, it

Table 1.2 Flow-definition

Integrated services	Single user activity
Connectionless approach	5-tuple[a]
Dynamic packet state	Single user activity
Caspian networks/Anagran	5-tuple
Feedback and distribution	Single user activity
Flow-based DiffServ	S-D pair + DS field
Flow-aware networking	5-tuple
Flow-State-Aware transport	5-tuple + DS field (or MPLS label)
Flow-Aggregate-Based services	5-tuple + DS field (or MPLS label)

[a]A 5-tuple is defined as follows: <source IPv4 address, destination IPv4 address, source port number, destination port number, transport protocol>

may also be defined by the multi-protocol label switching (MPLS) label. Therefore, the term flow in FSA may indicate either IP 5-tuple flows or aggregates of them.

Flow-Aggregate-Based Services is derived from the FSA transport technology and as such it uses the same definition of flows.

Table 1.2 summarizes how all flow-based QoS architectures actually see a flow. In three cases, i.e., IntServ, DPS and F&D, a flow is not explicitly defined, yet it is understood as a flight of packets forming a single transmission. The exact definition is not presented in these approaches, although from architecture descriptions we can deduce similarities with the common understanding of a flow. Therefore, 'Single user activity' entries in Table 1.2 mean that the definition is not explicitly specified and the technical details are up to the implementers of the solution.

Architectures such as: Connectionless Approach, Anagran and FAN use the standard 5-tuple of IP headers. FSA transport and its follower FAbS adopted a 5-tuple along with a DS field to identify a flow. Alternatively, they envisage using MPLS for signaling purposes. Finally, Flow-Based DiffServ uses only an S-D pair of IP addresses along with the DS field which, as explained, has its drawbacks, although it still introduces flow-awareness.

1.5 Classes of Service

A Class of Service (CoS) is one of the fundamental aspect of every QoS architecture, acting as a means to provide service differentiation. In general, a CoS represents a group of flows that are treated following class-specific rules. Depending on the solution, CoS may be defined thoroughly, presented as a set of rules or left entirely for the operator to define and implement.

1.5.1 Integrated Services

The Integrated Services model has three explicitly defined classes of service. They are as follows:

- *Guaranteed Service* (GS),
- *Predictive Service* (PS),
- *Best-effort Service* (BE).

The *Guaranteed Service* class provides a certain amount of ensured bandwidth, absolutely no losses of packets due to buffer overloads, and a perfectly reliable upper bound on delay of packets in the end-to-end relation. This service is designed for delay-intolerant real-time applications.

In the *Predictive Service* (also named in [1, 16, 18] as *Controlled Load*) the flow does not obtain strict QoS guarantees. Instead, the application receives a constant level of service equivalent to that obtained with the *Best-effort Service* at light loads. It means that even under severe congestion, the quality of transmission should not degrade. This class of service was planned for real-time applications, which tolerate occasional loss of packets (e.g., VoIP) or which may adjust to the level of service that is offered at the moment.

The third service level (de facto unclassified) is oriented towards classical data transmission, without any QoS guarantees. When congestion occurs, the quality of the transmission degrades. This service is designed for elastic applications, due to their adaptability to the offered level of service.

1.5.2 Connectionless Approach

The flow classification strategy is based on the method introduced in [9]. The classification for both TCP and UDP flows is performed on the basis of different treatment that is required by different traffic types. Therefore, all applications with similar service requirements are likely to fall under the same class. The classification process can also be enhanced by the port number information. However, it is not considered to be a sufficient source of information, but rather an addition to the data gathered dynamically.

In [9], six traffic classes are proposed: three for TCP flows, and three for UDP. The main idea behind dividing flows into these categories is to separate flows which require fast response times from those which are delay insensitive. Figure 1.4 presents all the six classes of service and the outline of the classification scheme. TCP flows may be classified as:

- *Interactive*,
- *Bulk Transfer With Reserved Bandwidth*,
- *Bulk Transfer With Best Effort*.

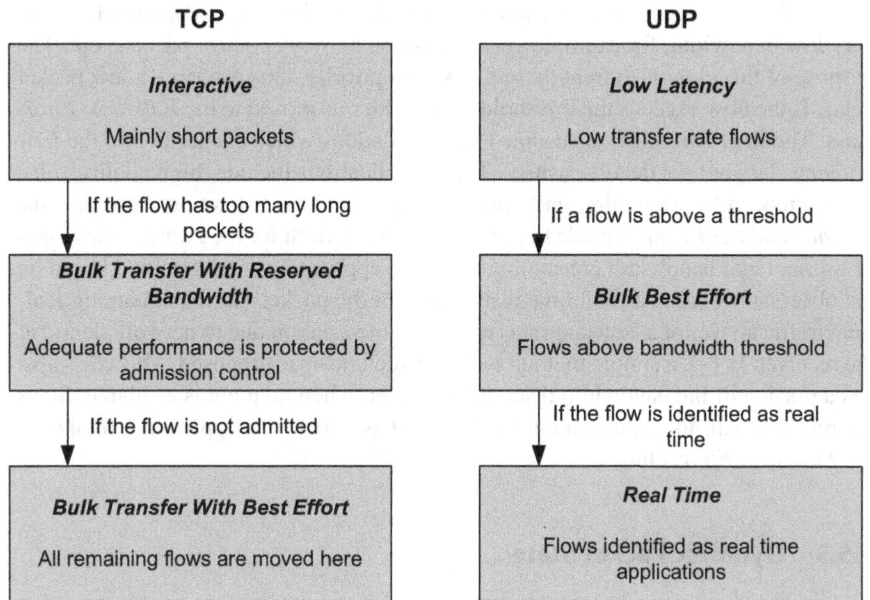

Fig. 1.4 Six flow classes with an outline of a classification scheme

The *Interactive* class is suited to applications which require short round trip times, such as Telnet, X-Windows or web browsing. These applications may last for a very long time, but they predominantly use short packets for transmission. For the purpose of classification, a short packet is defined to be no longer than 128 bytes. This is the first choice class for any new flow. However, when the flow exceeds some number of long packets (200) without an intervening string of two or more short packets, it is considered as bulk transfer and is no longer adequate for this class. To ensure a reasonable response time this class has a protected portion of the total allocated bandwidth.

If the TCP flow is not interactive, it is classified as a bulk transfer. If some portion of the reserved bandwidth is available, flows are moved to the *Bulk Transfer With Reserved Bandwidth* class, otherwise, the *Bulk Transfer With Best Effort* class is the last choice. Whenever the bandwidth becomes available, these flows may be moved to the reserved bandwidth class. Additionally, on each occurrence of two or more short packets, these flows are retained in the *Interactive* class.

UDP flows may belong to the following classes:

- *Low Latency*,
- *Real Time*,
- *Bulk Best Effort*.

Low Latency is the default class for UDP flows. This class contains flows of very low bandwidth, for example voice transfers, network control packets, etc. The purpose of this class is to treat these flows with priority, thus asserting a low packet delay. If the flow exceeds the threshold bandwidth it is moved to the *Bulk Best Effort* class. The *Real Time* class is designed for applications which cannot fit into the *Low Latency* class but are delay sensitive. These applications include: high quality voice connection, video streaming and conferencing, etc. The distinction between *Low Latency* and *Real Time* is made to preserve the bandwidth for the *Low Latency* class of traffic. High bandwidth consuming real-time applications are identified based on the observation of the arrival time distribution of the packets, as the streaming real-time traffic arrives at a constant rate (with a slight variation due to network delay) at the receiver. In [9], a simple method to detect such flows is proposed. This class also has a portion of the bandwidth reserved; however, when no more is available, flows are rejected. All flows that cannot be classified as a real-time application remain in the *Bulk Best Effort* class.

1.5.3 Dynamic Packet State

DPS, as reported in [46], was developed "to bridge this long-standing gap between stateless and stateful solutions in packet switched networks", with IntServ being stateful and DiffServ being stateless. DPS does not introduce any classes of service on its own. The method focuses on providing *Guaranteed Service* (GS), a CoS known from IntServ, but without using flow-state information in the core network.

The name GS is only used in DPS to provide an analogy to stateful solutions. Although one CoS is identified, service differentiation is still possible, as certain flow requirements are associated with each flow, namely the reserved rate and the deadline of the last packet that was served by a node. These parameters come from the Jitter Virtual Clock algorithm which is introduced in Sect. 1.6. Therefore, by changing the values of such parameters, DPS provides differential treatment of flows, although only one CoS is mentioned.

1.5.4 Caspian Networks/Anagran

Caspian Networks in [41] propose three types of service, namely: *Available Rate* (AR), *Maximum Rate* (MR), and *Guaranteed Rate* (GR). AR traffic does not have real-time requirements associated with the flow. Therefore, AR flows have very loose delay and jitter characteristics as well as relatively relaxed discard (loss) requirements. MR traffic, on the other hand, requires more rigid delay and jitter assurances and is more sensitive to traffic loss. Typically, MR flows will correspond to UDP-based real-time transmissions, such as voice or video.

GR traffic is similar to MR traffic with regard to its characteristics. It also has strict delay, jitter and loss requirements; however, the rate of the flow which is desirable by the end user is fed to the network prior to transmission, either by explicit signaling, examining the Real-Time Transport Protocol (RTP) type or by user-defined traffic profiles.

It needs to be noted, however, that these three classes of service are merely coarse characterizations of quantified state information that is associated with different types of transmissions. Within each CoS, multiple flows may receive similar yet differential treatment, including differences in delay variations and delay characteristics.

The above characteristics of CoS derived from Caspian Networks find their place in Anagran as well. Anagran supports AR and GR classes; however, new classes can be defined and created by network administrators.

1.5.5 Feedback and Distribution

The Feedback and Distribution method does not specify certain CoS. There is, however, a distinction between low-priority and high-priority traffic in the network. Profile meters measure each flow rate and send these measurements to markers. A marker sets a high priority to packets of flows whose rate is lower than the guaranteed rate and low priority to all other flows. When congestion occurs, surplus packets from the low priority flows are dropped, therefore the flow is shaped to the guaranteed rate. Although simple, this approach proves to be effective.

1.5.6 Flow-Based Differentiated Services

Flow-Based Differentiated Services operates on classes that were defined by DiffServ itself, providing flow-awareness. DiffServ envisages using the following classes of service: *Expedited Forwarding* (EF), *Assured Forwarding* (AF) and unclassified services.

The EF class ensures low packet delays and low packet latency variations. Additionally, traffic belonging to this class has a certain amount of link bandwidth reserved. The guaranteed EF rate must be settable by the network administrator. The AF class does not impose any guarantees. Instead, AF traffic is to be delivered with a probability no lower than a certain threshold. AF provides forwarding of IP packets in four independent AF subclasses. Each subclass consists of three levels of packet drop precedence. Best-effort traffic is covered under the unclassified service. A more detailed description of the EF and AF classes can be found in [22] and [19], respectively.

1.5.7 Flow-Aware Networking

All flows in FAN are divided into either a streaming or elastic type, hence two classes of service. The distinction is implicit, which means that the system categorizes the flows based on their current behavior. There is no need for a priori traffic specification as the classification is based solely on the current flow peak rate. All flows emitting at lower rates than the current fair rate (fair rate is one of the measured indicators of the outgoing link condition and is defined in Sect. 1.6) are referred to as streaming flows, and packets of these flows are prioritized. The remaining flows are referred to as elastic flows. Nevertheless, if a flow, first classified as streaming, surpasses the current fair rate value, it is degraded to the elastic flow category. Similarly, a flow is promoted to streaming, if it emits at a lower rate than the current fair rate at any time.

The assumption of FAN was to provide two classes of service. For low-rate flows which are typically associated with streaming transmissions, the streaming type is considered. All flows classified as streaming receive prioritized treatment—packets of these flows are sent through priority queues, hence, low delays and delay variations. For the remaining flows, proper fair queuing algorithms ascertain fair bandwidth sharing which cannot be assured with standard FIFO-based queueing disciplines. Finally, the distinctive advantage of FAN is that both streaming and elastic flows achieve a sufficiently good quality of service without any mutual detrimental effect.

1.5.8 Flow-State-Aware Transport

In FSA, the following four classes of service, referred to as service contexts, are defined: *Available Rate Service* (ARS), *Guaranteed Rate Service* (GRS), *Maximum Rate Service* (MRS), and *Variable Rate Service* (VRS).

ARS is similar to the ATM available bit rate (ABR), and it is typically used for data traffic flows. The requested rate is recommended to be set to the maximum rate that can be supported by the end equipment or application. The FSA nodes along the path are required to forward the request with the rate reduced to the rate they can support. Finally, the destination returns the value (possibly reduced) to the sender, which is then responsible for always maintaining the transmission at a rate no greater than the latest offered value. Otherwise, if the sending rate is sustained at a value above the offered rate, packet discards may be applied. Through signaling, the source is always updated with the latest rate offered.

GRS is similar to the guaranteed service class in IntServ and it is designed for applications that require guaranteed bandwidth for the entire duration of the flow. The source sends a request packet specifying the demands, while the network responds with an indication of the requested rate or a lower rate. The source must then confirm that the proposed rate is acceptable. Upon accepting, the flow is assigned to the 'discard last' packet discard priority, and is thus protected during local congestions. However, if the sending rate is sustained at a value above the guaranteed rate, packet discards may be applied. GRS is the only service context which requires the indication of starting (confirm packet) and terminating (close packet) the transmission.

Table 1.3 Classes of service in Flow-State-Aware transport

	Available rate service	Guaranteed rate service	Maximum rate service	Variable rate service
Requested rate meaning	Max. supported rate	Required rate	Maximum rate	Minimum rate
Offered rate meaning	Max. available rate	Guaranteed rate	Statistically guaranteed rate	Guaranteed rate
Renegotiations	Currently available rate	None	None	Requests for more bandwidth
Transmission start	After response	After confirmation	Immediately	After response

MRS is designed for video, voice, or other streaming media. As in GRS, the source specifies its bitrate demand, and it may be accepted, lowered or rejected. However, the difference is that MRS flows have the option of 'immediate transmission', i.e., they do not need to wait for the network response and can send traffic immediately after the request. Additionally, the admission decision is based on conditional guarantees of the requested rate with no reserved bandwidth. Again, packet discards may be applied if the transmission rate exceeds the offered rate.

VRS is a combination of MRS and ARS and is designed for obtaining a minimum response time for a transaction. The initial request rate is interpreted as the minimum (guaranteed) rate, i.e., policing is required to never reject packets sent at or below this rate. Subsequent request signals are interpreted as requests for bandwidth over this minimum rate. VRS flows are expected to be treated like ARS flows, except for their minimum guaranteed capacity which should be treated like MRS.

Table 1.3 summarizes and compares all four classes of service specified for FSA. The requested rate parameter, although required for all the classes, has a different meaning in each. Similarly, the network response, i.e., the offered rate, has different effects. For GRS, MRS and VRS it denotes the rate which should be guaranteed for the flows; however, for MRS, no strict reservations are made, only the source is statistically assured of the available bandwidth. In ARS and VRS, the current rate offer may be renegotiated, but for VRS, the offer must not drop below the initial request. Out of all classes of service, only MRS has the option of immediate start of transmission, while the remaining services must wait for a network response. Additionally, GRS needs to confirm its compliance with the network proposal prior to transmission.

1.5.9 Flow-Aggregate-Based Services

As stated by the authors in [25], one of the most significant contributions of FSA was its elaborate description of flows and classes of service provided. As such, FAbS also adopts all the classes of service proposed by FSA.

Table 1.4 Classes of service

Integrated services	GS, PS, BE
Connectionless approach	TCP: Interactive, BWRB, BWBE, UDP: *Low Latency, Real-Time*, BBE
Dynamic packet state	GS
Caspian networks/Anagran	AR, MR, GR
Feedback and distribution	Low-priority, High-priority
Flow-based DiffServ	EF, AF, BE
Flow-Aware Networking	Streaming, elastic
Flow-State-Aware transport	ARS, GRS, MRS, VRS
Flow-Aggregate-Based services	ARS, GRS, MRS, VRS

GS—*Guaranteed Service*, PS—*Predictive Service*, BE—*Best Effort*, BWRB—*Bulk With Reserved Bandwidth*, BWBE—*Bulk With Best Effort*, BBE—*Bulk Best Effort*, AR—*Available Rate*, MR—*Maximum Rate*, GR—*Guaranteed Rate*, EF—*Expedited Forwarding*, AF—*Assured Forwarding*, ARS—*Available Rate Service*, GRS—*Guaranteed Rate Service*, MRS—*Maximum Rate Service*, VRS—*Variable Rate Service*

1.5.10 Summary

Table 1.4 names all the classes of service that are identified by the QoS architectures under comparison. Additionally, in solutions such as IntServ, DPS, Caspian Networks, FSA, FAbS flows can receive differential treatment within each CoS. Connectionless Approach, Feedback and Distribution and FAN provide a certain CoS and assign flows to these classes according to their current behavior in the network, e.g., flow peak-rate, packet size, transport protocol, etc. In Flow-Based DiffServ, the CoS are divided into subclasses. This means that differentiated treatment within a class is provided, even though all flows within a subclass are treated identically.

1.6 Architecture

This section presents the means of providing QoS in each architecture and describes all the blocks that contribute to QoS provisioning, e.g., admission control, scheduling, meters, markers, etc. Additionally, some method-specific solutions are also presented in this section.

1.6.1 Integrated Services

Every router supporting the Integrated Services model must implement the following mechanisms of traffic control:

- packet scheduling,
- packet classification,
- admission control.

The packet scheduler is responsible for altering the order of datagrams in the outgoing queues. This procedure is necessary when congestion occurs, and it allows certain flows to be treated with a higher priority by assigning the correct QoS to them. The details of the scheduling algorithm may be specific to the particular medium of transmission. The packet scheduler is also responsible for dropping packets, should congestion take place.

One of the functions of the packet scheduler is traffic policing. The purpose of traffic policing is to ensure that a user does not violate its promised traffic characteristics. It would be natural to situate traffic policing at the edge of the network (like in ATM technology), but it would introduce additional complexity.

Each incoming packet must be mapped into some class of service. This is the role of the classifier module. The mapping may be performed based on the packets' header fields or other information. All packets in the same class are treated equally by the packet scheduler. One class of service may be assigned to one flow only, but it may also correspond to a broad category of flows. For example, all video streams or all voice transmissions may be assigned to a single class of service. A class is a local term, i.e., the same packet may be classified differently in each router along its path.

The admission control module is responsible for admitting or rejecting new flows. The decision is made based on whether admitting a new flow would negatively impact earlier guarantees. The admission control block operates on each node, and takes local accept/reject decisions. A new flow must find a path along which every node will be able to accept its requirements.

The last and the most important component of the Integrated Services framework is the reservation setup protocol, which is necessary to create and maintain resource reservations on every node along the path of transmission. The reservation protocol is presented in Sect. 1.7. The above description of IntServ components is brief and presented as such in official documents. Although it might not seem impressive, we need to bear in mind that IntServ was a pioneering endeavor and even such simple definitions were not obvious in 1994.

Figure 1.5 shows the placement and mutual cooperation of IntServ specific router components. The traditional IP router needs to be extended in order to fit into the Integrated Services model. The forwarding path is shown in part (a) of the figure, and part (b) presents the background mechanism. The forwarding path of the router must be executed for every packet, and therefore needs to be optimized. This path is divided into three parts: input driver, internet forwarder and output driver. The internet forwarder interprets the headers of the packets and assigns them to the appropriate output driver and the class of service. The classifier and routing mechanisms need to work in close cooperation due to efficiency issues. The output driver implements the packet scheduler.

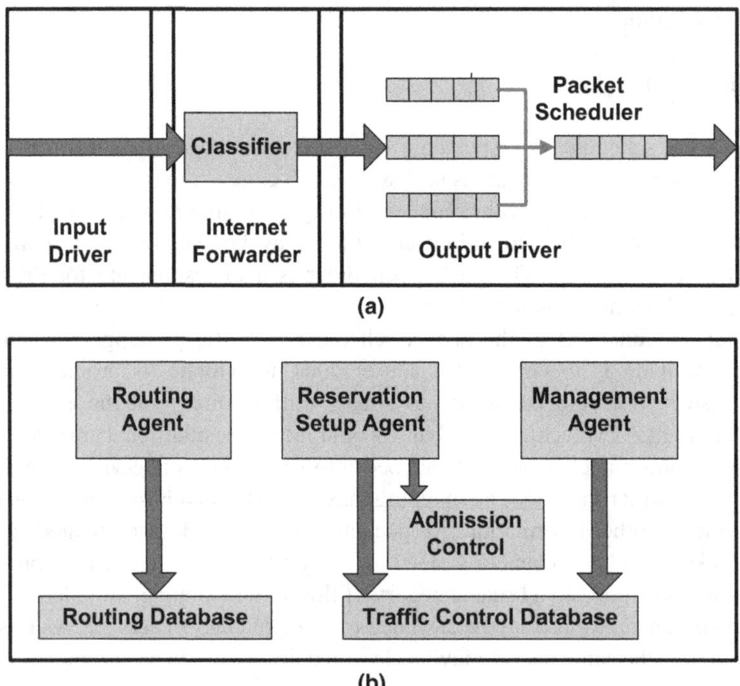

Fig. 1.5 Implementation reference model for IntServ routers: (a) the forwarding path; (b) the background mechanism

The background routine (Fig. 1.5b) creates the data structures which control the forwarding path. The routing agent and routing database are standard IP router mechanisms. The reservation setup agent is required for communicating with the reservation protocol and responding to its requests. The reservation setup agent cooperates with the admission control block, which accepts or rejects new flows. If a new flow is admitted, the changes are made to the traffic control database, which is then used by the classifier and the packet scheduler to implement the desired QoS. Finally, every router must support an agent for network management, which may modify the traffic control database to setup and maintain controlled link-sharing as well as creating new admission control parameters.

1.6.2 Connectionless Approach

The Connectionless Approach defines the traffic conditioner, a part of a router which performs flow-level service differentiation. The functional model of the traffic conditioner is presented in Fig. 1.6. Traffic conditioning is performed on flows, rather than on individual packets. Flows are maintained in a flow-list. If the flow

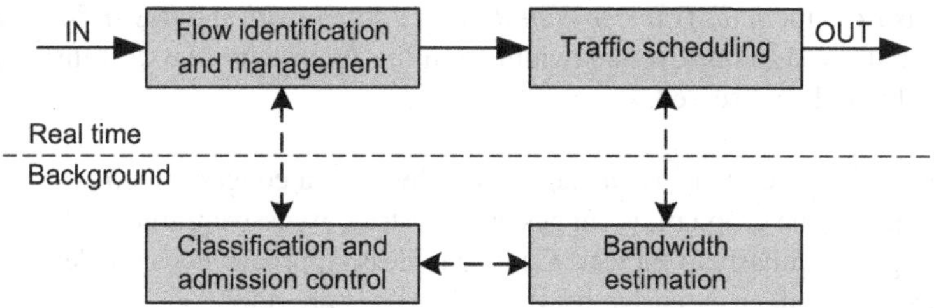

Fig. 1.6 Traffic conditioner functional blocks

associated with an arriving packet is not on a flow-list, a new flow entry is attached to the list.

Figure 1.6 also presents the real time and background operations of the router. The real-time data path has two major functions, i.e., to identify the flow for the input packet and to schedule the packet to the output. The background functions are supposed to: classify the flows, perform admission control and estimate the bandwidth of different classes of traffic. The classification is performed on-the-fly for each flow, based on its traffic characteristic. Admission control is necessary to regulate the load and to some extent to control the overall level of QoS that can be provided to the active flows. The role of the bandwidth estimator is to monitor the scheduling process and to provide information on bandwidth usage by each class to the admission control block.

Scheduling The scheduler is a key component in bandwidth management. Scheduling of previously classified flows is performed with two priorities: high and low. High priority traffic is scheduled without any delay and limited by the admission control mechanism, while low priority traffic is scheduled according to the set of rules. Flows in the *Real Time* and *Low Latency* classes are handled with high priority, whereas the rest are scheduled with low priority. The general rules of packet scheduling are presented in the following list.

1. All high priority packets are transmitted until there are no remaining packets in their queues. The queues are served in the round robin fashion.
2. Packets of the *Interactive* and *Bulk Transfer With Reserved Bandwidth* classes are served next, also in the round robin fashion.
3. Packets from the *Bulk Transfer With Reserved Bandwidth* class are transmitted only if the allocated bandwidth limitation for the class is not exceeded.
4. Packets from the *Interactive* class are transmitted even if the allocated bandwidth limitation for the class is exceeded but there are no packets waiting in the *Bulk Best Effort* or *Bulk Transfer With Reserved Bandwidth* classes.
5. Packets from the *Best Effort* classes are transmitted if there are no packets in any other class and bandwidth is available.

6. Packets from the *Bulk Transfer With Reserved Bandwidth* and *Best-Effort* classes are not allowed to borrow bandwidth from the *Interactive* class, as this portion must always be preserved.

Additionally, to effectively manage queue lengths, a congestion control mechanism, similar to the drop tail, is suggested to restrict excessive traffic for best effort classes. Again, similarly to IntServ, Connectionless Approach does not define exact algorithms. Instead, an extensive list of guidelines is provided.

1.6.3 Dynamic Packet State

In DPS, only edge routers perform per-flow management, whereas core routers do not. However, DPS provides end-to-end per-flow delay and bandwidth guarantees as defined in IntServ. To achieve this, two algorithms are proposed: one for the data plane to schedule packets, and the other for the control plane to perform admission control.

Scheduling

Scheduling in DPS is based on the Jitter Virtual Clock (Jitter-VC) algorithm, which is a non-work-conserving version of the Virtual Clock algorithm [52]. In Jitter-VC, each packet is assigned an eligible time and a deadline upon its arrival. The packet is held in the system until it becomes eligible, i.e., the system current time exceeds the packet eligible time. Then, the scheduler orders the transmission of eligible packets according to their deadlines, starting from the one with the closest deadline. This algorithm eliminates the delay variation of packets by forcing all packets to perceive the maximum allowable delay. It is claimed that Jitter-VC servers can provide the same guaranteed service as a network of Weighted Fair Queuing (WFQ) [10] servers [47].

For the purpose of realizing scheduling in the core, which is to be stateless, a variant of Jitter-VC, known as Core-Jitter-VC (CJVC), which does not require flow state at core nodes was proposed in [47]. It was shown that CJVC can provide the same guarantees as a network of Jitter-VC servers, hence the same as WFQ servers. The key idea behind CJVS is to have ingress nodes encode scheduling parameters in each packet header.

In CJVS, each packet carries three variables: the flow's reserved rate, the slack variable and the ahead-of-the-schedule variable. The last variable is inserted/updated by each node, while the first two are inserted by an ingress node and do not change. Based on these variables, every router is able to calculate the eligible time and the deadline for each packet. The mathematical side of the calculations can be found in [47] and [46], where, it is also shown that the deadline of a packet at the last hop in a network of CJVC servers is equal to the deadline of the same packet in corresponding networks of Jitter-VC servers.

Admission Control

In DPS, core nodes do not maintain any per-flow state. It is therefore difficult to decide whether a new flow may be admitted or not. To cope with this issue, each node in DPS keeps an aggregate reservation rate parameter for each outgoing link. Equation 1.2 presents the most straightforward condition that has to be met in order to admit a new flow.

$$R + r \leq C \tag{1.2}$$

where: R is the aggregate reservation rate, r is the rate reservation request and C denotes the link capacity. Unfortunately, the admission control scheme is not robust due to partial reservation failures, packet losses, and link and node failures. Therefore, DPS uses a more sophisticated approach, the upper bound of R is estimated and periodically recalibrated. Similarly, as in the scheduling algorithm, the exact mathematical formulas for implementing admission control in DPS are presented in [47] and [46].

1.6.4 Caspian Networks/Anagran

Caspian Networks, in [41], present a model of a network router which consists of an ingress micro-flow manager, an egress micro-flow manager and a memory. Figure 1.7 shows a detailed block diagram of the router's single line card. Although many blocks are visible, their operation is straightforward and there is nothing solution-specific, therefore they are not described here. More information can be found in [41]. Concerning the scheduling, Caspian Networks recommends using the Weighted Fair Queuing (WFQ) [10] algorithm. It is argued that with such extensive state information, the WFQ scheduler can be efficient.

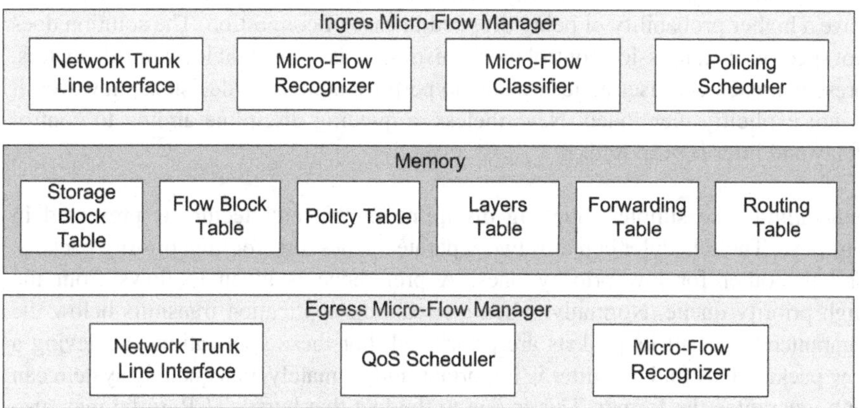

Fig. 1.7 Caspian Networks router linecard architecture

As for Anagran, the situation is similar, although the information is even less precise. This is due to the fact that Anagran is an existing technology incorporated in the FR-1000 router. The router provides the Intelligent Flow Discard (IFD) technology base on flow-based admission control. In case of congestion, packets to be dropped are not chosen randomly, but the minimum damage approach is envisaged. IFD ensures a constant quality by automatically invoking call admission control whenever an incoming stream threatens the quality of the existing streams. Additionally, it is possible to pre-empt of existing flows by higher priority flows for emergency services applications.

Anagran introduces another trademarked technology, i.e., Behavioral Traffic Control (BTC). This mechanism is responsible for constantly monitoring all active flows, and comparing their behavior against a simple set of operator-defined rules per flow class. BTC can identify 'suspect' flows based on: their duration, byte count, source/destination addresses, or other criteria. For flows which require some form of corrective or policing action, BTC can:

- reduce the allowed maximum rate of the flow,
- change the class of the flow (to lower or higher),
- forward the flow over different output port.

Unfortunately, available patents, i.e., [42] and [41] say little about these technologies, presenting instead a set of rules that should be followed. Therefore, all FR-1000 qualities that can be found are presented in a marketing oriented way and their descriptions lack details.

1.6.5 Feedback and Distribution

The Feedback and Distribution architecture defines a scheduling discipline which distinguishes high and low priority traffic. Packets that are treated as low priority have a higher probability of being dropped in case of congestion. The solution does not specify any admission control mechanism. It is assumed that local profile meters, present at each end-user node, are able to perform admission decisions; however, it is not explicitly mentioned. Nevertheless, a queuing discipline aiming to control delay and jitter is proposed.

Scheduling The simplest queuing discipline in this architecture is presented in Fig. 1.8a. The scheduler contains two separate queues: one for high priority packets, and the other for low priority ones. A preference is given to flows from the high priority queue. Normally, when a streaming application transmits below the guaranteed rate, all its packets are prioritized. For these applications, achieving a low packet delay and low jitter is important; unfortunately, this queuing system can only guarantee the former. This is due to the fact that bursty TCP traffic may also use the high priority queue for short periods of time. When a large volume of bursty traffic is put to the high priority queue at the same time, the following streaming

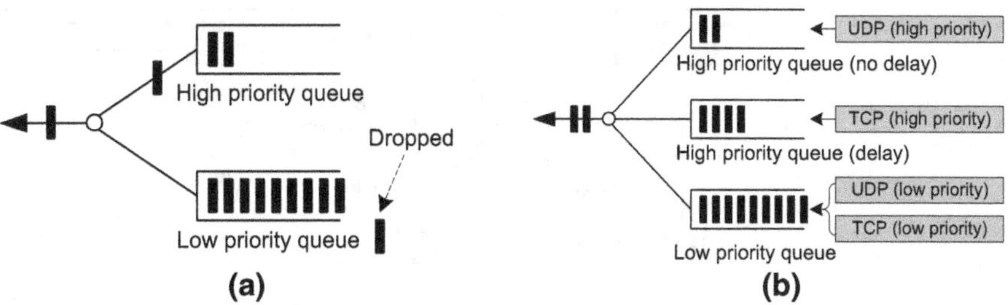

Fig. 1.8 Scheduling in the Feedback and Distribution method

packets are delayed resulting in jitter. This issue is considered significant, as the authors of [27] note that jitter vulnerability for interactive applications increases with their transfer rate, and as such it may become a more significant problem in the future.

Figure 1.8b shows a revised version of the scheduling mechanism in a dropper. Jitter is reduced by using a third queue and by classifying traffic into TCP and UDP. Two of the queues serve high priority traffic (separate for TCP and UDP) and one serves low priority traffic (for the remaining packets). In this method, burst-like TCP traffic does not interfere with UDP flows. This method, then, combines the low delay UDP service and burst-like TCP with bandwidth controlled for each flow.

Scalability of the architecture is not a problem, since traffic measurement is performed near the end-users. Busy servers do not need to provide measurements for multiple flows simultaneously. Instead, they only receive information from traffic meters and mark the packets accordingly. Additionally, routers do not need to maintain a per-flow state for each transmission, which simplifies their operation. Finally, the queuing discipline is easy but still efficient.

1.6.6 Flow-Based Differentiated Services

In order to change class-based DiffServ to a flow-based architecture, it is necessary to estimate the number of currently active flows in each class. This is performed by the flow number estimator. As such, Flow-Based DiffServ presents a method for proportional bandwidth and delay differentiation.

Router Architecture

Figure 1.9 presents the proposed mechanisms in a proportional flow-based DiffServ router. On entering the router, packets are assigned to an appropriate class by the *classifier* and then forwarded to the associated queue. Packets belonging to different flows in the same class are dispatched to the same FIFO queue, as only one instance of queue exists per class. The number of active flows in each class may be different and time-varying. This is an important indicator for handling traffic. To introduce flow-based differentiation, the number of active flows in each class is

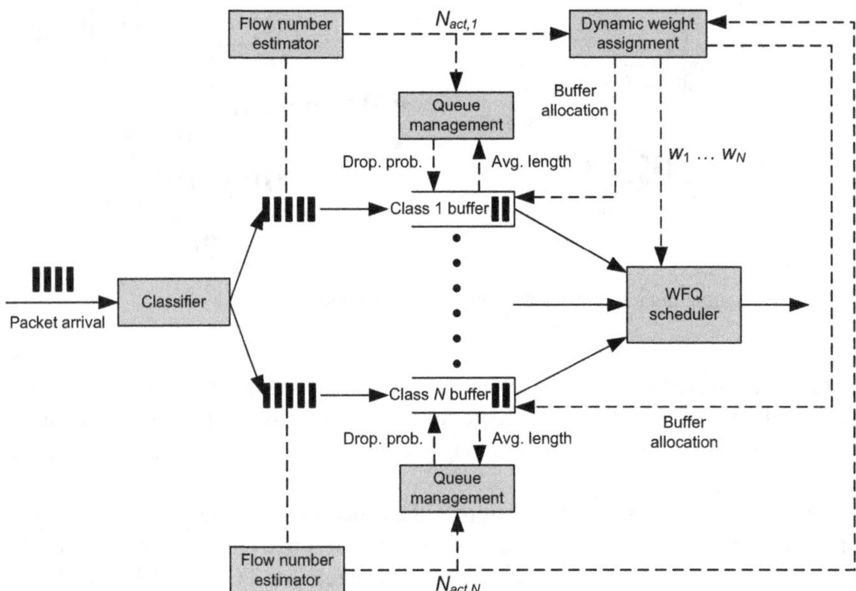

Fig. 1.9 Flow-based DiffServ router architecture

constantly monitored by the *flow number estimators*. According to these estimations the weights for each class in the WFQ algorithm can be dynamically adapted. Additionally, the flow number estimator feeds the *queue management* blocks which dynamically allocate buffers and control their queues. The dynamically adjusted *WFQ scheduler* is responsible for proportional flow-based bandwidth allocation among the classes, whereas queue management is employed to achieve proportional delay differentiation. The blocks provide flow-based proportional bandwidth and delay differentiation without maintaining per-flow state in the router.

Flow Number Estimator

The method of estimating the number of active flows is based on the Bloom filter [5]. The Bloom filter is a probabilistic data structure, used to test whether an element is a member of a certain set. Elements can be added to the set, but they cannot be removed. Commonly, these filters are used for quick and space-efficient spell-checking in word processing software. Similarly to checking whether the entered word is present in the dictionary, for flows, the filter checks whether the flow associated with an incoming packet is already accounted for.

Bloom filters are based on hash functions. Initially, each bin in a hash table is set to 0. When a packet arrives, the identity of its flow is hashed and the corresponding bin is set to 1. Whenever this procedure changes the value of a bin from 0 to 1, the counter of active flows in incremented. This method is not perfectly accurate because hash collisions and flow terminations may occur. The former issue appears when two or more flows are hashed to the same bin. It is solved by using a K-level hash table; it provides N^K virtual buckets for N bins in each of the K levels, meaning that up to N^K flows can be identified with NK bins only. This approach greatly reduces the probability of a hash collision, providing that a sufficiently extensive hash table is used. The latter problem (terminated flows) exists because of a property of the Bloom filter, i.e., elements cannot be removed from the set. Therefore, each flow that ends is not removed from the hash-table. To solve this, a concurrent operation of two hash-tables is proposed. Each is periodically reset (all the bins are set to 0) but never at the same time. After one hash-table is reset, the number of active flows is derived from the other and vice versa. Using two hash-tables is necessary to prevent warm-up effects which would appear after resetting a hash table, had there been only one.

Proportional Bandwidth and Delay Differentiation

To achieve proportional QoS differentiation between classes (Eq. 1.1) the actual bandwidth and delay must be adjusted proportionally to the defined quality ratio and the number of active flows in each class. Bandwidth allocation is performed by dynamically changing the weight of each class in a WFQ scheduler. The ratio of weights for two different classes is presented in Eq. 1.3, where w_i, $N_{act,i}$ and α_i are the WFQ weight, the estimated number of active flows and the bandwidth differentiation parameter for class i, respectively.

$$\frac{w_i}{w_j} = \frac{N_{act,i}}{N_{act,j}} \times \frac{\alpha_i}{\alpha_j} \tag{1.3}$$

To achieve both proportional bandwidth and delay differentiations simultaneously, a dynamic buffer allocator and a queue manager are also proposed. As in the case of bandwidth, the buffer allocator is used to dynamically adapt buffer sizes according to the number of active flows in each class. Queue management is based on the Random Early Detection (RED) mechanism which is also dynamically adjusted. The queue management block obtains information from the flow number estimator as well as from the queue (the average queue length) and adapts drop probabilities in RED in order to maintain the average queue length at a target value. By combining these two mechanisms, the proportional delay differentiation can be achieved.

1.6.7 Flow-Aware Networking

To present the architecture of FAN, we introduce the Cross-Protect router and describe the operation of the admission control and scheduling blocks.

Cross-Protect Router

To introduce FAN into a network, an upgrade of current IP routers is required. Figure 1.10 shows a concept diagram of a Cross-Protect router (XP router), the

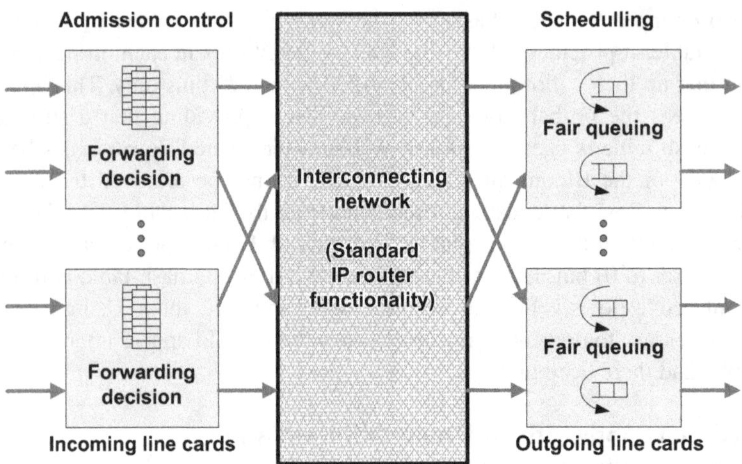

Fig. 1.10 Concept diagram of a Cross-protect router

standard interconnecting device in FAN. FAN adds just two blocks to the standard IP router, namely the admission control and scheduling blocks. The former is placed in the incoming line cards of the router, whereas the latter is situated in the outgoing line cards.

Admission control is responsible for accepting or rejecting incoming packets, based on current congestion status. The purpose of scheduling is twofold: it provides prioritized forwarding of streaming flows and assures fair sharing of residual bandwidth by all elastic flows.

Cross-protect routers are so named becasue they provide cooperation and protection simultaneously, between both additional blocks. The admission control block limits the number of active flows in a router, which improves the queuing algorithm functionality and reduces its performance requirements. It is vital that queuing mechanisms operate quickly, as for extremely high speed links the available processing time is strictly limited. On the other hand, the scheduling block provides admission control with information on the congestion status on the outgoing interfaces. The information is derived based on, for example, the current queues occupancy. Mutual protection contributes to the smaller protected flow list and active flow list sizes, which significantly improves FAN scalability.

Measurement-Based Admission Control

The admission control block implements the measurement based admission control (MBAC) functionality [28]. It is not class-based or user-based: each new flow receives the same treatment, and in case of congestion, all new flows are blocked. Such an approach may be considered as unfair service differentiation, since in congestion some flows are admitted and some are blocked. However, MBAC treats all flows equally, i.e., (a) the decision of whether to accept or reject the traffic affects

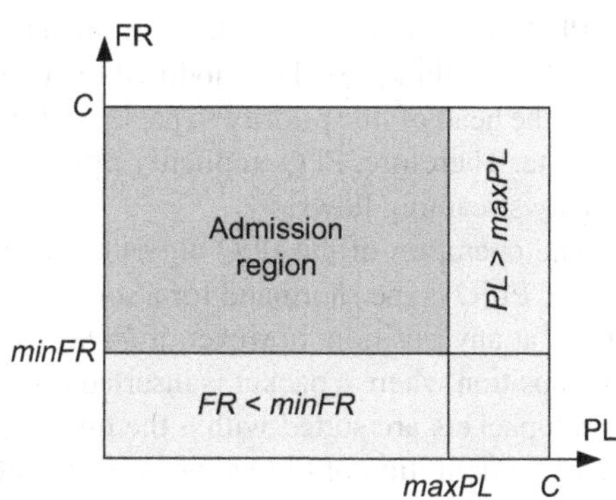

Fig. 1.11 Admission region in FAN

all new incoming flows, not just some of them, and (b) admission decisions are implicit, based on internal measurements only.

MBAC performs actions based on information derived from scheduling algorithms. Two parameters are constantly measured, i.e., fair rate (FR) and priority load (PL). Following [30], "fair rate is an estimation of the rate currently realized by backlogged flows", and represents the amount of link bandwidth which is guaranteed to be available for a single flow, should it be necessary. Similarly, "priority load is the sum of the lengths of priority packets transmitted in a certain interval divided by the duration of that interval", and shows the amount of data that is prioritized. The manner of calculating both indicators is a feature of the scheduling algorithm, and is presented in [30].

Figure 1.11 illustrates the admission decision in MBAC. Each router has two pre-defined threshold values of FR and PL which are to be maintained, namely: the minimum value of FR (minFR) and the maximum value of PL (maxPL). If current FR is lower than minFR or if the current PL is greater than maxPL, the incoming flow is blocked. Otherwise, when in the admission region, the new flow is admitted.

Scheduling

Queue management in FAN is realized in the scheduling block of an XP router. Fair queuing ensures that link bandwidth is shared equally, without relying on cooperative behavior of end-users. This is a different approach than in currently used IP routers, where the FIFO queue is usually implemented.

There are two per-flow fair queuing algorithms proposed for FAN: Priority Fair Queuing (PFQ) and Priority Deficit Round Robin (PDRR). Both algorithms have, logically, one priority queue and a secondary queuing system. They aim to implement fair sharing of link bandwidth to elastic flows and priority service to streaming flows. The latter (PDRR) was primarily suggested to accelerate commercial adoption since it improves the algorithm complexity from $O(log(N))$ to $O(1)$, where N is the number of currently active flows. However, it has been shown that both scheduling algorithms have similar performance [31].

PFQ, as proposed in [30], is an enhancement of the Start-Time Fair Queuing (SFQ) algorithm [15]. The modified queuing discipline differs from SFQ in that it gives the head of line priority to packets of flows whose rate is lower than the current fair rate. Therefore, PFQ implicitly prioritizes packets of low-rate flows, which are usually streaming flows.

The operation of the PFQ algorithm is based on the Push-In, First-Out (PIFO) queue. PIFO is the shorthand for a sorting algorithm that allows a packet to join the queue at any position; however, it always serves the packet at the head of the line. The position where a packet is inserted is determined by a time stamp, according to which packets are sorted within the queue. The calculation of the time stamps and the exact definition of PFQ along with pseudo-codes are presented in [30].

PFQ was the first queuing algorithm proposed for the FAN architecture. In fact, the simulations have shown that PFQ performs well, and cooperates with the admission control block correctly [30]. Furthermore, the scalability of PFQ has been demonstrated using trace driven simulations and analytical modeling in [29] and [31]. However, PFQ can be replaced by an adaptation of the Deficit Round Robin (DRR) [44] algorithm. An enhancement to DRR, known as Priority Deficit Round Robin (PDRR), is presented in [32].

PDRR retains the low complexity of DRR, and at the same time, provides low latency for streaming flows. PDRR complexity is constant ($O(1)$), therefore it does not increase with the growing number of active flows (PFQ complexity is logarithmic with respect to the number of active flows). PDRR enhances the DRR algorithm in that it introduces the priority queue, which is used for low rate flows. Similarly, as for PFQ, the exact definition of PDRR can be found in [32].

Regardless of the algorithm used, it has been shown in [29] that fair queuing in FAN is scalable since complexity does not increase with link capacity. Moreover, fair queuing is feasible as long as link loads are not allowed to attain saturation levels, which is asserted by admission control. More recently, another FAN architecture has been proposed in [13], based on the Approximate Fair Dropping [39] queuing algorithm. The new architecture is referred to as Approximate Flow-Aware Networking or AFAN for short, and aims to simplify the queuing processes further. As shown in [13], the enqueue and dequeue operations in AFAN are implemented in a simpler way than in the previous proposals of PFQ and PDRR.

1.6.8 Flow-State-Aware Transport

The recommendation [21], as its title implies, forms a set of rules that an FSA architecture should follow. For instance, exact numerical values needed for admission control decisions are not presented; however, the functions of the admission control block are described. Moreover, the guidelines for accepting flows from each CoS are formed. The guidelines include: the parameters that should be taken into account, the required decision time, possible treatment of flows, etc. The most comprehensive part of the recommendation is the description of flows and CoS which was presented in previous sections. Section 1.7 discusses signaling issues. As for the architecture, we need to describe flow treatment, supplementing the CoS and flow aggregation concepts.

Flow Treatment

In the network, flows are treated differently, according to flow specification parameters, such as:

- flow identity,
- class of service,
- requested rate,
- preference priority indicator,
- packet discard priority,
- burst tolerance,
- delay priority.

Flow identity is derived automatically from each packet. The remaining parameters must be signaled prior to transmission, except for the packet discard priority which is not included in the signaling information. The type of the proposed signaling in FSA is presented in Sect. 1.7.

The requested rate parameter has different meanings for different classes of service, and it is required for each one. The preference priority indicates the priority for admission decision, i.e., flows with a greater preference priority will be accepted first. If a high-preference priority flow arrives at a congested link, a pre-emption mechanisms may need to be implemented to remove active flows of a lower priority. The packet discard priority, on the other hand, is required to distinguish between at least two values, namely 'discard first' and 'discard last'. It is used for packet discard decisions upon congestion. Flows marked with the 'discard first' parameter are, naturally, dropped first. When congestion persists even after all such packets have been dropped, the networks should re-mark additional flows as 'discard first', starting from the lowest preference indicator value.

Typically, video and voice transmissions require lower delay variance than file transfers. To encompass a wide range of existing and future application needs, the delay priority parameter has been introduced. This may give additional information to the queuing disciplines in the FSA nodes on how to manage the packet scheduling process. Moreover, due to queuing procedures and the nature of Internet traffic, packets frequently arrive in bursts. It is therefore vital for FSA nodes to apply a level of tolerance (burst tolerance parameter) to rates that exceed the requested rate for a short duration.

Flow Aggregation

Ingress nodes may aggregate selected flows into fewer aggregates, based on certain criteria. MPLS is particularly useful for carrying a flow aggregate identifier. However, flow aggregation is not permanent and unconditional. For example, if one of the aggregated flows violates the contract, it can be automatically relocated to a different aggregate, where appropriate treatment will be applied. Where appropriate, signaling messages may also be aggregated and de-aggregated with the flows so they can follow the transmission regardless of the aggregation processes in the core. Practical guidelines for aggregation are not specified, although it is assumed that only flows of the same class of service can be aggregated. An aggregated flow becomes a new entity which must be set up and signaled in the FSA network, and should be treated as a single flow with proper QoS guarantees. Despite aggregation the network maintains per-flow treatment, because when single flows are aggregated into one instance, this new instance is subject to appropriate QoS constraints. For instance, in case of aggregated flows with a guaranteed rate, the reserved rate for an aggregate will be the sum of the reservations for each flow individually.

1.6.9 Flow-Aggregate-Based Services

As mentioned in Sect. 1.3, FAbS focuses on dealing with instantaneous congestion, sustainable congestion and providing congestion avoidance. The resolution of instantaneous congestion is based on Inter-Domain Flow Aggregation (IDFA), while sustainable congestion incorporates endpoint implicit admission control and endpoint rate limiting with DiffProbe delay measurement. Congestion avoidance is centered around MPLS traffic engineering, and it is left for future studies. The first two mechanisms are described below.

Inter-Domain Flow Aggregation

FAbS adopts flow aggregation mechanisms proposed in FSA. However, considering the fact that flows passed through the aggregation-deaggregation process can exhibit worse performance than if they would not have been put through it [24], flow aggregation should only be executed if it is possible to carry the aggregates across the network domain. This mechanism is referred to as Inter-Domain Flow Aggregation (IDFA). The domain is defined as a single administrative network domain in which the flow aggregation policy remains the same. The main principles of IDFA are as follows:

1. the starting point of the aggregation should be as close to the user-network interface as possible,
2. the aggregation region should be as large as possible,
3. in the end-to-end transmission, the number of aggregation processes with new flows should be as small as possible.

Figure 1.12 presents a possible implementation of IDFA. Let us consider two flow aggregates (FA), FA-i and FA-j, arriving at an ingress edge node. Some flows within both aggregates are destined to the same node in the network, say, FA-i-n and FA-j-m. Without knowing the aggregation policy in the previous node/network, these flows are likely to be aggregated together. However, following principle (3), IDFA may not aggregate the flows. An immediate consequence of IDFA is a much

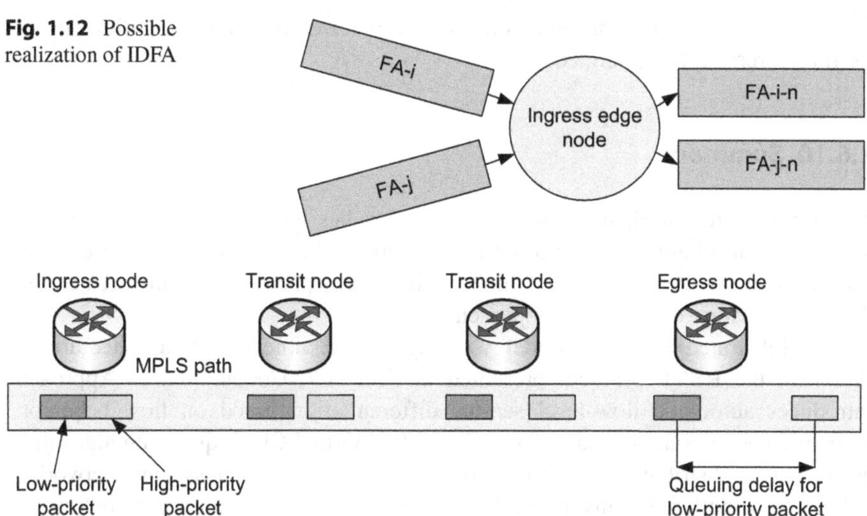

Fig. 1.12 Possible realization of IDFA

Fig. 1.13 The concept of DiffProbe

greater number of aggregates within a network and a lower number of flows per aggregate.

The main idea of IDFA is that flow membership should remain as unchanged as possible. To maintain flow aggregate membership, FA identification and membership information should be handed over from one network to the other. This can be done by either in-band or out-of-band signaling; however, in-band signaling is recommended where scalability is a limiting factor. The concepts of in-band and out-of-band signaling are presented in Sect. 1.7.

Endpoint Implicit Admission Control

The suggested admission control in FAbS checks the congestion status of the network using end-to-end delay measurement by using DiffProbe [45], as shown in Fig. 1.13. DiffProbe measures one-way delay of the target class of service using the interarrival time between the supreme class and the target class packets. The greater the difference between the packet arrivals, the greater congestion is assumed along the path. For DiffProbe to work, it needs to be assured that the DiffProbe packets and the new transmission will follow the same path. This can be guaranteed by MPLS.

Under low load states, service requests are accepted without any limitations. Should the network become congested, only high preference services (such as emergency connections) are admitted. Congestion detected through DiffProbe can also trigger rate control mechanisms at the endpoints. As mentioned, FAbS adopts classes of service from FSA. Therefore, for ARS and VRS service contexts, rate renegotiation procedures may be invoked. Finally, the preference priority from FSA can also be used to determine which flows are and which are not to be served at the moment. These are only guidelines as the precise admission conditions using DiffProbe remain to be defined.

1.6.10 Summary

The architectures of all flow-aware QoS approaches have been presented in this section. All mechanisms that do not fit into any of the remaining categories have also been shown here. Table 1.5 shows architecture-specific mechanisms, i.e., the distinctive feature of each QoS approach.

The Integrated Services model was the first complete QoS architecture in line with the RSVP protocol presented in Sect. 1.7. Connectionless Approach introduces automatic flow-level service differentiation based on flow behavior. Dynamic Packet State introduces the Core-Jitter Virtual Clock queueing algorithm as well as a distributed admission control scheme for stateless core networks. Additionally, both mechanisms use the fact that flow-state information is sent inside packet headers. Anagran introduces Intelligent Flow Discard and Behavioral Traffic Control, however, the exact operation of these algorithms is not revealed. The Feedback and Distributed architecture is based on putting profile meters near the user and feeding distant markers with the measured information.

Flow-Based DiffServ enhances the Differentiated Services architecture by introducing flow number estimator and proportional bandwidth and delay differentiation. Flow-Aware Networking proposes a cross-protect router which performs measurement-based admission control and scheduling based on either PFQ or PDRR queuing algorithms. Flow-State-Aware Transport is known for its extensive flow and CoS definition, as well as introducing flow aggregations into the network, while still retaining flow-aware QoS differentiation. Finally, Flow-Aggregate-Based Services introduces Inter-Domain Flow Aggregation and Endpoint Implicit Admission Control which uses DiffProbe to estimate congestion in the network.

Table 1.5 Architecture specific mechanisms

Integrated services	First complete QoS system, RSVP protocol
Connectionless approach	Automatic flow-level service differentiation
Dynamic packet state	Core-Jitter-VC algorithm, admission control in stateless core
Caspian networks/Anagran	Intelligent flow discard, behavioral traffic control
Feedback and distribution	Measurement and distribution method
Flow-based differentiated services	Flow number estimator, proportional bandwidth and delay differentiation
Flow-Aware Networking	Cross-protect router, measurement-based admission control, scheduling: PFQ, PDRR
Flow-State-Aware transport	Extensive flow definition, flow aggregation
Flow-aggregate-based services	Inter-domain flow aggregation, endpoint implicit admission control + DiffProbe

1.7 Signaling

The essence of signaling is grounded in the following question: how do we feed the network with information on specific treatment of flows? In other words, how do we inform the nodes whether a new flow should be treated with priority? The task is not trivial and numerous approaches to the problem are known.

1.7.1 Integrated Services

For the purpose of implementing Integrated Services, IETF specified the Resource Reservation Protocol (RSVP) [6, 8, 34], described its interoperation with IntServ networks [50], extensions [20, 38], and additional procedures [26]. The IntServ model is not strictly associated with the RSVP protocol. IntServ may interoperate with various reservation protocols, and RSVP is an instance of such a protocol (although it is the sole example). This section describes the basic concepts and mechanisms of the RSVP protocol. For more detailed information, see relevant IETF documents.

The RSVP protocol is used by a host to request a specific QoS from the network for a particular data stream, prior to the transmission. This protocol is also used by the routers to transport QoS requests to all nodes along the path of the flows and to create and maintain the state providing the requested service.

During the setup of the reservation, an RSVP request is passed onto two local decision modules in every router, namely *admission control* and *policy control.* Admission control decides whether there are sufficient resources to supply the request, while policy control determines whether the user has the administrative permission to make the reservation.

The RSVP protocol has the following features:

1. RSVP is receiver oriented,
2. RSVP transports traffic control and policy control parameters that are opaque to RSVP,
3. RSVP is simplex-oriented,
4. RSVP operates for both unicast and multicast connections,
5. RSVP maintains *soft state* in routers and hosts,
6. RSVP depends upon and cooperates with routing protocols,
7. RSVP provides several reservation models and styles,
8. RSVP provides a transparent operation mode through routers that do not support it,
9. RSVP supports both IPv4 and IPv6.

ad. (1) The receiver (all of them in the case of multicast transmission) of the transmission initiates and maintains resource reservation procedures.

ad. (2) RSVP transfers traffic control and policy control data to appropriate control modules for interpretation. The reservation protocol itself does not need to understand them, which renders its implementation much simpler. The structure and contents of the QoS parameters are specified in [50].

ad. (3) RSVP requests resources only for simplex flows. If guarantees for bidirectional transmission are necessary, two separate negotiation procedures are required.

ad. (4) RSVP (as well as IntServ) was designed to support both unicast and multicast communication. This feature is significant, since real-time applications are often implemented to operate in the multicast mode (e.g., multimedia conferencing, video streaming).

ad. (5) RSVP establishes the *soft state*, which means that periodic refresh messages are sent to maintain the state along the reserved path. In the absence of the refresh messages, the state is automatically deleted.

ad. (6) RSVP itself is not a routing protocol. It processes information from local routing databases to obtain routes. RSVP is designed to operate with current and future routing protocols.

ad. (7) The available reservation models and styles are presented in [8].

ad. (8) The RSVP protocol may operate on routers that do not support it—they simply pass the protocol datagrams with information.

The reservation process (Fig. 1.14) is initiated by the sender that constructs a special *Path* message and transmits it to the receiver. A certain route is chosen by routing protocols, and the transmission will follow this path. The *Resv* message (initiated by the receiver) is sent in the opposite direction. Moreover, it must follow exactly the same route as the *Path* message, even though the path chosen by the routing protocol in this direction may differ. To re-create the original path, the IP address of the previous hop router is carried in the *Path* message, and stored locally in each node. Therefore, the reservation messages should always find the correct path (solid arrows) and make the correct reservations.

The basic RSVP reservation model is known as one pass. This means that when a receiver sends a reservation request, each node along the path either accepts or rejects the request. There is no indication of the available resources, should the application settle with a lower quality service level. Therefore, the RSVP supports enhancement to the one-pass service known as One Pass With Advertising (OPWA). With OPWA, the control packets are created and sent to the receiver in order to gather information which may be used to predict the end-to-end QoS. These control packets, named *advertisements*, may be used by the receiver to construct an appropriate reservation request.

RSVP uses a *soft state* fashion to managing the reservations in routers and hosts. The soft state is created and maintained by the *Path* and *Resv* messages. Every reservation must be either periodically refreshed or is automatically terminated. This approach has both pros and cons. When a route dynamically changes, the *Path* and *Resv* messages establish guarantees in the new nodes, while previously used reservations (due to the lack of refreshment) terminate automatically. Moreover, periodic

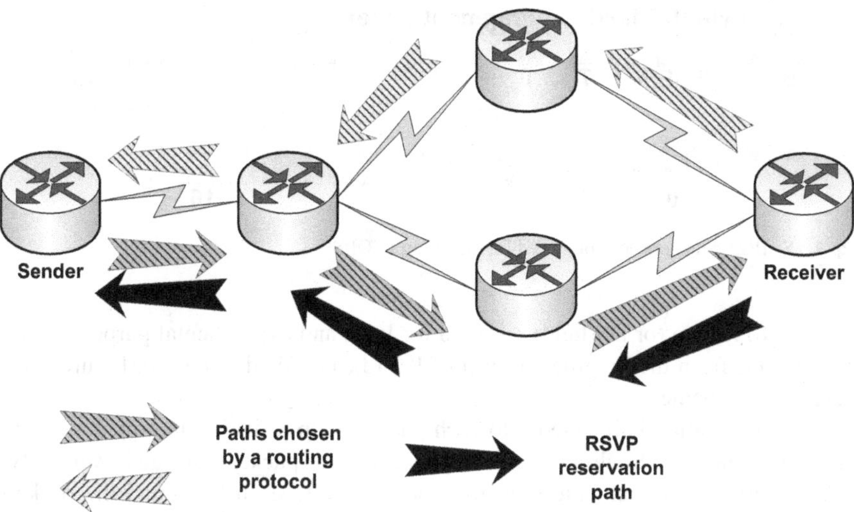

Fig. 1.14 RSVP reservation process

transmissions of refresh packets handle the occasional loss of RSVP messages. This feature is important, since RSVP messages are transmitted unreliably and without confirmation.

Unfortunately, RSVP refresh messages increase the traffic in the network. This growth is strictly proportional to the number of existing paths, and therefore it becomes a significant problem while dealing with multicast transmissions. The soft state approach also increases router overloading, decreasing standard CPU time for basic routers' actions. Moreover, every router needs to store and process a high volume of information. All this renders the RSVP protocol unscalable.

1.7.2 Connectionless Approach

In the Connectionless Approach, all decisions in the nodes are taken based on current flow characteristics. Therefore, they operate independently, and as such the solution does not require any kind of signaling. This is a great advantage of the architecture, since signaling usually involves scalability problems.

1.7.3 Dynamic Packet State

DPS encapsulates flow-state information within packets. This information is then used by core routers to treat flows according to their requirements. As core nodes read state information from packet headers, they do not need to remember it, hence the stateless core paradigm. For carrying state information, 4 bits from the Type of

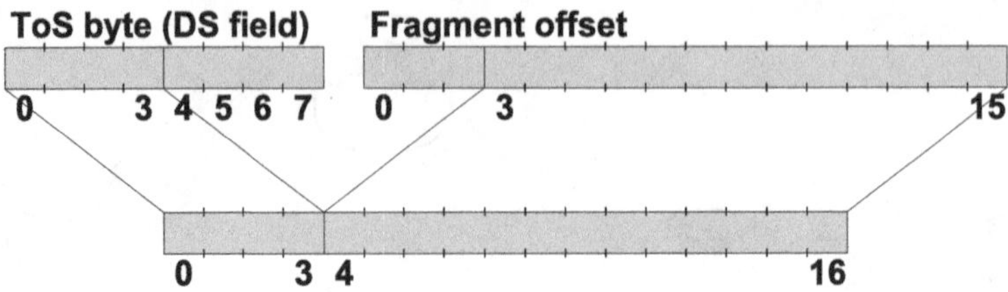

Fig. 1.15 IPv4 packet header bits used for signaling in DPS

Service (ToS) byte (or DS field) reserved for local and experimental purposes, and up to 13 bits from the Fragment Offset of IPv4 header fields are used. Figure 1.15 presents the scheme.

State information is injected into each packet upon arrival in the ingress node. Each subsequent node along the path processes the packet state and eventually updates both its internal state (general, not specific to each flow) and the packet state before forwarding it. The egress node removes the state from the packet header. Although end-users do not observe any difference in the protocol stack, the network devices have to deal with minimum incompatibility with IPv4 due to imposed changes in understanding certain packet header fields. Unfortunately, this triggers another problem with the implementation, as in order for DPS to operate, all nodes in the network must be DPS aware.

Additionally, for the purpose of admission control, DPS considers a lightweight signaling protocol, such as RSVP, to be used within the domain. The utilization of RSVP is, however, different than in case of IntServ, as here nodes do not need to keep per-flow states. Instead, only the aggregate reservation rate for each outgoing link is maintained. The use of an explicit signaling protocol is another reason why all nodes within the network must be DPS aware.

1.7.4 Caspian Networks/Anagran

Neither Caspian Networks nor Anagran specify a signaling method to be used. Most of the work is done by the device which measures the flow's traffic and assigns it to a certain CoS. However, for the Guaranteed Rate class, the rate needs to be fed to the network prior to transmission. In [41], it is stated that any kind of explicit signaling can be used, e.g., RSVP or ATM/Frame Relay signaling. Additionally, some information can be derived from examining the RTP protocol type, or user-defined traffic policies.

Although the exact signaling method is not directly specified, both Caspian Networks and Anagran propose in-line signaling. The former suggests including QoS requirements within the first packet of each new flow. Routers need to remember this information while the flow lasts. In case of Anagran, in the commercially available router FR-1000, the TIA-1039 [3] signaling protocol is used. TIA-1039 is an in-band signaling protocol which adds a small amount of extra information to each

TCP header. This allows a sender to communicate the rate of traffic that can be sent over the incoming TCP connection, and also allows the requestor to either accept this rate or request a lower rate.

1.7.5 Feedback and Distribution

Profile meters (see Fig. 1.2) measure the traffic for each end user and then feed the information to markers. Once they have this information, markers can assign certain packets to high or low priority (high when a flow does not exceed the guaranteed rate, and low otherwise). In case of congestion, packets with low priority are dropped first.

Given that the authors do not specify how certain blocks communicate with each other, it can be assumed that the communication is based on regular TCP/IP transmissions. It is true that putting profile meters close to the end users make them feasible; however, the volume of signaling data that needs to be sent through the network is significant. Therefore, Feedback and Distribution reduces the need to measure and maintain flow-state information on core routers at the cost of increased network load due to extensive signaling associated with each flow.

1.7.6 Flow-Based Differentiated Services

In Flow-Based Differentiated Services, much as in plain DiffServ, the signaling is embedded into packet headers. For this purpose, the Type of Service (ToS) field in the IPv4 packet header has been transformed into a DiffServ field (or DS field) [36]. A fixed number identifying a certain class is inserted into this field. It should be noted that flows do not communicate their specific QoS requirements. Instead, they choose one of the pre-defined classes (or the operator makes the choice) which most closely suit their needs.

In the original DiffServ, all packets having the same DS field number are treated as one instance, therefore they receive identical treatment. In Flow-Based DiffServ, the volume of reserved resources also varies according to the number of active flows in one class, hence the flow-awareness.

1.7.7 Flow-Aware Networking

For the same reasons as in Connectionless Approach, FAN does not require any kind of signaling, which is a significant advantage of this technology.

1.7.8 Flow-State-Aware Transport

ITU-T allows for the use of in-band or out-of-band signaling in FSA; however, in-band signaling is strongly recommended wherever possible. In-band signaling means that the messages are within the flow of the data packets and follow the path tied to the data packets. They are routed only through nodes that are in the data path. Out-of-band signaling means the messages are not in the same flow of data packets and may follow a different path. They usually visit other nodes in the network, either deliberately or not. Signaling packets and data packets must be recognizable by each FSA node; however, the exact method is yet to be specified.

Every signaling packet determines one of the signaling types. Recommendation [21] specifies five types of in-band signaling packets as follows:

- request,
- response,
- confirm,
- renegotiate,
- close.

Table 1.6 shows which types of signaling packets are required for preparing and managing the transmission of packets belonging to different classes of service in FSA. The *request packet* is the start of the signaling process, specifying the source demands. The FSA nodes answer with the *response packets*. For the GRS class, the *confirm packet* is necessary to inform the nodes that a source agrees to the offered rate, and to define the volume of bandwidth that should be reserved along the path. When the transmission is finished, GRS flows must close the session with the *close packet*, while for ARS, MRS and VRS, the nodes should time out the flow if no packets are seen for a given period of time. Finally, for ARS and VRS flows, the *renegotiate packets* are used to change the offered rate during the transmission.

1.7.9 Flow-Aggregate-Based Services

In general, FAbS adopts the signaling approach from FSA, i.e., in-band and out-of-band signaling. Authors of [25] claim that the signaling complexity of their solution,

Table 1.6 Flow setup signaling in FSA

	Request	Response	Confirm	Renegotiate	Close
ARS	✓	✓	×	✓	×
GRS	✓	✓	✓	×	✓
MRS	✓	Optional	×	×	×
VRS	✓	✓	×	✓	×

ARS—*Available Rate Service*, GRS—*Guaranteed Rate Service*, MRS—*Maximum Rate Service*, VRS—*Variable Rate Service*

Table 1.7 Signaling in flow-oriented approaches

Integrated services	RSVP
Connectionless approach	None
Dynamic packet state	Embedded into packet headers + RSVP
Caspian networks/Anagran	Not specified/TIA-1039
Feedback and distribution	Not specified
Flow-based DiffServ	DS field
Flow-Aware Networking	None
Flow-State-Aware transport	Extra messages within the flow of packets
Flow-aggregate-based services	Extra messages within the flow of packets + DiffProbe

FAbS, is better than FSA, although their arguments are unclear. The foundations may lie in the concept of DiffProbe signaling and in IDFA, which can reduce the amount of required signaling by smart aggregations. Nevertheless, since the technology is in its infancy, further analysis is required in the future.

1.7.10 Summary

Table 1.7 summarizes the signaling approaches in flow-aware QoS architectures. Two solutions, namely Connectionless Approach and FAN, do not use any signaling, which is one their greatest advantages. IntServ, FSA, FAbS provide detailed descriptions on how to use signaling. DPS and Flow-Based DiffServ propose embedding information inside the packet headers. Finally, Caspian Networks / Anagran and Feedback and Distribution noticed the need for signaling, although the precise means of providing it are not mentioned.

1.8 Summary

Flow-awareness as a method of providing QoS to IP networks has been a hot topic since the pioneering IntServ architecture was proposed by IETF. Several new approaches have been developed since. They use different methods to make it possible to differentiate traffic based on a flow entity. This is supported by the requirements of new applications, as they become more and more demanding, not only in terms of bandwidth. This section presents the most important and original suggestions and key features.

1.8.1 Complexity and Scalability Assessment

Since IntServ, it has become apparent that QoS architectures need to be assessed not only by the differentiation they can provide, but also by their complexity and

Table 1.8 Complexity and scalability assessment

Architecture	Data handling complexity	Signaling complexity	Scalability
Integrated services	High	High	Very Low
Connectionless approach	Medium	None	High
Dynamic packet state	High	Medium	Medium
Caspian networks/Anagran	High	Medium	Low
Feedback and distribution	Low	Medium	Medium
Flow-based differentiated services	Medium	Low	High
Flow-Aware Networking	Low	None	High
Flow-State-Aware transport	Medium	High	Medium
Flow-aggregate-based services	Medium	High	Medium

scalability. Complex architectures may be difficult to set-up and maintain, as well as being expensive while unscalable ones may not work in large-scale networks. Table 1.8 subjectively assesses all architectures with respect to data handling complexity, signaling complexity, and scalability.

Integrated Services are known to be complex and not scalable, mainly due to the need to maintain the flow-state in each node along the path. Additionally, the RSVP signaling protocol has been shown to be unscalable. Connectionless Approach does not use signaling between nodes, which contributes to its high scalability. Although each node operates independently, they need to perform complex measuring operations, which contributes to their medium data handling complexity. The Dynamic Packet State seems to be a scalable approach, since the core routers do not maintain state information. However, they need to be able to modify each packet on-the-fly which may be challenging.

Caspian Networks and Anagran maintain per-flow state in each router and perform complex measurements, which does not seem optimistic while assessing scalability. Nevertheless, the solution is on the market. The Feedback and Distribution data handling complexity is low, and its signaling may be a limiting factor on scalability. Flow-Based DiffServ retains a high scalability of standard DiffServ and low signaling complexity.

Flow-Aware Networking does not use signaling and proposes lightweight scheduling algorithms, which makes FAN a highly scalable QoS approach. Flow-State-Aware Transport technology is relatively similar to IntServ, although seems to be more scalable and less complex, mainly due to aggregations. Finally, Flow-Aggregate-Based Services improve FSA by introducing additional mechanisms. Authors of [25] claim that signaling complexity of FAbS is lower than that of FSA; however, the argumentation is unclear, especially in light of introducing DiffProbe.

1.8.2 Pros and Cons

Table 1.9 summarizes the pros and cons of all presented architectures.

IntServ is the first QoS architecture for IP networks, and its developers focused on providing diverse service differentiation options. This makes IntServ a model architecture in terms of QoS guarantees. However, the strong assurances came with the price of very low scalability. Connectionless Approach went in the opposite direction, by providing no signaling in the architecture while the nodes attempt to recognize flows on-the-fly. The lack of signaling, however, precludes on-demand service differentiation; in other words, users are not able to pay for better service. Additionally, automatic flow recognition does not always work. The architecture is not robust, as users may try to imitate other traffic types to get better treatment.

DPS relieves core routers from maintaining flow-state information which significantly contributes to the solution's scalability. However, data handling is complex since it involves modifications of the packet header in each node (even in the core), the CJVC algorithm, and distributed admission control with a relevant signaling protocol. Additionally, the architecture cannot be introduced gradually into the network as it requires slight changes in the IP functionality.

Anagran is a working technology, although its technical side lacks a detailed description. On the downside, routers need to maintain and constantly monitor the flow-state of each instance. This may be an easy task for small networks, although this approach is not suitable for high-speed core networks.

The Feedback and Distribution method simplifies the operation of core nodes, as they do not need to perform measurements. Instead, they read the information provided within the marked packets and perform actions accordingly. Profile measurements are performed only at the edge, which is feasible; however, this

Table 1.9 Pros and cons

Architecture	Pros	Cons
Integrated services	Real guarantees	Low scalability
Connectionless approach	No signaling	Implicit differentiation, user misbehavior vulnerability
Dynamic packet state	Stateless core	Complex data handling
Caspian networks/Anagran	Available product	Per-flow state and complex measurements in each node
Feedback and distribution	Simple core operations	Per-flow signaling, weak service differentiation
Flow-based differentiated services	DiffServ scalability	Fixed classes
Flow-Aware Networking	No signaling, simple	Weak service differentiation
Flow-State-Aware transport	Great service differentiation options	Complex signaling
Flow-Aggregate-Based services	Great service differentiation options	Complex signaling

information must be constantly fed to the network for each flow, which does not scale well. Additionally, only two classes of service are proposed (low priority and high priority), which does not provide service differentiation options such as those offered by IntServ or FSA.

Flow-Based Differentiated Services maintain the scalability of the original DiffServ, which is a significant advantage. Despite the fact that flow-based treatment is retained even inside fixed classes of service, DiffServ specific difficulties remain, such as a limited number of CoS, difficulties in carrying service across domains, admission control issues, and complexity of operation.

Flow-Aware Networking is a solution with many advantages. First of all, it does not require signaling, it is simple and efficient, and it can be introduced gradually into a network. Additionally, neither inter-operator nor user-operator agreements are needed. It provides differentiation based on the current flow peak rate and protects low-rate flows. However, in terms of congestion, the admission control block may force new flows (even those that should be prioritized) to wait for the network resources to become available again. Certain mechanisms mitigating this issue are presented in [12,23] and [11]. One weakness, resulting from the lack of signaling is poor service differentiation. Flows are divided only on low-rate and high-rate flows and treated accordingly.

Both FSA and FAbS provide high service differentiation. There are numerous parameters to be assigned to each flow and multiple classes of service. However, the signaling is relatively complex limiting the scalability. Fortunately, due to flow aggregations these architectures appear to be more scalable than IntServ.

1.8.3 Perspectives

All the flow-aware architectures presented are well thought-out, and they all have pros and cons, although their future is unclear as none have been widely implemented. Why have none become the dominant QoS architecture? To answer this question we need to look at the big picture of QoS. Xiao, in [51], shows that it is commercially difficult to introduce QoS into a network which works satisfactorily mainly due to over-provisioning. Currently, even highly demanding applications can achieve sufficiently good QoS, providing that access networks are not congested (core networks are never congested according to most major networks operators).

This situation has two consequences. First of all, it does not put pressure on telecom operators to introduce any differentiation mechanisms whatsoever. They argue that when a network works fine, it should be left at that, with additional bandwidth thrown occasionally. This approach is typical for most operators who believe that "bandwidth is infinite" and more capacity can always be provided. Secondly, in an uncongested network it is at least difficult to convince users to buy extra services while the standard service works just fine.

The lack of commercial revenue prospects inhibits the development of QoS architectures, not only flow-aware ones. Moreover, the network neutrality (NN) debate may become crucial in the future. NN is the vision of networks in which operators are not allowed to discriminate the traffic of certain users or applications in favor of others. Both proponents and opponents have strong arguments on their sides, as well as very influential allies. The outcome of the debate is unclear, although it is certain to impact the future QoS development. Therefore, QoS architectures are being assessed with respect to their neutrality, for instance Flow-Aware Networks in [14].

Does this mean that QoS architectures do not have a future? Not necessarily. We note that the progress in access network capacities is far greater than in core networks. The proposals of Fiber-To-The-Home (FTTH), Passive Optical Networks (PON) and other broadband access technologies provide increased bandwidth to end users, and the bandwidth is always consumed. In late 1980s when 155 Mbit/s links were first introduced, operators wondered whether they would ever need such capacity in the core. Today, we can see how wrong they were. In light of this fact, there may come a time when networks start to be congested on a regular basis, and the efficient and feasible QoS technology may become needed.

1.9 Conclusion

In the introduction, the flow-aware approach is explained and the time frames of different architectures are defined. In this survey, nine flow-aware QoS architectures have been presented and compared. Instead of presenting them one by one, we chose to compare certain important aspects of QoS architectures in general. Therefore, after a brief introduction of each architecture, we compared the understanding of a flow, proposed classes of service, mechanisms that provide service differentiation, and, finally, the signaling. In the summary, we identified the pros and cons of each architecture, as well as their complexity and scalability.

Based on this information, we conclude that it is difficult to single out a solution and claim that it is best suited to current and the future networks, as all proposals have their strong and weak sides.

1.10 Check Your Knowledge

1. Which QoS architecture was the first to be proposed for IP networks?
2. Define the 5-tuple.
3. Which protocol can be used for signaling in IntServ?
4. Give the names of the defined classes of service in the Flow-State-Aware Transport architecture.
5. How does Flow-Based DiffServ make the original architecture flow-aware?
6. Which flow-aware QoS architectures do not require signaling?
7. How is the traffic classified in the Connectionless Approach?
8. How are flows classified in Flow-Aware Networking?
9. Explain what is the main disadvantage of IntServ.
10. How does Dynamic Packet State provide signaling?

References

1. V. Alwayn, *Advanced MPLS Design and Implementation* (Cisco Press, Indianapolis, IN, USA, 2002)
2. Anagran, Eliminating Network Congestion Anywhere with Fast Flow Technology from Anagran, http://www.anagran.com, 2005, white Paper, downloaded on 10th June 2009
3. T.I. Association, *QoS Signaling for IP QoS Support*, Telecommunications Industry Association Std. TIA-1039, May 2006, recommendation TIA-1039
4. S. Blake, D. Black, M. Carlson, E. Davies, Z. Wang, W. Weiss, An Architecture for Differentiated Services, IETF RFC 2475, December 1998
5. B. Bloom, Space/time trade-offs in hash coding with allowable errors. Commun. ACM **13**, 422–426 (1970)
6. R. Braden, L. Zhang, Resource ReSerVation Protocol (RSVP)—Version 1 Message Processing Rules, IETF RFC 2209, September 1997
7. R. Braden, D. Clark, S. Shenker, Integrated Services in the Internet Architecture an Overview, IETF RFC 1633, June 1994
8. R. Braden, L. Zhang, S. Berson, S. Herzog, S. Jamin, Resource ReSerVation Protocol (RSVP)—Version 1 Functional Specification, IETF RFC 2205, September 1997
9. A. Chapman, H.T. Kung, Automatic quality of service in IP networks, in *Proc. Canadian Conference on Broadband Research, CCBR 1997*, Ottawa, Canada, pp. 184–189, April 1997
10. A. Demers, S. Keshav, S. Shenker, Analysis and simulation of a fair queueing algorithm, in *Proc. ACM SIGCOMM 1989* (ACM, New York, NY, USA, 1989), pp. 1–12
11. J. Domzal, A. Jajszczyk, The flushing mechanism for mbac in flow-aware networks, in *Proc. Next Generation Internet Networks NGI 2008*, pp. 77–83, 2008
12. J. Domzal, A. Jajszczyk, New congestion control mechanisms for flow-aware networks, in *Proc. IEEE International Conference on Communications ICC 2008*, Beijing, China, May 2008
13. J. Domzal, A. Jajszczyk, Approximate flow-aware networking, in *Proc. IEEE International Conference on Communications ICC 2009*, Dresden, Germany, June 2009
14. J. Domzal, A. Jajszczyk, Qos-aware net neutrality, in *Proc. First International Workshop on Neutral Access Networks (NEUTRAL)*, Cannes, France, August 2009
15. P. Goyal, H.M. Vin, H. Cheng, Start-time fair queuing: A scheduling algorithm for integrated services packet switching networks. IEEE/ACM Trans. Netw. **5**, 690–704 (1997)
16. J. Gozdecki, A. Jajszczyk, R. Stankiewicz, Quality of service terminology in IP networks. IEEE Commun. Mag. **41**(3), 153–159 (2003)
17. R. Guerin, S. Blake, S. Herzog, Aggregating RSVP-based QoS Requests, IETF Internet draft, November 1997
18. F. Halsall, *Computer Networking and the Internet* (Pearson Education Limited, Harlow, England, 2005)
19. J. Heinanen, F. Baker, W. Weiss, J. Wroclawski, Assured Forwarding PHB Group, IETF RFC 2597, June 1999
20. S. Herzog, RSVP Extensions for Policy Control, IETF RFC 2750, January 2000
21. ITU-T Recommendation Y.2121, Requirements for the support of flow-state-aware transport technology in an NGN, January 2008
22. V. Jacobson, K. Nichols, K. Poduri, An Expedited Forwarding PHB, IETF RFC 2598, June 1999
23. A. Jajszczyk, R. Wojcik, Emergency calls in flow-aware networks. Commun. Lett. IEEE **11**(9), 753–755 (2007)
24. J. Joung, Feasibility of supporting real-time traffic in DiffServ architecture, in *Proc. 5th International Conference on Wireless/Wired Internet Communications, WWIC 2007*, vol. 4517, Coimbra, Portugal, pp. 189–200, May 2007
25. J. Joung, J. Song, S.S. Lee, Flow-based QoS management architectures for the next generation network. ETRI J. **30**, 238–248 (2008)

26. K. Kompella, J. Lang, Procedures for Modifying the Resource reSerVation Protocol (RSVP), IETF RFC 3936, October 2004
27. R. Kuroda, M. Katsuki, A. Otaka, N. Miki, Providing flow-based quality-of-service control in a large-scale network, in *Proc. 9th Asia-Pacific Conference on Communications, APCC 2003*, vol. 2, Penang, Malaysia, pp. 740–744, September 2003
28. A. Kortebi, S. Oueslati, J. Roberts, MBAC algorithms for streaming flows in cross-protect, in *Proc. Next Generation Internet Networks EuroNGI Workshop*, Lund, Sweden, June 2004
29. A. Kortebi, L. Muscariello, S. Oueslati, J. Roberts, On the scalability of fair queueing, in *Proc. Third Workshop on Hot Topics in Networks, ACM HotNets-III 2004*, San Diego, USA, November 2004
30. A. Kortebi, S. Oueslati, J.W. Roberts, Cross-protect: implicit service differentiation and admission control, in *Proc. High Performance Switching and Routing, HPSR 2004*, Phoenix, AZ, USA, pp. 56–60, 2004
31. A. Kortebi, L. Muscariello, S. Oueslati, J. Roberts, Evaluating the number of active flows in a scheduler realizing fair statistical bandwidth sharing, in *Proc. International Conference on Measurement and Modeling of Computer Systems, ACM SIGMETRICS 2005*, Banff, Canada, June 2005
32. A. Kortebi, S. Oueslati, J. Roberts, Implicit service differentiation using deficit round robin, in *Proc. 19th International Teletraffic Congress, ITC 2005*, Beijing, China, August/September 2005
33. J.-S. Li, C.-S. Mao, Providing flow-based proportional differentiated services in class-based DiffServ routers. in *IEE Proceedings on Communications*, vol. 151, pp. 82–88, February 2004
34. A. Mankin, F. Baker, B. Braden, S. Bradner, M. O'Dell, A. Romanow, A. Weinrib, L. Zhang, Resource ReSerVation Protocol (RSVP)—Version 1 Applicability Statement Some Guidelines on Deployment, IETF RFC 2208, September 1997
35. B. Nandy, N. Seddigh, A. Chapman, J.H. Salim, A connectionless approach to providing QoS in IP networks, in *Proc. 8th Conference on High Performance Networking, IFIP 1998*, Vienna, Austria, September 1998
36. K. Nichols, S. Blake, F. Baker, D. Black, Definition of the Differentiated Services Field (DS Field) in the IPv4 and IPv6 Headers, IETF RFC 2474, December 1998
37. S. Oueslati, J. Roberts, A new direction for quality of service: Flow-aware networking, in *Proc. 1st Conference on Next Generation Internet Networks - Traffic Engineering, NGI 2005*, Rome, Italy, 2005
38. J. Polk, S. Dhesikan, A Resource Reservation Protocol (RSVP) Extension for the Reduction of Bandwidth of a Reservation Flow, IETF RFC 4495, May 2006
39. K. Psounis, R. Pan, B. Prabhakar, Approximate fair dropping for variable-length packets. Micro IEEE **21**, 48–56 (2001)
40. L. Roberts, Internet founder ponders the web's future. IT Professional **2**, 16–20 (2000)
41. L. Roberts, Micro-Flow Management, US Patent US 2007/0 115 825 A1, May 24, 2007, caspian Networks, INC, US patent application no. 2007/0115825 A1
42. L. Roberts, A. Henderson, System, Method, and Computer Program Product for IP Flow Routing, US Patent 2007/0 171 825 A1, July 26, 2007, anagran, INC., US patent application no. 2007/0171825 A1
43. J. Roberts, S. Oueslati, Quality of service by flow aware networking. Philos. Trans. R. Soc. Lond. **358**, 2197–2207 (2000)
44. M. Shreedhar, G. Varghese, Efficient fair queuing using deficit round-robin. IEEE/ACM Trans. Netw. **4**, 375–385 (1996)
45. J. Song, S. Lee, Y.S. Kim, DiffProbe: one way delay measurement for asynchronous network and control mechanism in BcN architecture, in *Proc. 8th international conference on Advanced Communication Technology, ICACT 2008*, vol. 1, Phoenix Park, Republic of Korea, pp. 677–682, February 2006
46. I. Stoica, Stateless Core: A Scalable Approach for Quality of Service in the Internet, Ph.D. dissertation, Carnegie Mellon University, Pittsburgh, USA, December 2000

47. I. Stoica, H. Zhang, Providing guaranteed services without per flow management, in *Proc. ACM SIGCOMM 1999*, New York, NY, USA, pp. 81–94, 1999
48. I. Stoica, S. Shenker, H. Zhang, Core-stateless fair queueing: achieving approximately fair bandwidth allocations in high speed networks. ACM SIGCOMM Comput. Commun. Rev. **28**(4), 118–130 (1998)
49. R. Wójcik, A. Jajszczyk, Flow oriented approaches to QoS assurance. ACM Comput. Surv. **44**(1), 5:1–5:37 (2012)
50. J. Wroclawski, The Use of RSVP with IETF Integrated Services, IETF RFC 2210, September 1997
51. X. Xiao, *Technical, Commercial and Regulatory Challenges of QoS: An Internet Service Model Perspective* (Morgan Kaufmann Publishers, San Francisco, CA, USA, 2008)
52. L. Zhang, Virtual clock: a new traffic control algorithm for packet switching networks, in *Proc. ACM SIGCOMM 1990* (ACM, New York, NY, USA, 1990), pp. 19–29

Flow-Aware Networking

2

QoS is . . . Quite often Stupid!

— James Roberts

The success of the Internet lies in its simplicity; however, this comes at a cost of only best effort non-differentiated service. For years, institutions such as the IETF have been trying to introduce a QoS architecture to the current IP network. Unfortunately, the proposed QoS models, i.e., IntServ [6] and DiffServ [4, 37], are not suitable for the Internet as a whole. To provide a service at a reasonable level, under the terms of congestion, some priorities and discriminations must be imposed. The aforementioned architectures propose the use of a reservation protocol and a packet marking scheme, respectively; however, these solutions require proper inter-domain agreements, complex router implementations, and, most of all, end-user compliance. Besides IntServ and DiffServ, many other QoS architectures have been proposed for IP networks.

An efficient and robust QoS architecture for IP networks requires that the user-network interface remains the same as today, no signaling protocol or packet marking is introduced, and no new user-operator or operator-operator agreements are signed. These constraints are very strict, yet they have been met. This chapter introduces a novel approach to achieving QoS guarantees in the Internet—Flow-Aware Networking, or FAN for short.

The description of FAN starts with Sect. 2.1 which shows why the new QoS architecture is needed. Sect. 2.2 describes the basic concepts of FAN. Sections 2.3 and 2.4 introduce the flow-aware approach and a Cross-Protect (XP) router, respectively. Section 2.5 describes one of the FAN-specific mechanisms i.e., measurement-based admission control, while fair queuing algorithms are presented and compared in Sect. 2.6. Section 2.7 briefly surveys other mechanisms and architectures which have been proposed for Flow-Aware Networks.

J. Domżał et al., *Guide to Flow-Aware Networking*, Computer Communications and Networks, https://doi.org/10.1007/978-3-030-57153-5_2

2.1 The Need for a New QoS Architecture

IETF introduced two ideas on how to assure QoS. Chronologically, the first was Integrated Services. IntServ has many advantages, such as real (as opposed to statistical) assurances, easy control in nodes, use of a reservation protocol, and the option to create various traffic profiles. However, there are certain disadvantages, which make IntServ unsuitable for larger networks. These include maintaining information about all flows in every node and demanding that end-users explicitly define required transmission parameters. These pros and cons make IntServ a good solution for dealing with a small network, where all the end-users are known, traffic is mostly defined, and every router in the network can be easily configured by a single network operator.

To overcome the scalability issue, IETF introduced a new idea—the Differentiated Services. At the cost of certain constraints, DiffServ avoids the problems that eventually halted the development of its predecessor. That is why in DiffServ the assurances are statistical and the admission control blocks are only placed at the borders of each DiffServ domain. Moreover, the inner nodes do not keep the flow information, which suits it better to larger networks; however, the scalability issue is not completely overcome. Still, all routers in a domain must be pre-configured so that the per-hop behavior matches the actual classes of service which are provided inside the domain. Although DiffServ is more flexible and scalable than its predecessor, it still has features which make it unsuited for extra large networks like the Internet.

It can be said that IntServ and DiffServ represent a trade-off between fine service granularity and scalability. Over the years, many attempts to alleviate this relationship have been proposed, including: combined use of IntServ and DiffServ, or new and better congestion control mechanisms cooperating with the service isolation provided by DiffServ. However, no solution has attracted enough attention to be widely implemented and used.

2.2 Basic Concepts of FAN

Flow-Aware Networking is a new direction for QoS assurance in IP networks. The original idea was initially introduced by J. Roberts et al. in [5,43] and then presented as a complete system in 2004 [32, 42]. Their intention was to design a novel QoS architecture that would be possible to use in networks of all sizes, including the global IP network—the Internet. In [38] the belief that adequate performance can be assured much more simply than in classical QoS architectures, and more reliably than in over-provisioned best effort networks is expressed.

The goal of FAN is to enhance the current IP network by improving its performance under heavy congestion. To achieve this, certain traffic management mechanisms to control link sharing are proposed, namely measurement-based admission control [38] and fair scheduling with priorities [31, 32]. The former

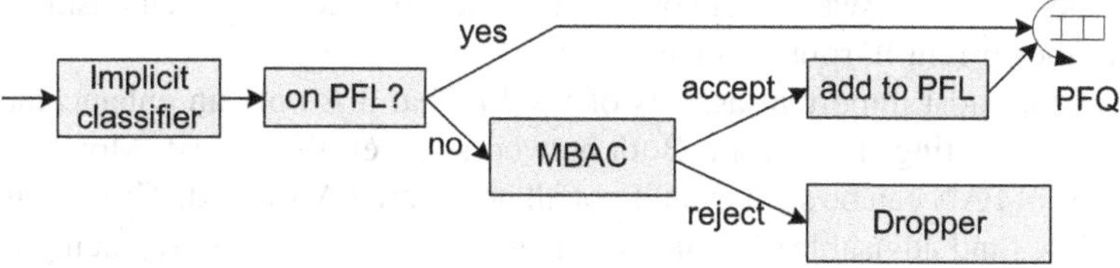

Fig. 2.1 Operation of FAN

is used to keep the flow rates sufficiently high to provide a minimal level of performance for each flow in case of overload. The latter realizes the fair sharing of link bandwidth while ensuring negligible packet latency for flows emitting at lower rates. All the new functionalities are performed by a unique router, named the Cross-Protect router. This device alone is responsible for providing admission control and fair queuing.

Figure 2.1 illustrates the operation of FAN. All incoming packets are first classified into flows. The flow identification process is implicit and its goal is not to divide flows into different classes, but only to create an instance on which the service differentiation will be performed. Then, all the flows that are currently in progress, i.e., are present on the Protected Flow List (PFL), are forwarded unconditionally, whereas all new flows are subject to admission control. The admission control in FAN is measurement based (MBAC) which implies that the accept/reject decisions are based only on the current link congestion status. If a new flow is accepted, it is put onto the PFL list and then all successive packets from this flow are forwarded without checking the status of the outgoing link by MBAC.

In FAN, admission control and service differentiation are implicit. In classic explicit service differentiation architectures, user requirements are signaled to the network and the nodes perform differentiation actions based on the information received. For example, the provision of better quality is a consequence of the explicit identification of a certain transmission. On the contrary, implicit service differentiation performs differentiation actions based on traffic characteristics and network measurements.

In FAN, there is no need for *a priori* traffic specification, as well as no class of service distinction. Both streaming and elastic flows achieve the necessary QoS without any mutual detrimental effect. Nevertheless, streaming and elastic flows are implicitly identified inside the FAN network. This classification, however, is based solely on the current flow peak rate. All flows emitting at lower rates than the current fair rate are referred to as streaming flows, and the packets from those flows are prioritized. The remaining flows are referred to as elastic flows.

FAN is intended to be suited even to the whole Internet. This is due to a number of constraints that have been imposed by the designers. First of all, nodes do not need to exchange any information among themselves; they do not even need any explicit information about the flows. All information is gathered through local measurements. Flow-Aware Networking is based on the XP mechanism, which enhances the current IP router functionality.

One of the most important aspects of FAN is that it is only an enhancement of the currently existing IP network. Both networks can easily coexist. Moreover, the advantages of FAN can be seen even if not all nodes are FAN based. This means that it is possible (and advisable) to improve the network gradually by replacing nodes, starting with those that are attached to the most heavily congested links.

2.3 Flow-Aware Approach

FAN is flow oriented. This means that traffic management is based on user-defined flows. The definition of a flow in Flow-Aware Networking comes from [38]: "By flow we mean a flight of datagrams, localized in time and space and having the same unique identifier". The datagrams are localized in space as they are observed at a certain interface (e.g., on a router) and in time, as they must be spaced by no more than a certain interval, which is usually a few seconds. The space localization means that a typical flow has many instances, one at every interface on its path.

The identifier is obtained from certain IP header fields, including IP addresses and some other fields, e.g., the IPv6 *flow label*. One idea is to allow users to freely define flows that correspond to a particular instance of some application. The intention is to allow users as much flexibility as possible in defining what the network should consider as a single flow. Such an approach is surely beneficial for the user; however, it always introduces the possibility of malicious behavior. A flow label may also be deduced from IPv4 header fields. Typically, it could be a standard 5-tuple, though this approach limits the flexibility, allowing users no control in defining their flows.

All flows in FAN are divided into either streaming or elastic, hence two classes of service. This distinction is implicit, which means that the system categorizes the flows based on their current behaviour. There is no need for *a priori* traffic specification as the classification is based solely on the current flow peak rate. All flows emitting at lower rates than the current fair rate[1] are referred to as streaming flows, and packets from those flows are prioritized. The remaining flows are referred to as elastic flows. The association of a flow with a certain class is not permanent. If a flow, initially classified as streaming, surpasses the current fair rate value, it is degraded to the elastic flow category. Analogously, a flow is promoted to streaming if at any time it emits at a lower rate than the current fair rate. Note that both factors, i.e. flow bitrate and current fair rate, can change.

The assumption of FAN was to provide two classes of service. For low-rate flows which are typically associated with streaming transmissions, the streaming type is considered. All flows classified as streaming receive prioritized treatment—packets of those flows are sent through priority queues, hence, small delays and

[1] Fair rate is one of the measured indicators of the link condition and is defined in Sect. 2.6.

delay variations. For the rest of the flows, proper fair queuing algorithms provide fair bandwidth sharing which cannot be assured with standard FIFO-based queuing disciplines. Finally, the distinctive advantage of FAN is that both streaming and elastic flows achieve sufficiently good QoS without any mutual detrimental effect.

2.4 Cross-Protect Mechanism

To install FAN in a network, an upgrade of current IP routers is required. Figure 2.2 shows the concept diagram for an XP router, the standard interconnecting device in FAN. FAN adds only two blocks to the standard IP router, namely the admission control and scheduling blocks. The former is placed in the incoming line cards of the router, whereas the latter is situated in the outgoing line cards.

Admission control is responsible for accepting or rejecting the incoming packets based on the current congestion status. The purpose of scheduling is twofold: it provides prioritized forwarding of streaming flows, and assures fair sharing of the residual bandwidth by all elastic flows. If a packet is allowed, the flow associated with it may be added to the PFL, and then all forthcoming packets from this flow will be accepted. The admission control block realizes the measurement based admission control functionality which is described in Sect. 2.5. The scheduler is responsible for queue management. It is a very important block as it has to ascertain that all flows are treated equally. All flows that currently have at least one packet in a queue are added to the Active Flow List (AFL). Detailed information on the scheduling algorithms is provided in Sect. 2.6.

Naming FAN devices as "Cross-Protect routers" is a consequence of the mutual cooperation and protection which exist between both extra blocks. The admission control block limits the number of active flows in a router, which essentially

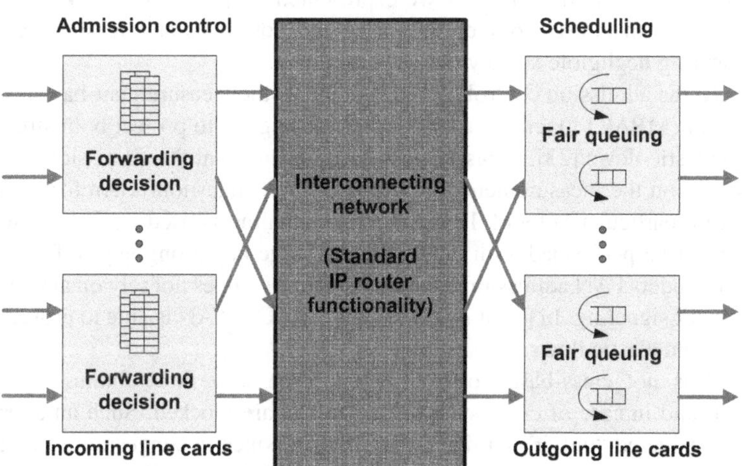

Fig. 2.2 Concept diagram of a Cross-Protect router

improves the queuing algorithm functionality, and reduces its performance requirements. It is vital that queuing mechanisms operate quickly, as for extremely high speed links the available processing time is strictly limited. On the other hand, the scheduling block provides admission control with information on the congestion status on the outgoing interfaces. This information is derived based on, for example, current occupancy of the queues. This mutual protection contributes to a smaller protected flow list and active flow list sizes, which significantly improves FAN's scalability.

The advantage of XP routers is that they may be introduced progressively, starting from the most heavily loaded links. In this scenario, the overall network efficiency will gradually improve. However, obviously, for the best performance, all nodes in a network should be FAN-aware. Incremental replacement is possible because each XP router operates independently and transparently to other standard IP routers. There is no need for a signaling protocol, end-user compliance or any inter-network agreements. Moreover, in [38], the belief that in FAN there is "virtually no requirement for standardization" with an exception only for an "agreed convention for defining the flow identifier" is expressed. The lack of standardization is possible because of the local nature of the XP router functionality. As long as nodes perform well and maintain their functions, the exact method of their operation is insignificant. Lastly, once developed and implemented, the proposed mechanisms are thought to be particularly inexpensive.

2.5 Measurement-Based Admission Control

Admission control is a mechanism which allows blocking of some portion of traffic should congestion occur. This ensures that the quality of currently realized transmissions will not deteriorate below a certain threshold. The benefits of using admission control in IP networks were presented in [2, 35] and [44]. In FAN, admission control is used to keep the maximum flow rates at a reasonable level, while ensuring negligible latency for low-rate flows.

In FAN, the admission control block implements the measurement-based admission control (MBAC) functionality [26], and is designed to protect both streaming [27] and elastic flows [23]. Measurement-based means that the admission decision relies solely on the measurements of outgoing link congestion. Therefore, MBAC is local to a particular network link. Since no signaling is used in FAN networks, MBAC must be performed with minimal knowledge about ongoing traffic. All of the above renders FAN admission control implicit, as it does not rely on any explicit user-network signaling. In [3], it is shown that MBAC in FAN is able to protect both streaming and elastic flows.

MBAC is not class-based or user-based: each new flow obtains the same treatment, and in case of congestion all new flows are blocked. Such an approach may be considered "unfair" service differentiation, since in congestion some flows are admitted and some are blocked. However, MBAC treats all flows equally, i.e. (a) the decision to accept or reject the traffic affects all new incoming flows, not just some of them, and (b) admission decisions are implicit, based only on internal measurements.

MBAC performs actions based on information derived from the scheduling algorithms. Two parameters are constantly measured, i.e., fair rate (FR) and priority load (PL). Following [32], "fair rate is an estimation of the rate currently realized by backlogged flows", and represents the amount of link bandwidth guaranteed to be available for a single flow, should it be necessary. Similarly, "priority load is the sum of the lengths of priority packets incoming to the router in a certain interval divided by the duration of that interval", and shows the amount of data that is prioritized. The manner of calculating both indicators is a feature of the scheduling algorithm, and is presented in Sect. 2.6 where fair queuing algorithms, suitable for FAN, are described.

Figure 2.3 illustrates the admission decision in MBAC. Each router has two predefined threshold values for FR and PL which are to be maintained, namely: the minimum value of FR (minFR) and the maximum value of PL (maxPL). If the current FR is lower than minFR or if the current PL is greater than maxPL, the incoming flow is blocked. Otherwise, when in the admission region, the new flow is admitted.

The user-defined flows discussed earlier appear as the most appropriate entity on which the admission control should be performed. Admitted flows and those currently in progress are registered in PFL. If the flow identity of a newly arriving packet is already on the PFL, the packet is forwarded. If not, the flow is subject to admission control. If the outgoing link is congested, the packet is simply discarded. In the absence of congestion, the packet is forwarded, and its flow may be added to the PFL. This decision on whether to include the flow on the PFL or not is probabilistic. The flow is added with the probability p, e.g., $p = \frac{1}{10}$. This procedure aims to decrease the size of the PFL, as with high probabilities very short flows (a few packets) will not be added to the PFL. Flows with tens of packets and more will be added to the PFL eventually.

In the simplest example, the admission criteria could rely only on PL and FR measurements. For instance, FR and PL thresholds could be set to 0.1 and 0.7,

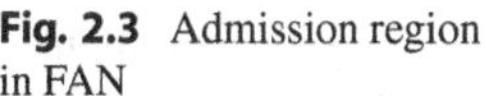
Fig. 2.3 Admission region in FAN

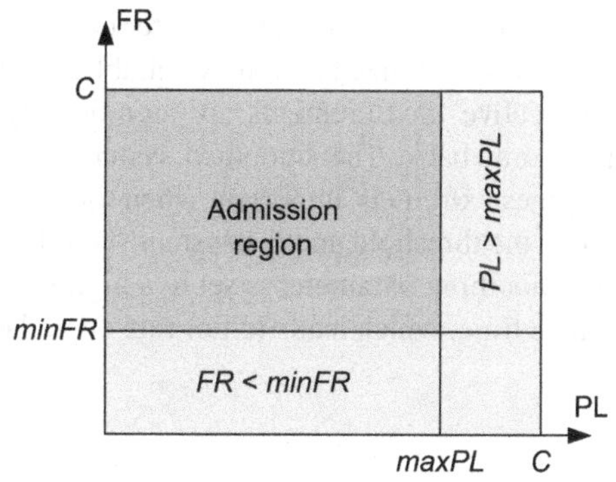

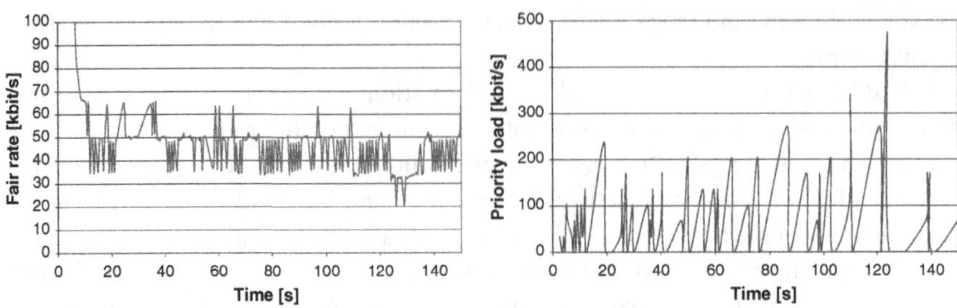

Fig. 2.4 FR and PL measurements; no exponential smoothing

respectively. This means that packets of flows not registered in the PFL are discarded if the current FR is lower than 10% of the link capacity or if the amount of priority traffic exceeds 70% of the link capacity. However, the MBAC algorithm may also be based on some additional factors. In [27], such an algorithm is proposed. This algorithm also takes into account the measured aggregate load which should be less than a predefined threshold for new flows to be admitted. The ns-2 [36] simulations have shown that high link utilization can be achieved while maintaining a low packet delay and loss rate.

Figure 2.4 shows examples of FR and PL measurements in FAN-based routers, over time, using the Priority Fair Queuing scheduling algorithm. The experiment is performed over a 1 Mbit/s link with the offered load exceeding the link capacity by almost double. Strong variations in the values measured can easily be observed. These appear due to the extremely dynamic nature of packet-based transmission. In order to make the measurements more reliable, the notion of exponential smoothing was proposed in [30] and [27]. The smoothing formula is presented in Eq. 2.1, in which α represents the smoothing parameter.

$$\text{new value} = \alpha \times \text{old value} + (1 - \alpha) \times \text{new measurement} \tag{2.1}$$

Figures 2.5 and 2.6 show the same measurements as in Fig. 2.4, but with the additional use of a smoothing parameter of 0.5 and 0.9, respectively. The measurements seem to be stabilized and more reliable, because the amplitude differences between consecutive measurements are significantly decreased. However, smoothing also has a drawback. The smoothed system reacts much more slowly to changes. This becomes extremely important when the currently measured values of fair rate drop below the threshold and the system should start to block incoming new flows. When the smoothing parameter is set to a high value, the system is not able to respond for quite a time, which leads to fair rate degradations.

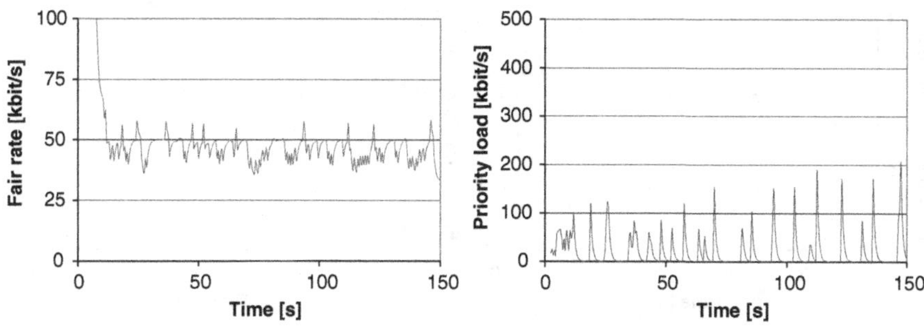

Fig. 2.5 FR and PL measurements; exponential smoothing $\alpha = 0.5$

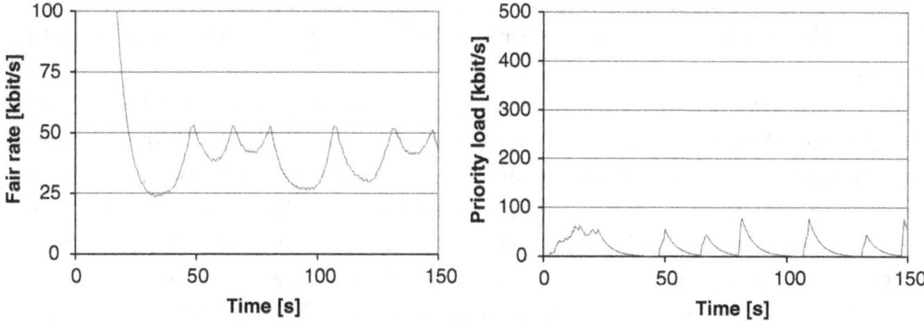

Fig. 2.6 FR and PL measurements; exponential smoothing $\alpha = 0.9$

2.6 Fair Queuing with Priority

Queue management in FAN is realized in the scheduling block of the XP router. Fair queuing (FQ) ensures that link bandwidth is shared equally, without relying on cooperative behavior by end users. This is a different approach to that currently used in IP routers, where, usually, a FIFO queue is implemented. The FIFO queuing discipline does not ensure fair sharing of the link bandwidth. Instead, all flows are limited to the same percentage of their nominal rates. Figure 2.7 shows the behavior of FIFO and FQ queues when two flows struggle for link resources.

The bottleneck link capacity is 3 Mbit/s, and the red and blue UDP flows[2] have nominal rates of 2 Mbit/s and 4 Mbit/s, respectively. Between the 4th and 8th second of the simulation time, both flows are in progress. The FIFO queue limits the rates of both flows to approximately 50% of their desired rates, allowing the faster flow to utilize almost twice as much bandwidth as its competitor. The FQ discipline, which is represented in this example by Priority Fair Queuing, limits both flows to the same rate: 1.5 Mbit/s, which is exactly half of the total link capacity. It should be noted

[2]UDP flows were chosen as they are only shaped by the queuing algorithms, and not by the protocol behavior. This allows us to present solely the features of the queuing disciplines.

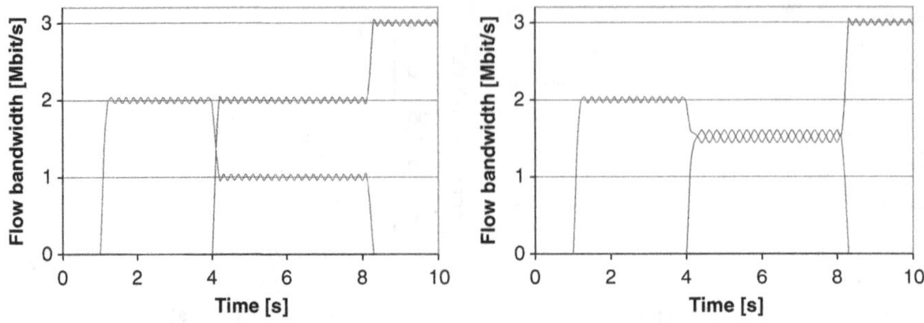

Fig. 2.7 FIFO (left) and FQ (right) scheduling comparison

that the order in which flows appear on the link is irrelevant to the outcome of fair queuing.

There are two per-flow fair queuing algorithms proposed for FAN: Priority Fair Queuing (PFQ) and Priority Deficit Round Robin (PDRR) . Both algorithms have, logically, one priority queue and a secondary queuing system. They are intended to realize fair sharing of link bandwidth to elastic flows and priority service to streaming flows. The latter (PDRR) was primarily suggested to speed up commercial adoption since it improves the algorithm complexity from $O(\log(N))$ to $O(1)$, where N is the number of currently active flows. However, it has been shown that both scheduling algorithms achieve a similar performance [29].

Regardless of the algorithm used, it has been shown in [28] and [29] that fair queuing in FAN is scalable, since the complexity does not increase with link capacity. Moreover, fair queuing is feasible as long as link loads are not allowed to attain saturation levels, which is asserted by admission control. The latest FAN architecture has been proposed in [16], based on the Approximate Fair Dropping [41] queuing algorithm. This architecture is referred to as Approximate Flow-Aware Networking or AFAN for short, and aims at further simplifying the queuing processes. As shown in [16], the enqueue and dequeue operations in AFAN are realized in a simpler way than in the previous proposals for PFQ and PDRR.

2.6.1 Priority Fair Queuing

A large number of queuing algorithms have been proposed in the literature. The Start-time Fair Queuing (SFQ) [24] is particularly well suited to the FAN architecture. However, in [32], an enhancement of the SFQ algorithm is proposed. This modified queuing discipline is referred to as Priority Fair Queuing. PFQ differs from SFQ by the fact that it gives head of line priority to packets of flows whose rate is lower than the current fair rate. Therefore, PFQ implicitly prioritizes packets of low-rate flows, which are streaming flows in FAN.

The PFQ algorithm is based on the Push-In, First-Out (PIFO) queue. PIFO is the shorthand for a sorting algorithm that allows a packet to join the queue at any

```
1  if PIFO congested, reject packet at head of longest backlog
2  if F ∈ flow_list
3  begin
4      backlog (F) += L
5      if bytes ≥ MTU
6          push {packet, flow_time_stamp} to PIFO
7      else begin
8          push {packet, virtual_time} to PIFO behind P; update P
9          (counter of priority bytes += L)
10         bytes (F) += L
11     end
12     flow_time_stamp(F) += L
13 end
14 else begin
15     push {packet, virtual_time} to PIFO behind P; update P
16     (counter of priority bytes += L)
17     if flow_list is not saturated
18     begin
19         add flow F
20         flow_time_stamp(F) = virtual_time + L
21         backlog (F) = L
22         bytes (F) = L
23     end
24 end
```

Fig. 2.8 PFQ packet arrival operations [32]

position and always serves the packet at the head of the line. The position that a packet is inserted into is determined by a time stamp, according to which packets are sorted within the queue. Therefore, every element in the PIFO queue has the form *packet, time stamp*, where *packet* represents the data relating to the packet (e.g., a memory location pointer), and *time stamp* is a packet "start tag" determined by the PFQ algorithm.

Figure 2.8 shows the pseudocode that is executed on each packet arrival, as proposed in [32]. First, it is necessary to test whether the queue is congested, and if so, which packet should be dropped. Dropping the packet at the head of the longest backlog is one proposal, although different criteria are possible. If a flow is active (line 2), its *backlog* is increased by the size of the packet (L). The packet is given priority when the cumulative volume of transmitted bytes is lower than the maximum transfer unit (MTU) (lines 7–11). Then, the packet is enqueued with the $time\_stamp$ of $virtual\_time$, which is essentially the head of the queue. When the transmitted byte count is greater than MTU, the packet is placed in a PIFO queue, according to its nominal place. Lines 14–24 represent the situation in which the arriving flow is not active. Then, the packet is given a priority (line 15), and providing that the PFL is not saturated (line 17), the flow is added to the PFL (lines 18–23).

```
1   if PIFO is now empty
2       remove all flows from flow_list
3   else begin
4       backlog (F) − = L
5       serve packet at head of line
6       next_time_stamp designates time stamp of this packet
7       if next_time_stamp ≠ virtual_time
8       begin
9           virtual_time = next_time_stamp
10          for all flows f ∈ flow_list
11          begin
12              if flow_time_stamp(f) ≤ virtual_time
13                  remove f from flow_list
14          end
15      end
16  end
```

Fig. 2.9 PFQ packet departure operations [32]

Figure 2.9 shows the operations performed after each packet departure. If the PIFO queue is empty, obviously all flows must be removed from the PFL (lines 1–2). Otherwise, the next packet in the queue is prepared (lines 4–6): the flow backlog is reduced and the $next\_time\_stamp$ is set to this packet's $time\_stamp$. If $virtual\_time$ is equal to the $next\_time\_stamp$ (line 7) no further operations are required, as $virtual\_time$ has not changed since the last packet departure. If it has changed (lines 8–15), the $virtual\ time$ is updated, and flows that become inactive (i.e., their $flow\_time\_stamp$ is less than or equal to the new value of the $virtual\_time$), are removed from the PFL.

To provide the admission control block with a proper congestion status, PL and FR indicators are measured periodically. An estimation of the priority load is derived from Eq. 2.2. Variables $pb(t)$ represent the values of a counter, incremented on the arrival of each priority packet by its length in bytes, at time t. (t_1, t_2) is a measured time interval (in seconds), and C is the link bit rate. The priority load, therefore, represents the sum of the lengths of priority packets incoming to the router in a certain time interval, divided by the duration of that interval, and normalized with respect to the link capacity.

$$PL = \frac{(pb(t_2) - pb(t_1)) \times 8}{C(t_2 - t_1)} \tag{2.2}$$

The smoothing parameter α is applied such that:

$$PL(n) = \alpha \times PL(n-1) + (1-\alpha) \times measured\_PL(n)$$

where $PL(n)$ is the value of PL in the n-th iteration and the $measured\_PL$ is the value calculated from the formula (2.2) in the n-th iteration.

Equation 2.3 is used to calculate the fair rate, which is an estimation of the rate currently realized by backlogged flows. To estimate the fair rate, a fictitious flow emitting single byte packets is considered. In an idle period, the fictitious flow could transmit at the link rate. Otherwise, the number of bytes that could have been transmitted is given directly by the evolution of virtual time. In Eq. 2.3, $vt(t)$ is the value of virtual time at time t, (t_1, t_2) is the measurement interval, S is the total idle time during the interval, and C is the link bit rate.

$$FR = \frac{max\{S \times C, (vt(t_2) - vt(t_1)) \times 8\}}{t_2 - t_1} \tag{2.3}$$

The smoothing parameter β for calculating the values of FR is used in a similar way to the α parameter for PL.

When the measured link is lightly loaded, the first term of the max$\{\dots\}$ formula is significant, as the fictitious flow uses all residual link capacity. When the link is busy, the second term becomes important, as it approximately measures the throughput achieved by any flow that is continuously backlogged in this time interval.

As mentioned, both congestion indicators are calculated periodically. Considering the extremely dynamic variations in priority packet occurrence, the period between two consecutive measurements of the priority load is advised to be several milliseconds, whereas a several-hundred-millisecond period is sufficient for estimating the fair rate. Regarding frequent measurements of the congestion indicators in PFQ, the complexity may be an issue, especially in the core. However, all the mathematical calculations in Eqs. 2.2 and 2.3 are very simple, and not time consuming. Moreover, the complexity of enqueuing and dequeuing operations of PFQ, like SFQ, is logarithmic with respect to the number of active flows, which is essentially limited by the admission control block.

2.6.2 Priority Deficit Round Robin

PFQ was the first queuing algorithm proposed for FAN. In fact, simulations have shown that PFQ performs well and cooperates with the admission control block correctly [32]. Furthermore, the scalability of PFQ has been demonstrated by means of trace driven simulations and analytical modeling in [28] and [29]. However, PFQ can be advantageously replaced by an adaptation of the Deficit Round Robin (DRR) [45] algorithm. An enhancement to DRR, called Priority Deficit Round Robin, is presented in [31].

PDRR retains the low complexity of DRR, while at the same time providing low latency for streaming flows. PDRR complexity is constant (O(1)); therefore, it does not increase with the growing number of active flows (PFQ complexity was logarithmic with respect to the number of active flows). PDRR enhances the DRR algorithm in that it introduces the priority queue, which is used for low rate flows. Figure 2.10 shows the operations performed by PDRR on each packet arrival.

```
1   on arrival of packet P
2   if no free buffers left then
3       FreeBuffer()
4   i = ExtractFlow( P)
5   if (i ∉ PFL)
6   begin
7       add i to PFL
8       DC_i = 0
9       ByteCount_i = Size( P)
10      Enqueue( PQ, P)
11  end
12  else begin
13      ByteCount_i + = Size( P)
14      if (ByteCount_i ≤ Q_i) then
15          Enqueue( PQ, P)
16      else
17          Enqueue( Queue_i, P)
18  end
```

Fig. 2.10 PDRR packet arrival operations [31]

Initially, if the buffer for incoming packets is full, a certain packet must be selected for dropping (lines 1–3). PDRR does not specify which dropping mechanism should be used. One policy would be to drop packets at the head of the flow with the longest backlog; however, this approach is not mandatory. If packet P does not belong to an active flow, a new flow is added to PFL, the Deficit Count (DC) and Byte Count counters are properly initiated, and the packet is forwarded to the priority queue (PQ) (lines 5–11).

If an arriving packet belongs to a flow currently on the flow list, it may be placed at the end of his flow queue (line 17) or in the priority queue, providing that $ByteCount\_i \leq Q\_i$ (lines 14–15). The variable $ByteCount\_i$ holds the number of bytes inserted in the queue for flow i, while Q_i represents flow quantum: the cumulative number of bytes allowed for transmission after every cycle of the algorithm. Although DRR allows for differentiation in resource allocation, by means of assigning different quanta Q_i for different flows, the FAN fairness concept implies that the same quanta should be used for each flow.

In PDRR, the FR is computed from the following formula:

$$FR = \frac{max\{S \times C, fair\_bytes \times 8\}}{t_2 - t_1} \tag{2.4}$$

where *fair_bytes* is the number of bytes which could be sent by a fictitious permanently backlogged flow during the time interval (t_1, t_2), S is the total length of inactivity in the transmission during the (t_1, t_2) period, and C is the link bit rate.

The PL is estimated in the same way as in the PFQ. Moreover, the smoothing parameters are used in a similar way to that in the PFQ.

```
1   while TRUE do
2   begin
3      while PQ not empty do
4      begin
5          P = Dequeue( PQ)
6          i = ExtractFlow( P)
7          Send( P)
8          DC_i − = Size( P)
9      end
10     if AFL is not empty then
11     begin
12         get head of AFL, say flow i
13         DC_i + = Q_i
14         while (DC_i ≥ 0) and (Queue_i not empty) do
15         begin
16             PacketSize = Size(Head( Queue_i))
17             if (PacketSize ≤ DC_i) then
18             begin
19                 Send(Dequeue(Queue_i))
20                 DC_i − = PacketSize
21             end
22             else
23                 break ; (*skip while loop *)
24         end
25         RemoveActiveList( i)
26         if Queue_i is not empty then
27             add i to AFL
28     end
29  end
```

Fig. 2.11 PDRR packet departure operations [31]

Figure 2.11 shows the dequeue operations in the PDRR algorithm. The priority queue is served, whenever it is not empty (lines 3–9). When a packet is sent through the priority queue, the deficit counter of its flow is decreased by the size of the packet. This operation prevents serving more than one quantum in a single round. When there are no packets in the priority queue, and the active flow list (AFL) contains some flows, the flow at the current head of the AFL cycle is selected for service (line 12). The deficit counter for this flow is incremented by one quantum (line 13), and packets at the head of this flow's queue are prepared for being serviced (lines 14–24). The flow may emit up to DC_i bytes. At the end of the cycle, the AFL is rebuilt, i.e., completely erased (line 25) and re-created (lines 26–27).

The congestion indicators are measured differently than in PFQ. To measure the fair rate, we count the number of bytes that a fictitious and permanently backlogged flow could emit in a certain time interval and divide that value by the duration of the interval. This procedure is very easy to implement. The algorithm maintains one fictitious flow and treats it as a normal transmission, except that it does not transmit any packets. Therefore, the value of the deficit counter, which is regularly increased by the quantum, represents the theoretical amount of data that could be emitted by that flow. Since this flow is permanently backlogged, it does not disappear from the AFL, and thus its *DC_i* value is sustained. The priority load measurements are even simpler and are performed by averaging the emitted bit rate from a priority queue over a suitable time interval.

The introduction of a priority queue in PDRR results in situations in which flows with empty queues, i.e., flows whose packets are forwarded only via the priority queue, may exist. This implies that the dequeue procedure complexity is not strictly O(1). However, according to [31], this can be corrected by modifying the AFL, to be a list for non-empty queues only. This list would be updated, whenever a new flow receives more that its quantum in the initial round.

The enqueuing module complexity depends on the speed of detecting the presence of a flow in the AFL (line 5 in Fig. 2.10). In order to maintain the O(1) complexity, Content-Addressable Memory (CAM) must be used. CAM is a special kind of memory designed to search its entire contents in a single operation, but hardware implementation issues require that the size of AFL be small enough. However, the ns-2 based simulations have shown [31] that the required size of AFL is relatively small and, most importantly, does not increase with the link speed.

2.6.3 PFQ and PDRR Comparison

PDRR and PFQ are similar queuing algorithms. Although their operation is quite different, they realize the same objectives. The only advantage of PDRR over PFQ is simplicity. As mentioned before, the complexity of queuing disciplines in PFQ is logarithmic with respect to the number of active flows, whereas the same complexity is constant, and does not depend on the AFL size in PDRR.

Figures 2.12 and 2.13 show a comparison between the measured congestion indicators by PFQ and PDRR algorithms, namely: fair rate and priority load, respectively. The ns-2 simulation scenario was identical for both scheduling disciplines. Two UDP flows of 1 Mbit/s and 2.5 Mbit/s nominal bit rates struggled to utilize the

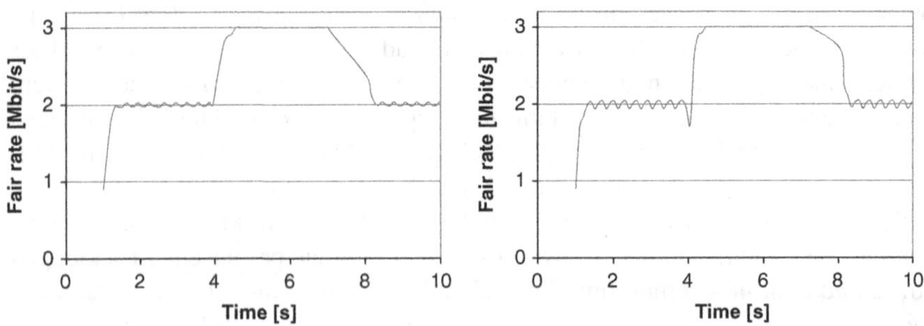

Fig. 2.12 Fair rate measurements; PFQ (on the left) and PDRR (on the right)

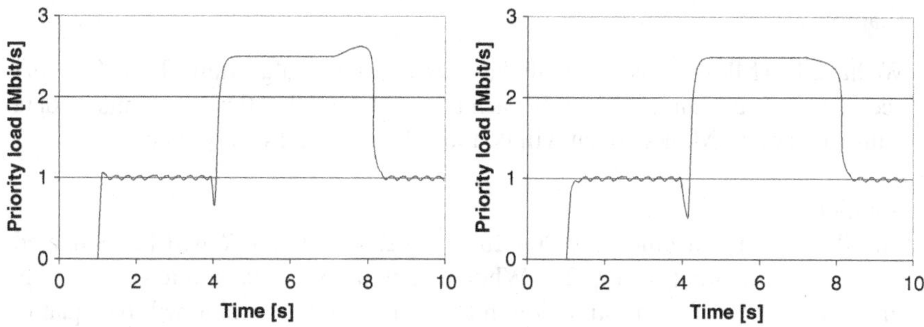

Fig. 2.13 Priority load measurements; PFQ (on the left) and PDRR (on the right)

3 Mbit/s bottleneck link. Between the 4th and 7th second, only the latter flow was active.

According to the fair rate definition (see Sect. 2.5), its value should be 100% of the link capacity when only one flow is active, as that flow could emit at the link maximum bitrate, should it be necessary. When both flows are in progress, a 2 Mbit/s FR value is also expected. 1 Mbit/s flow is not backlogged, as it emits through the priority queue constantly (its rate is always below FR). Therefore, 2 Mbit/s is left for backlogged flows, but since only one more flow is in progress, 2 Mbit/s is the value of FR.

Priority load is the amount of data that is prioritized by the schedulers. When both flows are in progress, as mentioned previously, FR is equal to 2 Mbit/s. Therefore, a 1 Mbit/s flow is below FR, and its packets constantly go through the priority queue, whereas a 2.5 Mbit/s flow is above FR and always utilizes normal queuing. However, when only a 2.5 Mbit/s flow is in service, FR is equal to 100% of link capacity and the flow's packets use the priority queue, as the flow's rate is below the current FR. Therefore, the measured PL values are 1 Mbit/s in the former case, and 2.5 Mbit/s in the latter.

As expected, no major differences between the measured values by both scheduling disciplines exist. This confirms the previous statement that the difference between PFQ and PDRR lies only in complexity issues. Although minor differences can be observed, they are insignificant to the overall behavior of admission control for which these indicators are used.

Example 2.1

We have 100 Mbit/s FAN link with the PFQ scheduling algorithm. Two 50 Mbit/s access links are connected to it. In each access link a TCP flow transmits its data. What will the FR value be in a steady state?

Solution

The bandwidth in the FAN link will be divided in a fair manner for those TCP flows. Therefore the FR value will be 50 Mbit/s.

Example 2.2

We have 100 Mbit/s FAN link with the PFQ scheduling algorithm. Two 50 Mbit/s access links are connected to it. In each access link a UDP flow transmits its data with a rate of 10 Mbit/s. What will be the FR value in a steady state?

Solution
The flows will consume only 20 Mbit/s. Therefore the FR will be estimated based on the first part of Eq. 2.3. While data will not be transmitted in the FAN link during 80% of each estimation interval of the FR, its value will be equal to 80 Mbit/s.

2.6.4 Approximate Flow-Aware Networking

The queuing and dequeuing operations in two well known FAN architectures, with PFQ and PDRR scheduling algorithms, are quite complex. It is necessary to analyze the virtual tags of each flow in PFQ. The position of the pointer provided for separating the packets in streaming and elastic flows in the PIFO queue has to be analyzed each time the packet is selected for transmission. In PDRR, it is necessary to implement many FIFO queues, individual for each elastic flow, and one for packets of streaming flows. In both versions, the AFL is used for selecting packets to be sent.

Packet transmission is usually more effective if the network architecture is as simple as possible. In this section the third FAN architecture, known as Approximate Flow-Aware Networking (AFAN), introduced in [16], is presented. This solution ensures fair transmission of packets which belong to elastic flows through one FIFO queue and prioritizing possibilities by using a separate FIFO queue for streaming flows. The pseudo-code for enqueuing the packets in AFAN is presented in Fig. 2.14. There is no need to implement AFL or additional objects.

Admission Control Operation in AFAN

Each packet P incoming to the FAN router has to be analyzed in the admission control block. If its flow ID is written to the PFL the packet is selected for queuing (lines 3–4). On the other hand, if packet P represents a new flow it must be dropped in overload (lines 5–6). In a congestionless state it may be accepted and its flow ID is written to the PFL with probability $P1$ (line 7). This probability may be low. As a result, the IDs of short flows will not be added to the PFL. The congestion state is noticed based on the values of the FR and the PL parameters estimated in the scheduler block. The admission control mechanism works exactly the same as in the FAN versions with PFQ and PDRR algorithms. However, different methods for estimating the values of the parameters mentioned above are used.

To estimate the PL in AFAN a counter incremented on the departure of each priority packet by its length in bytes has to be maintained. Let $pb(t)$ be the value of

```
######### Admission control module: #########
on arrival of packet P
if flow ID ∊ PFL then
    accept P for queuing
else if congestion is noticed then
        drop P
    else accept P with probability P1
######### Enqueuing module: #########
on packet P accepted in MBAC
if flow_bytes ≤ Q then
begin
    Enqueue(PQ, P)
    flow_bytes = flow_bytes + size(P)
end
else compute ABS of elastic FIFO queue
if ABS ≥ max_th then
begin
    drop P
    count = 0
end
if min_th ≤ ABS < max_th then
begin
    count = count + 1
    draw packet D from the elastic FIFO queue
    if flow ID(P) = ID(D) then
    begin
        drop D
        calculate probability P2
        drop P with probability P2
        if P is dropped then
            count = 0
        else P is selected for queuing
    end
    else P is selected for queuing
end
if ABS < min_th then
begin
    P is selected for queuing
    count = −1
end
if flow_bytes > Q and P is selected for queuing then
begin
    Enqueue(EQ, P)
    flow_bytes = flow_bytes + size(P)
end
```

Fig. 2.14 AFAN packet arrival operations [16]

this counter at time t, (t_1, t_2) is the measurement interval (in seconds) and C is the link bit rate. An estimate of the *PL* is:

$$PL = \frac{(pb(t_2) - pb(t_1)) \times 8}{C(t_2 - t_1)} \tag{2.5}$$

As a result, we estimate the value of the PL based on the transmitted packets. This method is more precise than the one used in PFQ or PDRR (where incoming packets are encountered and which later may be dropped).

The *FR* is computed by the following formula:

$$FR = \frac{max\{S \times C, FB \times 8\}}{t_2 - t_1} \tag{2.6}$$

where *FB* is the number of bytes sent by elastic flows during the time interval (t_1, t_2) divided by the number of elastic flows in the PFL, *S* is the total length of inactivity in the transmission during the (t_1, t_2) period, *C* is the link bit rate.

In this method we do not need to use any fictitious flow (which is used in PFQ or PDRR). As a result, this method is less complex.

Enqueue Operation

If the accepted packet belongs to a flow, which has less than or equal to Q (flow quantum usually set to the value of MTU) bytes in the buffer, it is enqueued to the priority queue (lines 9–13). In the other case, the value of the ABS (*Approximate Buffer Size*) parameter is estimated (line 15) from the following formula:

$$\begin{cases} ABS = (1 - w_q)ABS + w_q q & \text{if the queue is nonempty} \\ ABS = (1 - w_q)^m ABS & \text{if the queue is empty} \end{cases} \tag{2.7}$$

where w_q is queue weight, q is the current buffer size and m represents the number of packets that could be sent when the line was free [22] and is computed from the following formula:

$$m = (time - q\_time)/s \tag{2.8}$$

where $time$ is the current time, q_time is the start time of the buffer idle time and s is the transmission time of the packet.

If the ABS is greater than or equal to the maximum threshold set for the buffer (*max_th*), the incoming packet must be dropped and the counter $count$, which means the number of incoming packets since the last dropping operation is set to zero (lines 16–19). If the ABS is greater than or equal to the minimum threshold set for the buffer (min_th) and lower than the *max_th* the *count* parameter is incremented by one and the flow ID of randomly selected packet *D* from the elastic FIFO queue is compared with the flow ID of incoming packet *P* (lines 21–24). In practice, we do not draw a packet but a byte from the buffer and then search the

```
1   ######### Dequeuing module: #########
2   while PQ is not empty do
3   begin
4       P = Dequeue(PQ)
5       Send(P)
6       flow_bytes = flow_bytes − size(P)
7   end
8   if elastic FIFO queue is not empty then
9   begin
10      P = Dequeue(EQ)
11      Send(P)
12      flow_bytes = flow_bytes − size(P)
13  end
```

Fig. 2.15 AFAN packet departure operations [16]

packet it belongs to. This allows for proper transmission of flows with variable-length packets. If both packets represent the same flow, packet *D* is dropped and packet *P* is dropped with probability *P2* (lines 25–29). If *P* is dropped, *count* is set to zero, if not *P* is selected for queuing (lines 30–32). Packet *P* may also be queued if its flow ID is different from the flow ID of packet *D*, or ABS is lower than *min_th* (lines 36–38). In the latter case the value of the *count* parameter is set to minus one (the initial value of the algorithm) (line 39). If the number of bytes in the flow the packet *P* belongs to is greater than Q, the packet is queued in the elastic queue (lines 41–44).

Dequeue Operation

The process of selecting a packet for sending is very simple. The pseudo-code for such an operation is presented in Fig 2.15. If there are any packets in the priority queue the first of them is selected to be served (lines 2–6). If the PQ is empty, the first packet from the elastic queue is sent (lines 8–12).

Complexity

Admission control complexity is the same as in the FAN implementations with PFQ and PDRR. The enqueue operation is less complex in AFAN. We need to compute the *ABS* for the elastic flows, but in fact this is a fraction of the current buffer size estimated in each FAN version. There is also a need for random selection of packet *D* from the elastic queue to compare it with the incoming elastic packet *P*. In the well known versions of FAN, it is necessary to check the buffer load and whether it is full (in almost every case) to find the longest flow and drop its last packet. The complexity of queuing the elastic packets is the same in all FAN versions. The advantage of AFAN is visible when we compare the enqueuing process for streaming flows. In the versions of FAN with PFQ and PDRR these are served in the same way as elastic flows. In AFAN the packets of streaming flows are queued immediately without any additional operation. This is possible because in this solution it is impossible to overload the buffer. The real gain in algorithm complexity may be seen in AFAN while comparing the dequeuing operations for each FAN version. In this proposal, we only have to check whether there are any packets in the priority queue and if so serve them as first. There is no need to maintain an additional structure like the AFL implemented in both known versions of FAN. We do not need to find a flow before sending a packet and update the content of AFL. All the arguments presented in this section confirm that AFAN is less complex than its predecessors. We can assume that it is also easy to implement in routers.

Calculation of the AFAN Parameters

New parameters, which have to be set in routers are provided in AFAN. In this proposal a low-pass filter to calculate the ABS is used (see formula (2.7)). This method is taken from the RED (*Random Early Detection*) queuing algorithm [22] and ensures insignificant changes in the ABS in spite of bursty incoming traffic. The weight w_q represents the time constant of the low-pass filter. The proper value of this parameter affects the effectiveness of the whole algorithm. If it is too large, the transient congestion may not be noticed in the router. On the other hand, if w_q is too low the mechanism may react to changes in the queue too slowly. As a result, the router may be unable to detect some symptoms of congestion. Based on the analysis presented in [22] we can assume that the value of the w_q parameter should be set in the range from 0.001 to 0.0042. In the simulation experiments presented in the following section, we used the value of 0.002, which ensured the achievement of the assumed goals.

min_th and max_th are the key parameters for AFAN. Their optimal values affect buffer occupation and allow for fair and efficient transmission in the links. If the traffic is fairly bursty, the value of min_th should be set to a value large enough to ensure link utilization at an acceptable level. On the other hand, it ought not to be too large because of packet delay demands. Following [22], the difference max_th-min_th should be larger than the typical increase in the estimated ABS in one roundtrip time. In practice, max_th should be set to at least twice min_th. We set the min_th parameter to 40 kB and max_th to 90 kB in the experiments. The buffer size was set to 100 kB.

Two methods for computing *P2* are proposed in [22]. Method 2 called "uniform random variables" is described as the better one. *P2* is calculated from the following formula:

$$P2 = P2_{temp}/(1 - count \cdot P2) \tag{2.9}$$

The $P2_{temp}$ is calculated as the function of ABS and estimated from:

$$P2_{temp} = max_p(ABS - min\_th)/(max\_th - min\_th) \tag{2.10}$$

where max_p is the maximum allowed value of $P2_{temp}$. It is important to set the proper value for the max_p parameter to estimate $P2$ efficiently.

The expected value for this method is estimated from:

$$E[X] = 1/(2P2) + 1/2 \tag{2.11}$$

This means that if we set max_p to 0.02 (as we did in the simulation experiments), and the ABS is halfway between min_th and max_th an average of one out of fifty arriving packets is dropped in the router. The value of max_p should be set to values which allow for slow changes in the $P2$ probability. This is needed for minimizing the fluctuations in the ABS.

Simulation Experiments of AFAN

In this section we present the results of simulation experiments in the ns-2 simulator [36]. They show that AFAN is very simple in implementation and works similarly to the FAN versions with PFQ and PDRR. We evaluated AFAN performance by analyzing the traffic parameters during transmission in an overloaded AFAN link.

The experiments were provided for a single FAN link with many source and destination nodes. The topology is presented in Fig. 2.16. It is simple, yet adequate to analyze traffic performance in Flow-Aware Networks. The reasoning behind this is that all nodes in FAN operate independently and all the decisions are taken without any information from the network.

The nodes S_{E1}-S_{En} are the sources of the elastic traffic, while the nodes S_{S1}-S_{Sm} are the sources of the streaming traffic. The nodes D_{E1}-D_{En} and D_{S1}-D_{Sm} represent the destination nodes for the elastic and streaming traffic, respectively.

To provide credible simulations it is important to set proper values for the simulation parameters. The capacity of the FAN link was set to 100 Mbit/s. Of

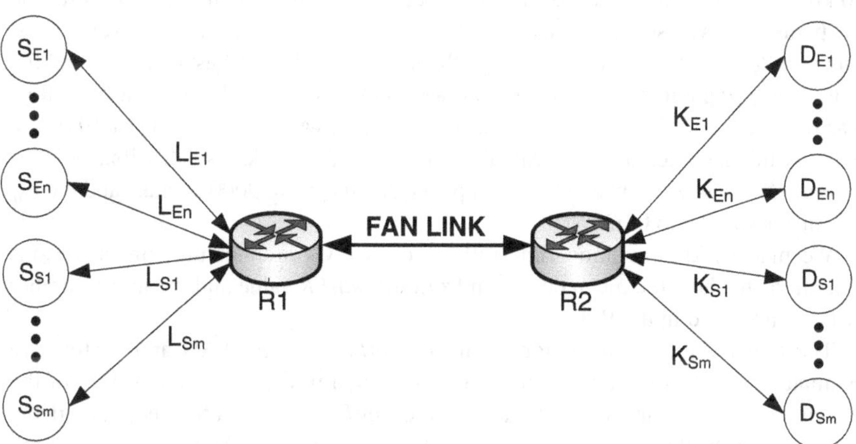

Fig. 2.16 The basic simulation topology

course, this value is too low when considering core links; however, the obtained results are scalable. The only reason to make simulations for a low capacity core link is the time needed to conduct the experiments. In our conditions, one simulation run took about an hour. The capacity of other links was set to 1 Gbit/s.

Based on the simulation parameters presented in [1], the buffer size for a 50 Mbit/s link should be set to a value of 100 packets. The buffer is sized to absorb approximately one delay bandwidth product. For a 100 Mbit/s link (used in the simulation runs for this book) a reasonable value is 1000 packets. This allows for low packet delays and jitter.

All observations of simulation parameters should be provided in a steady-state. The setting of an appropriate value for the warm-up period is a key element for the credibility of simulation results. There are many methods for estimating the value of this parameter [40]. One of these is based on the assumption that the values of the observed variable stop moving in one direction and start oscillating. In another, the steady-state is noticed at the point at which the value is neither the minimum nor the maximum of the remaining observations. The warm-up for all simulations experiments described in this section, based on several observations of the results obtained, was assumed to be 20 s.

The other simulation parameters were set as follows. The traffic pattern was provided with Pareto distribution for calculating the volume of traffic to be sent by each of the elastic flows in the FAN link ($k = 1.5$, mean size of elastic flow was set to 150 Mbit). We used exponential distribution for generating the time intervals between beginnings of the transmissions of the elastic flows (mean inter-arrival time was set to 0.1 s) and 20 streaming flows (mean inter-arrival time was set to 1 s). We made our simulation runs under various conditions changing the number of elastic flows from 200 to 600. The duration of each simulation run was set to 1200 s. The packet size for the elastic flows was set to 1000 bytes, while that for the streaming flows was set to 100 bytes. The transmission rate of streaming flows was set to 80 kbit/s (as in a typical Skype VoIP connection). The measurement interval for the *PL* parameter was set to 50 ms while the *FR* values were estimated every 0.5 s. The *maxPL* parameter was set to 70%, the *minFR* parameter was set to 5% and the *flow_time_out* parameter was set to 20 s, which means that the ID of an inactive flow was removed from PFL after 20 s. Each experiment was repeated at least 10 times. 95% confidence intervals were calculated by using the Student's t-distribution.

For AFAN, min_th was set to 4000 packets, max_th to 9000 packets and the w_q parameter was set to 0.02.

We made 150 simulation runs (50 for each FAN architecture) under various conditions to show the mean deviation from the *minFR* value and the mean number of flows accepted in the PFL.

The mean values of deviation from the *minFR* for each FAN architecture are estimated as part of the link capacity and presented in Fig. 2.17. The values of the *FR* change in time and oscillate around the *minFR*. The situation is better if the deviations from the *minFR* are lower. We can see that for AFAN and FAN with PDRR the analyzed mean deviation is lower than for FAN with PFQ. This means that the former two versions are more stable than the latter one.

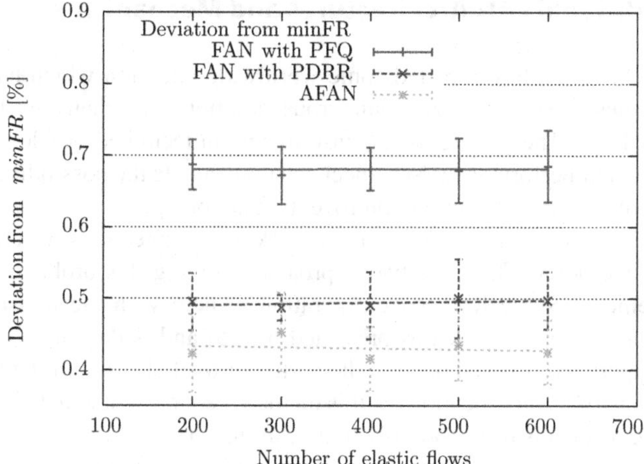

Fig. 2.17 The mean deviation from the *minFR*

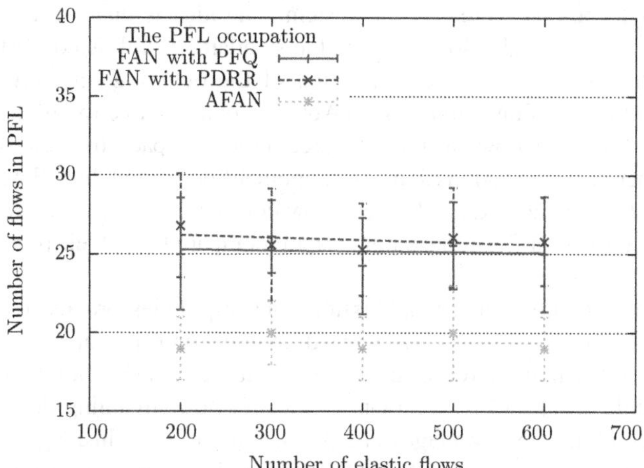

Fig. 2.18 The PFL occupation in various FAN architectures

We analyzed the mean flow count in the PFL in the same simulation scenarios. Based on the results shown in Fig. 2.18 we may conclude that the number of active flows in AFAN is slightly lower than in the other FAN architectures. The difference is not great. We can see that all three versions work similarly, giving an equal possibility for each flow accepted in the admission control block to transmit its traffic with a rate more or less equal to the *FR*. However, we should remember that the AFAN architecture is less complex than FAN with PFQ or PDRR.

2.7 Additional FAN Architectures and Mechanisms

The FAN architecture has attracted some worldwide attention which has resulted in many studies. Over the years, numerous additional mechanisms have been proposed for FAN. These were in response to certain technical problems with the implementation or performance. New mechanisms evaluate the possibilities of using FAN in certain scenarios or simply improve its functioning.

When the link is congested, XP routers block new connections which increases their acceptance delay. There are two approaches solving this problem. One is to use the scheme of Static Router Configuration to help with the transmission of emergency calls. This method was presented in [25] and is described in Chap. 7. The second approach is based on periodic partial or total clearing of the PFL list in an XP router. Various modifications of this method were presented in [12–14, 19, 21] and [20]. The mechanisms are described in detail in Chap. 4.

The notion of Multilayer Flow-Aware Networking (MFAN) was introduced in [34], and later presented as a complete approach in the PhD dissertation of V. López in 2010 [33]. In this study, it is shown that FAN can be extended by including an optical layer to be considered by the system. The idea is that a FAN router can request additional optical resources once the standard IP link is congested. Under normal circumstances, upon the congestion of the outgoing link, FAN starts to block new incoming connections. In MFAN, the router is able to utilize additional resources and redirect flows to that resource, creating space for new flows to be admitted. There are three admission control policies deciding which flows are to be redirected to the optical link, i.e., Newest Flow Policy, Oldest Flow Policy and Most-Active Flow Policy. In [34], those policies are compared and their performance is evaluated.

In [17], the authors compare admission control policies proposed for MFAN. As a result of the comparison, a new admission control strategy is proposed. The solution inherits the advantages of the already established admission control proposals while ensuring fast acceptance times for new streaming flows. It is also possible to combine the advantages of MFAN with those of flushing mechanisms. That work was continued under the BONE EU project, where the authors showed the differences between the admission control strategies proposed for IP-level FAN and MFAN.

In [18], a multi-layer recovery strategy for the MFAN nodes is presented. The authors propose using the Enhanced Hold-Off Timer (EHOT) algorithm [11], known from RPR networks, to control network operation after link or node failure. Network performance after failures is also presented in [15] where the authors measure the impact of proposed congestion control mechanisms in the case of network overload. The results show that the acceptance times for streaming flows are acceptable even with the presence of network failures, provided that proper congestion control mechanisms are used. Both papers essentially show that FAN networks have great resilience.

FAN was also tested in the Grid environment. In [8], the authors show the impact of DiffServ and FAN on the Grid traffic, and compare the efficiency of those architectures in providing QoS assurances. Further, in [7, 9] and [10], the performance of FAN in the Grid environment is evaluated. It is shown that FAN outperforms DiffServ in the average GridFTP session delay and the average GridFTP session goodput under increasing offered load.

FAN does not interfere with IP protocol functionality, including routing procedures. However, it is possible to introduce a new routing scheme—one which would cooperate with FAN. In [39], such a scheme is proposed. Adaptive routing clearly improves network performance especially in overload and failure conditions.

2.8 Check Your Knowledge

1. We have a 100 Mbit/s FAN link with the PFQ scheduling algorithm. The *minFR* is equal to 5 Mbit/s. The measurement interval for the *FR* parameter was set to 0.5 s. In 2.5 s FR was equal to 4.93 Mbit/s, while in 3.0 s it was equal to 4.98 Mbit/s. At 3.35 s the video flow wants to begin transmission with rate 1 Mbit/s. Will this flow be accepted immediately?
2. Are PFQ and PDRR the only scheduling algorithm which may be used in FAN?
3. Are packets in FAN marked?
4. In which block of an XP router are the values of FR and PL estimated?
5. The TCP flow wanted to begin transmission in 5 s, but the link was congested. The congestion was eliminated in 10 s. Was the TCP flow accepted immediately?
6. On a 3 Mbit/s FAN link, there are 2 UDP flows: 1 Mbit/s and 2 Mbit/s. What are the values of Fair Rate and Priority Load?
7. On a 5 Mbit/s FAN link, there are 2 UDP flows: 1 Mbit/s and 2 Mbit/s. What are the values of Fair Rate and Priority Load?
8. On a 3 Mbit/s FAN link, there are 3 UDP flows: two 1 Mbit/s and one 2 Mbit/s. What are the values of Fair Rate and Priority Load? What is the rate of each flow?
9. When are new flows admitted on a link?
10. What does it mean when a flow is on a PFL list?
11. What are the differences between the queuing algorithms designed for FAN?
12. How are flows identified in FAN?
13. What are the names of classes of flows in FAN?
14. How do FAN nodes know which class a flow belongs to?
15. Can flows belong to two classes at the same time?
16. Can flows change their class over time?
17. What is the difference in treating flows of different classes?
18. Can a UDP flow be an elastic flow?
19. Can a TCP flow be a streaming flow?
20. Can current FR drop below the *minFR*?

21. Can current PL exceed the *maxPL*?
22. When are flows removed from the PFL list?

References

1. J. Auge, J. Roberts, Buffer sizing for elastic traffic, in *Proceedings of 2nd Conference on Next Generation Internet Design and Engineering, NGI 2006*, Valencia, Spain, April 2006
2. N. Benameur, S.B. Fredj, F. Delcoigne, S. Oueslati-Boulahia, J. Roberts, Integrated admission control for streaming and elastic traffic, in *Proc. Second International Workshop on Quality of Future Internet Services, QofIS 2001*, Coimbra, Portugal, September 2001
3. N. Benameur, S.B. Fredj, S. Oueslati-Boulahia, J. Roberts, Quality of Service and flow level admission control in the Internet. Computer Networks **40**, 57–71 (2002)
4. S. Blake, D. Black, M. Carlson, E. Davies, Z. Wang, W. Weiss, An Architecture for Differentiated Services, IETF RFC 2475, December 1998
5. T. Bonald, S. Oueslati-Boulahia, J. Roberts, IP traffic and QoS control, in *Proc. World Telecommunications Congress, WTC 2002*, Paris, France, September 2002
6. R. Braden, D. Clark, S. Shenker, Integrated Services in the Internet Architecture an Overview, IETF RFC 1633, June 1994
7. C. Cárdenas, M. Gagnaire, Evaluation of Flow-Aware Networking (FAN) architectures under GridFTP traffic. Future Gener. Comput. Syst. **25**, 895–903 (2009). [Online]. Available: http://portal.acm.org/citation.cfm?id=1550955.1551007
8. C. Cardenas, M. Gagnaire, V. Lopez, J. Aracil, Admission control for grid services in IP networks, in *Proc. Advanced Networks and Telecommunication Systems, ANTS 2007*, Bombay, India, December 2007
9. C. Cardenas, M. Gagnaire, V. Lopez, J. Aracil, Performance evaluation of the Flow-Aware Networking (FAN) architecture under grid environment, in *Proc. IEEE Network Operations and Management Symposium, NOMS 2008*, Paris, France, pp. 481–487, April 2008
10. C. Cárdenas, M. Gagnaire, V. Lopez, J. Aracil, Admission control in Flow-Aware Networking (FAN) architectures under GridFTP traffic. Opt. Switch. Netw. **6**, 20–28 (2009)
11. J. Domzal, N. Ansari, A. Jajszczyk, Recovery, fairness and congestion mechanisms in RPR networks, in *12 th Polish Teletraffic Symposium PSRT*, Poznan, Poland, September 2005. [Online]. Available: http://citeseerx.ist.psu.edu/viewdoc/summary?doi=10.1.1.98.3023
12. J. Domzal, N. Ansari, A. Jajszczyk, The flushing mechanism for MBAC in Flow-Aware Networks, in *Proc. 4th EURO-NGI Conference on Next Generation Internet Networks, NGI 2008*, Krakow, Poland, pp. 77–83, April 2008
13. J. Domzal, N. Ansari, A. Jajszczyk, New congestion control mechanisms for Flow-Aware Networks, in *Proc. IEEE International Conference on Communications ICC 2008*, Beijing, China, May 2008
14. J. Domzal, N. Ansari, A. Jajszczyk, The impact of congestion control mechanisms for Flow-Aware Networks on traffic assignment in two router architectures, in *Proc. International Conference on the Latest Advances in Networks, ICLAN 2008*, Toulouse, France, December 2008
15. J. Domzal, R. Wojcik, A. Jajszczyk, The impact of congestion control mechanisms on network performance after failure in Flow-Aware Networks, in *Proc. International Workshop on Traffic Management and Traffic Engineering for the Future Internet, FITraMEn 2008, Book: Traffic Management and Traffic Engineering for the Future Internet, Lecture Notes on Computer Science 2009*, Porto, Portugal, December 2008
16. J. Domzal, N. Ansari, A. Jajszczyk, Approximate Flow-Aware Networking, in *Proc. IEEE International Conference on Communications ICC 2009*, Dresden, Germany, June 2009
17. J. Domzal, R. Wojcik, A. Jajszczyk, V. Lopez, J. Hernandez, J. Aracil, Admission control policies in Flow-Aware Networks, in *Proc. 11th International Conference on Transparent Optical Networks, ICTON 2009*, Azores, Portugal, pp. 1–4, July 2009

18. J. Domzal, R. Wojcik, K. Wajda, A. Jajszczyk, V. Lopez, J. Hernandez, J. Aracil, C. Cardenas, M. Gagnaire, A multi-layer recovery strategy in FAN over WDM architectures, in *Proc. 7th International Workshop on Design of Reliable Communication Networks, DRCN 2009*, Washington, USA, pp. 160–167, October 2009
19. J. Domzal, R. Wojcik, A. Jajszczyk, Reliable transmission in Flow-Aware Networks, in *Proc. IEEE Global Communications Conference GLOBECOM 2009*, Honolulu, USA, pp. 1–6, December 2009
20. J. Domzal, N. Ansari, A. Jajszczyk, Congestion control in wireless Flow-Aware Networks, in *IEEE ICC 2011*, Kyoto, Japan, June 2011
21. J. Domżał, R. Wójcik, V. López, J. Aracil, A. Jajszczyk, EFMP—a new congestion control mechanism for flow-aware networks. Trans. Emerg. Telecommun. Technol. **25**(11), 1137–1148 (2014)
22. S. Floyd, V. Jacobson, Random early detection gateways for congestion avoidance. IEEE/ACM Trans. Netw. **1**, 397–413 (1993)
23. S.B. Fredj, S. Oueslati-Boulahia, J. Roberts, Measurement-based admission control for elastic traffic, in *Proc. 17th International Teletraffic Congress, ITC 2001*, Salvador, Brasil, December 2001
24. P. Goyal, H.M. Vin, H. Cheng, Start-time fair queuing: A scheduling algorithm for integrated services packet switching networks. IEEE/ACM Trans. Netw. **5**, 690–704 (1997)
25. A. Jajszczyk, R. Wojcik, Emergency calls in flow-aware networks. Commun. Lett. IEEE **11**(9), 753–755 (2007)
26. Y. Jiang, P. Emstad, A. Nevin, V. Nicola, M. Fidler, Measurement-based admission control for a Flow-Aware Network, in *Proc. 1st Conference on Next Generation Internet Networks - Traffic Engineering, NGI 2005*, Rome, Italy, pp. 318–325, April 2005
27. A. Kortebi, S. Oueslati, J. Roberts, MBAC algorithms for streaming flows in Cross-protect, in *Proc. Next Generation Internet Networks EuroNGI Workshop*, Lund, Sweden, June 2004
28. A. Kortebi, L. Muscariello, S. Oueslati, J. Roberts, On the scalability of fair queueing, in *Proc. Third Workshop on Hot Topics in Networks, ACM HotNets-III 2004*, San Diego, USA, November 2004
29. A. Kortebi, L. Muscariello, S. Oueslati, J. Roberts, Evaluating the number of active flows in a scheduler realizing fair statistical bandwidth sharing, in *Proc. International Conference on Measurement and Modeling of Computer Systems, ACM SIGMETRICS 2005*, Banff, Canada, June 2005
30. A. Kortebi, L. Muscariello, S. Oueslati, J. Roberts, Minimizing the overhead in implementing Flow-Aware Networking, in *Proceedings of Symposium on Architectures for Networking and Communications Systems, ANCS 2005*, Princeton, USA, October 2005
31. A. Kortebi, S. Oueslati, J. Roberts, Implicit service differentiation using deficit round robin, in *Proc. 19th International Teletraffic Congress, ITC 2005*, Beijing, China, August/September 2005
32. A. Kortebi, S. Oueslati, J.W. Roberts, Cross-protect: implicit service differentiation and admission control, in *Proc. High Performance Switching and Routing, HPSR 2004*, Phoenix, AZ, USA, pp. 56–60, 2004
33. V. Lopez, End-to-end quality of service provisioning in multilayer and multidomain environments, Ph.D. dissertation, Universidad Autonoma de Madrid, 2010
34. V. Lopez, C. Cardenas, J.A. Hernandez, J. Aracil, M. Gagnaire, Extension of the Flow-Aware Networking (FAN) architecture to the IP over WDM environment, in *Proc. 4th International Telecommunication Networking Workshop on QoS in Multiservice IP Networks*, Venice, Italy, February 2008
35. L. Massoulie, J. Roberts, Arguments in favour of admission control for TCP flows, in *Proc. 11th International Teletraffic Congress, ITC 1999*, Edinbourg, June 1999
36. Network Simulator ns-2, Available at http://nsnam.isi.edu/nsnam
37. K. Nichols, S. Blake, F. Baker, D. Black, Definition of the Differentiated Services Field (DS Field) in the IPv4 and IPv6 Headers, IETF RFC 2474, December 1998

38. S. Oueslati, J. Roberts, A new direction for quality of service: Flow-aware networking, in *Proc. 1st Conference on Next Generation Internet Networks - Traffic Engineering, NGI 2005*, Rome, Italy, 2005
39. S. Oueslati, J. Roberts, Comparing flow-aware and flow-oblivious adaptive routing, in *Proc. 41st Annual Conference on Information Sciences and Systems, CISS 2007*, Baltimore, MD, USA, March 2007
40. K. Pawlikowski, Steady-state simulation of queueing processes: A survey of problems and solutions. ACM Comput. Surv. **22**(2), 123–170 (1990)
41. K. Psounis, R. Pan, B. Prabhakar, Approximate fair dropping for variable-length packets. Micro IEEE **21**, 48–56 (2001)
42. J. Roberts, Internet traffic, QoS and pricing, in *Proc. the IEEE*, vol. 92, pp. 1389–1399, September 2004
43. J. Roberts, S. Oueslati, Quality of service by Flow Aware Networking. Philos. Trans. R. Soc. Lond. **358**, 2197–2207 (2000)
44. J.W. Roberts, L. Massoulie, Bandwidth sharing and admission control for elastic traffic, in *Proc. ITC Specialist Seminar*, Yokohama, October 1998
45. M. Shreedhar, G. Varghese, Efficient fair queuing using deficit round-robin. IEEE/ACM Trans. Netw. **4**, 375–385 (1996)

3 Flow-Aware Networking for Net Neutrality

Any provider that blocks access to content is inviting customers to find another provider. And that's just bad business.

— Ed Whitacre

The Future Internet will greatly depend on the results of the net neutrality[1] debate, which has attracted an enormous amount of attention over the last few years and is widely covered in technical, economical and legal literature. The nature of the debate is controversial, i.e., there are several parties involved, and each has its own view on the matter. Unfortunately, this is not the whole story. Some of the major participants are the telecom operators, large companies with substantial market power and visibility. They have chosen to take an active part in the dispute, often not to present their 'objective' opinions but to protect their interests, as the possible legal outcome of the debate would introduce certain new regulations and restrictions aimed directly at them. Obviously, such behavior is characteristic for all parties who advance their interests. As a result, the literature on net neutrality must be read with caution, as there are positions which do not present objective statements and conclusions, but rather formulate false claims for the benefit of the authors' employers.

The literature is, therefore, complex to read, to say the least. After all, as the subject concerns us all, everyone is bound to evolve their own opinion on the matter, which does not contribute much to objectivity. The only even-handed approach to discussing the problem is to show it from a very wide perspective, presenting the ideas and opinions from all major parties involved. This is why we present a comprehensive view of the network neutrality debate and its possible impact on the Future Internet. Most parts of the discussion concern the debate carried out in the

[1] Although *network neutrality* is usually referred to as *net neutrality*, for short, both terms convey exactly the same meaning. Throughout this book both terms will be used interchangeably.

J. Domżał et al., *Guide to Flow-Aware Networking*, Computer Communications and Networks, https://doi.org/10.1007/978-3-030-57153-5_3

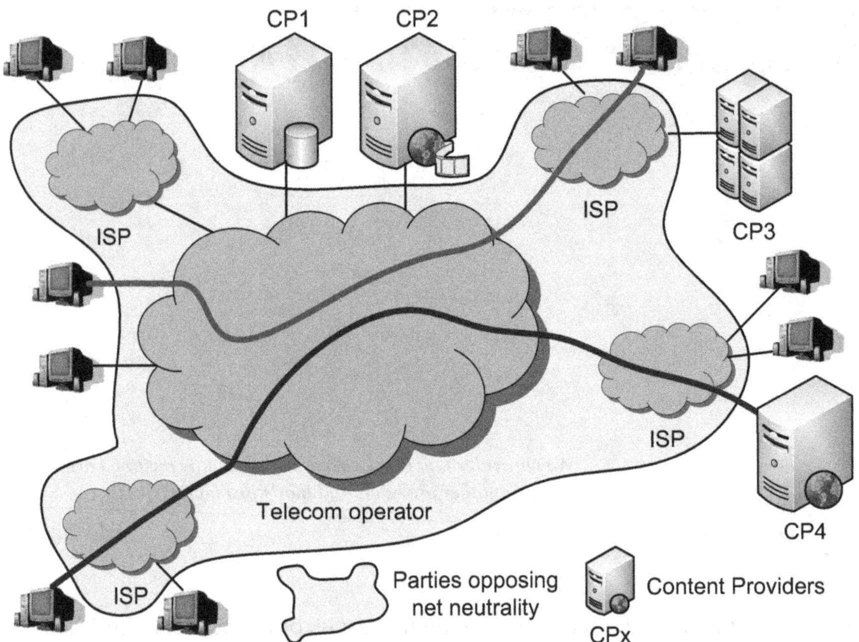

Fig. 3.1 The net neutrality debate players: the network perspective

US, where it is loudest. The rest of the world carefully monitors the dispute and tries to participate. Nevertheless, the sole values conveyed by network neutrality apply to all networks worldwide.

Figure 3.1 shows the net neutrality issue from the network perspective. Companies provide data transport services—they charge their customers for access to the network. These companies range from nationwide telecom operators, through big Internet Service Providers (ISPs), content providers (CPs) to the smallest firms which connect people. In the debate, these companies, in general, oppose the concept of network neutrality. Sometimes, there is friction associated with the debate between large telecom operators and ISPs. However, the debate usually concerns the operators as a whole and content providers.

Content providers sit on the other side along with the largest group of Internet users. They are the users of networks—networks which are owned and managed by telecom operators and ISPs. The users, in general, want to access all possible services and content on the Internet. As data transfers almost always involve multiple operators, the users want to be sure that they will not block or degrade their connection. This is why the users and content providers in general opt for network neutrality.

It needs to be mentioned that not all these parties can be categorized as strict proponents or opponents of net neutrality. Moreover, even within a broad category, such as content providers or ISPs, not every firm presents the same view. Regardless, this chapter presents the most common views on net neutrality as observed by players' actions.

3.1 Definition of Net Neutrality

Gilbert Held in [12] opens the discussion with the sentence: "*Net neutrality represents one of a few telecommunications terms that, while very difficult to precisely define, can cause a large amount of conversation on both sides of the issue.*" This observation is, obviously, true. Most of us perceive 'neutral' as a positive term, and agree that the Internet should be neutral in some way. However, if you ask various parties about the meaning of 'the neutral Internet', you are likely to receive different answers. This ambiguity (or lack of precision) has sparked many unnecessary discussions and accusations. Net neutrality consists of various propositions, rather than being just a single concept. Therefore, there are multiple possible meanings of the phrase 'net neutrality'.

The most common—if somewhat biased—understanding of the term can be found on the savetheinternet.com website. This is an American web page which consolidates the nationwide movement to legalize neutral Internet. Their definition is as follows: "*Net Neutrality is the guiding principle that preserves the free and open Internet. Net Neutrality means that Internet service providers may not discriminate between different kinds of content and applications online. It guarantees a level playing field for all Web sites and Internet technologies.*" The website authors say that the Internet should remain open (meaning that it is available to every user or company) and free (everybody should be free to use it however they like). It does not mean, and never has, that users should not pay for access to the Internet. It is only natural that people pay fees to their ISPs to gain access, with the quality provided proportional to what they pay.

The second part of the definition is more important. It states that the telecom operators should not be allowed to differentiate traffic based on its content, application, source or destination. In other words, the operators should be prohibited from doing this in order to:

1. provide better QoS for certain applications or users,
2. prevent them from charging more for using certain applications.

The reasons for such statements lie in the fact that telecom operators might manipulate the traffic in their networks for their own benefit. In the net neutral reality, the network's only function is to transmit data—not to choose which data should be privileged with a higher quality of service. Net neutrality wants the operators to be only 'carriers' of data, and their sole responsibility should be to transmit data from one side of the globe to the other, without caring what is inside the packets. These proposed regulations are based on past examples when Internet providers tampered with user traffic in order to obtain monetary benefits, by blocking or restricting the access to some services otherwise publicly available.

Table 3.1 Definition of network neutrality by all interested parties

Debate side	How do they see net neutrality?	Vote
Telecom operators	Unnecessary regulations (market rules are sufficient)	No
Content providers	Fair competition, no double payments	Yes
Technically aware users	Challenging, yet important step	Yes/No
Technically unaware users	Freedom	Yes

Table 3.2 The expected effects of possible network neutrality law enforcement through the eyes of all interested parties

Debate side	How do they see the effects?
Telecom operators	Regulation will lessen revenues, therefore, hindering the development of the networks
Content providers	Regulation will ensure fairness and promote development
Technically aware users	Regulation will promote fairness but may make network management more challenging
Technically unaware users	Regulation will enforce a free and fair Internet

Presented in this way, the debate might seem two-sided: network operators against everybody else. Of course, the issue is much more complicated, and it therefore leaves room for elaborate discussions. In the course of these discussions, more groups heavily interested in their outcome have emerged. In simple terms, the defending side is represented by large nationwide telecom operators (e.g., AT&T, Verizon), ISPs and other network traffic carriers, while the other side consists of content providers (e.g., Google, Skype) and regular users of the Internet. The defending side is mostly unanimous in their views. Unfortunately, the other side is not. This is partly due to the fact that it is represented by many groups: standard Internet users, networking specialists, politicians, lawyers, economists, businessmen and small to large companies. In the US, many thousands of statements have been filed with the Federal Communications Commission (FCC) showing a great diversity of opinion. Furthermore, among these groups there are people who are aware of how networking works, and those who propose sound solutions but with no possible implementation in reality. Jon Crowcroft says, "Much of what I have read on the subject of net neutrality by economists is technically naive and simplistic" [4].

The definition of the term 'net neutrality' differs between the sides. Tables 3.1 and 3.2 summarize the most common perceptions of each interested party. The telecom operators are obviously against any resolutions which would impose new regulations upon them. They feel that the free market mechanisms are sufficient guardians of the existing status quo, and that new regulations would only hinder further development. On those grounds, telecom operators are against putting the network neutrality principles into law. Content providers are on the opposite side of the debate. They argue that only by law can those large influential companies be forced to provide fair competition. Large content providers fear that they might be forced to share significant amounts of their revenues simply to be able to exist on the Internet. Small, innovative start-up companies are afraid that they might not be able to sell their ideas effectively (and hence develop them) if they are forced to pay substantial fees from the start. The general public opinion on the matter is that possibly unfair behavior of the telecom industries may prevent the development of small Internet-based businesses worldwide.

The last group in the discussion is the users of the Internet. Those with no background in networking feel that a neutral Internet is the only fair solution and should be preserved. People associate net neutrality with freedom of speech and freedom of choice of application or service. They also believe that if the Internet works well now, there should not be any changes in the future, apart perhaps from increasing speeds. To some extent, this line of reasoning seems rational. However, there are certain aspects of this which make the proposed network neutrality demands seem risky. Specialists in networking argue that, for example, only by looking into the payloads of carried packets can operators protect users from certain types of attack. Therefore, while the group's standing is divided, most technically aware users feel that the network neutrality principles are valid and important. However, their enforcement must be carried out with the utmost caution and rationality.

There are other aspects of net neutrality. The authors of [11] present an analysis of major search engine policies. They argue that this is a similar problem to net neutrality. For example, search engines can prefer certain content and present it in the search results on top of the page. Of course, usually, content owners pay for better treatment. The authors of the cited paper suggest that this part of a network should also be neutral. The paper is concluded with the statement that users may be harmed with the search bias.

3.2 History and Past Research

The American philosopher Georges Santayana once said, "*Those who do not study history are doomed to repeat it.*" Although net neutrality might seem like a relatively new concept, due to its possible legislative restrictions it is important to be aware of how similar regulations have impacted companies in the past.

The debate over network neutrality and the possible upcoming regulations are often compared to previous legislative motions in the US, i.e., regulation of the postal service and the telephone companies. Fred Schneider says, "*The 1984 breakup of AT&T radically changed the telephone business in the US. More than a quarter-century later, the action has shifted from telephone voice networks to wireless networks and the Internet*" [22]. The reasoning behind such a comparison is twofold. First, the regulations concern large companies with substantial market power, usually with monopolistic (or close to monopolistic) inclinations. And second, the proposed resolution revolves around the 'common carrier' approach which now governs the telephone companies.

Reference [20] presents a comparison of the current network neutrality debate with previous attempts to regulate commerce and the telephone companies. The author points out the failures of the previous legislative motions and shows their consequences. He says that in the past, "*In many cases, consumers would have been better off without regulation. The starkest evidence: deregulation of airlines, trucking and most rail rates actually produces lower prices*" [20].

The authors of [21] present arguments for and against the net neutrality law. They also propose some recommendations which cover effective control of internet resources by network operators and content providers, and new price and quality differentiation models for more transparent network management systems. The authors conclude that the security aspects should also be considered in the debate on net neutrality rules.

The net neutrality debate also concerns pricing of Internet access. The authors of [25] say that a plausible solution to the debate might benefit from an in-depth understanding of economic processes inside the user-ISP hierarchy. The analysis, based on game theory, presented in [5], shows that if transport prices are set by a regulator who wishes to maximize social welfare, those prices should be as low as possible. In other words, the current status of the Internet, where content providers do not pay extra for data they transmit, maximizes social welfare and should be a goal to reach or maintain. The economists Economides and Tag in [7] present a two-sided market analysis, a mathematical model to assess network neutrality. Even though certain assumptions are made, the authors claim that net neutrality is good for overall welfare.

Several authors, e.g., [23], worry that without net neutrality, operators may try to leverage their market power or monopoly by charging content providers for preferential treatment or simply for accessing their network. In [3] the authors consider several aspects of the role of pricing models in the net neutrality debate. They present a mathematical model, which is used to illustrate the economic relationships between ISPs and content providers. It is shown that side payments may lead to unfairness of revenue sharing, and that content providers may be the only winners of side payments.

The authors in [1] present a model for achieving sustainable growth of computing e-infrastructures, and say that network neutrality regulations will attract a growing fraction of the population to use the e-infrastructure. An analysis of aspects of net neutrality with regard to wireless networks is presented in [14]. The author of this article proposes a set of regulations which limits the ability of ISPs to restricting access to applications offered on wireless networks. It is suggested that the interface between transport and network layers should be open in wireless networks. For example, the author says that the QoS guarantees ought to be provided for all voice or video services, independent on who offers such services in the ISP's infrastructure.

It is also argued that regulated commerce is much less innovative than that of the monopolist. The author claims, "*Bell Labs was a famous source of invention, but AT&T was a ponderous and reluctant innovator*" [20]. To some extent this may be true, but many would disagree. It is true that monopolists, due to their almost infinite funding, can also conduct research on technologies or services which only have a small chances of success. In the competitive market, only research leading to financial reward is conducted, if any. However, the competitive market develops much faster and constantly probes the market to find new solutions because companies feel the breath of the competition. Apart from that monopolists on a global scale fail to satisfy consumers on other levels of their operations. The final thought, on which everybody agrees, is that when creating new laws for the preservation of the neutral Internet, the experiences of the past must be carefully considered.

3.3 Spectrum of Net Neutrality Violations

Figure 3.2 presents actions regarded as traffic management which are considered to be in-line (to the left) or against (to the right) network neutrality principles. There is also a grey area showing actions which are perceived differently by the parties. Best-effort, i.e., no traffic management, cannot violate network neutrality. Assigning certain services higher or lower priorities can be tolerated by net neutrality proponents, provided that all applications inside a certain service will receive that treatment. Such an approach to network neutrality is described by the US FCC report on Preserving the Free and Open Internet and is described in Sect. 3.5.3. For example, an operator may prioritize voice, however, all voice related services must be treated equally. Blocking unlawful content is seen as a necessary action, yet people fear that in searching for illegalities, the operators may violate privacy.

Deep packet inspection techniques, i.e., looking into the payload of the IP packets to gain information on data content is considered harmful. However, the operators argue that they need to do it occasionally to protect the network from certain types of attacks. Throttling or degrading certain types of traffic might look similar to prioritizing whole services, but it is more controversial. Let us consider P2P traffic which is often the subject of discrimination. Today, P2P traffic carries data,

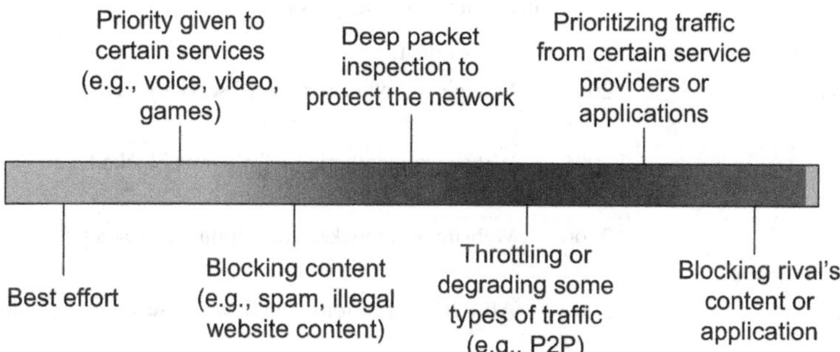

Fig. 3.2 Traffic management through the eyes of net neutrality

voice, video, gaming and many more services. Therefore, degrading P2P traffic discriminates only a part of video providers, voice providers, etc.

The last two actions are clearly against the net neutrality principles. In the proponents view, the operators should be prohibited from prioritizing certain services over others, as it creates unfair competition in the market, and, above all, threatens the development of the Internet. This point is especially important if the operator, using its power, wants to block rival content and behave as a monopolist.

3.4 Net Neutrality Violations from the Past

The fact that network neutrality has become such a widely discussed topic has its roots in the past, when certain telecom companies violated net neutrality principles. Table 3.3 shows only the most well-known instances of acts against neutrality. However, such violations happen every day everywhere; it is just that they are either not exposed or not publicly recognized.

The first significant dispute occurred in 2004, when Madison River, a telephone company and ISP from North Carolina, blocked the Vonage VoIP service from their customers. The Vonage service competed with the standard PSTN telephone service offered by the operator, and was constantly stealing some of their revenues. One year later, Canada's second largest ISP, Telus, blocked access for its users to the website run by a member of the Telecommunications Workers Union (TWU). At that time, Telus and the TWU were engaged in a harsh labor dispute.

Possibly one of the most widely recognized conflicts was that involving Comcast, the second largest Internet provider in the US, and the P2P environment, represented by Vuze, a BitTorrent application. Beginning around May 2007, Comcast began to block certain Internet communication protocols, including the P2P protocols BitTorrent and Gnutella. At first, Comcast denied taking any action. However, in February 2008 Comcast Executive Vice President David Cohen said at an FCC public hearing, "*Comcast may on a limited basis temporarily delay certain P2P*

Table 3.3 Documented violations of net neutrality principles [8, 27]

Operator content provider	Year	Discrimination
Madison river Vonage	2004	Vonage and other rival VoIP services were blocked
Telus TWU	2005	Website sympathetic to TWU was blocked
AOL www.dearaol.com	2006	Website was blocked for critiquing AOL's policies
Comcast P2P, Vuze	2007	All P2P connections shut down or severely degraded

TWU: Telecommunications Workers Union

traffic when that traffic has or is projected to have an adverse effect on other customers' use of the service." They claimed that their networks were not designed to provide BitTorrent services and that such services deteriorates other services in the network. Instead of investing in the development of their network, a simpler solution was to block the unwanted protocol. However, there is more to this than meets the eye. By blocking BitTorrent, Comcast got rid of Vuze, an application which legally delivered television content to end-users based on the P2P protocol and threatened Comcast's traditional cable-based content delivery.

In 2006, America On-Line (AOL) blocked a website which had posted some negative opinions about AOL's new pay-to-send email scheme. Similarly, in 2007 Verizon Wireless denied certain messages to be rightfully forwarded through their network. This incident concerned GSM networks and not the Internet; however, the actions taken resemble general carrier neutrality issues.

These violations of network neutrality principles happened in the past and attracted enough public attention to be recognized worldwide. However, such malpractices happen more often than we can imagine. The fact that an ISP favors its own service over competing services is not uncommon. For example, one of the Polish ISPs favors its VoIP connections over all other kinds of traffic, which at times of congestion results in a better quality of their service. The possibilities are endless. In many publications, e.g., in [10] and [12], the reader can find more examples of possible violations of network neutrality principles.

3.5 The Debate

The previous section showed the reasons behind the discussion and how the debate started. From what can be observed, a large body of Internet users, despite being strongly interested, are underrepresented in the discussion. This is because operators and large content providers such as Google or Yahoo are able to make their voices heard. For example, in 2006, Ebay.com emailed over 1 million of their customers urging them to support the legislation. Similarly, Google CEO Eric Schmidt wrote an open letter to Google users asking them to take active steps to protect Internet freedom. However, at the same time, it is estimated that telecom and cable companies in the US have been spending one million dollars per week on advertisements to oppose moves towards network neutrality legislation. Against this background, the users' voice is represented only on websites such as savetheinternet.com.

3.5.1 The Proponents' Perspective

Although the exact demands of various network neutrality proponents are not identical, the Internet Freedom Preservation Act of January 2007, introduced by eight US senators—including senators Barack Obama and Hillary Clinton—

enumerates many of them. The restrictions are summarized in [6]. According to the document, a broadband service provider:

1. may not block, impede, discriminate or degrade the ability of any person to use a broadband service to access, use, send, post or offer any lawful content, application or service available on the Internet,
2. cannot prevent users from attaching a physical device to the network, as long as the device does not degrade or damage the network,
3. must provide clear terms of service to their subscribers, explaining the access type, speed and limitations applied,
4. cannot impose a charge on the basis of the usage of the network,
5. cannot charge for prioritization of traffic,
6. cannot require a subscriber to purchase additional services to receive certain content.

The telecom companies refuse to meet these demands arguing that the fact that the Internet works so well is a result of unregulated competition on the market. The laws of the market, in the eyes of telecom syndicates, will be sufficient to protect consumer rights. AT&T chairman Ed Whitacre in March 2006 said, "*Any provider that blocks access to content is inviting customers to find another provider. And that's just bad business.*"

Unfortunately, as shown in [27], for a number of reasons this is not the case. Firstly, if all network providers block the same applications, there will be no-one to switch to—and the choice is not that great to begin with. Secondly, customers do not have an incentive to switch if they do not realize that their operator interferes with the traffic. Thirdly, switching to another ISP requires significant time, effort and money, as most consumers will have signed fixed-term contracts. Finally, if tampering with the users' traffic is such 'bad business,' why do operators argue that they need to do it to develop the infrastructure with the resulting revenue? This argument essentially concedes that ISPs have an incentive to discriminate in order to increase their profits.

3.5.2 The Opponents' Perspective

As any possible regulations related to network neutrality will be inconvenient, to say the least, for the network operators, they are opposed to network neutrality. Some say that the values of net neutrality are worth respecting, but putting them into law will break the Internet [19].

Telecom operators explain that network neutrality should not be legalized because:

1. broadband service providers should be allowed to control traffic inside their own network as they wish for the benefit of the users,

2. the Internet is not neutral today: QoS is and needs to be applied for certain applications to work,
3. the additional stream of revenues from providing differentiated treatment will allow for more investments in the infrastructure which, in turn, will result in overall better quality for all the users,
4. broadband competition is increasing and users are free to switch to another operator if they are not satisfied with the enforced traffic policies,
5. network administrators need to be able to inspect packet payloads in order to defend against certain network attacks,
6. market competition is sufficient for the operators to refrain from any bad behavior.

Most of the arguments mentioned above do not satisfy users and content providers. Andrew Odlyzko in [18] criticizes telecom operators for convincing people that they need additional revenues to build the Future Internet and that those funds will not come if network neutrality principles are enforced. The argument that the market rules are sufficient to maintain fairness can simply be overruled by the examples of network neutrality violations from the past. If the market laws did not apply then, we should not hope for them to apply in the future.

In their views, network providers often overlook the fact that content providers are the ones that increase demand on network services. Without content providers, the demand on network capacity will plummet, along with network operators' revenues. Therefore, it is in their best interests to foster the development of content providers, rather than to impede it by collecting additional charges.

Very often the position of the proponents is displayed as if they had asked for total net neutrality, i.e., the lack of a possibility to even discard viruses, spam or other malicious traffic. Although such extreme views used to appear from time to time, these ideas are no longer in the mainstream. Recalling them is merely an attempt to make net neutrality look absurd. In reality, users fear that ISPs will gain the power to completely model everybody based on their behavior on the Internet by collecting information stored in our transmissions [13].

3.5.3 The Government Perspective

In the US, the FCC has been deliberating the subject of network neutrality for a number of years now. After an extensive public debate, a report on "Preserving the Free and Open Internet" was adopted on 21 December, 2010 [2]. This document contains three rules for an open Internet: transparency, no blocking, and no unreasonable discrimination. Transparency forces fixed and mobile broadband providers to disclose their network management practices, performance characteristics, and the terms and conditions of their broadband services. The no-blocking rule prohibits fixed broadband providers from blocking any lawful content, applications, services, or non-harmful devices. At the same time, mobile broadband providers may not block lawful websites, or block applications that compete with their voice or video telephony services. As can be seen, the proposed regulations are less strict towards mobile broadband providers. The third rule establishes that fixed broadband providers may not unreasonably discriminate in transmitting lawful network traffic over a consumer's broadband Internet access service. This report was a firm step in the network neutrality debate. It presented the perspective and guidelines for the future.

According to the FCC report, telecom operators are able to manage their networks and carried traffic, as long as they inform their clients about the actions, and as long as the actions themselves are not discriminatory. They are able to engineer their traffic and provide quality of service to those applications which need it. Therefore, in accordance with net neutrality, assigning certain services higher or lower priorities can be tolerated, provided that all applications inside a certain service receive that treatment. Such an approach is reasonable. Currently, some network operators provide better treatment to certain voice applications for the sake of their quality. To maintain neutrality, equal actions must be carried out on all voice applications.

We should realize that the broadband market situation is not the same in every country. The authors of [4, 9, 15, 17] and [16] show the differences in telecommunications regulations and local broadband markets in Korea, the UK, and the European Union. In [17], we read that: "*... the landscape in Europe looks different than in the U.S. and is likely to remain so in the foreseeable future: fewer competing infrastructures, but more market players (...).*" While it is true that we will not be able to produce a 'one size fits all' resolution to the network neutrality problem, we can always learn from predecessors' mistakes and only slightly adjust our solutions.

3.6 Flow-Aware Networking: A Feasible Solution

The lack of commercial revenue prospects inhibits the development of QoS architectures. Moreover, the network neutrality debate will become decisive for the future of QoS. If network neutrality is the vision in which the network operator is not allowed to discriminate traffic of certain users or applications and favor others, many QoS architectures are simply unusable. Although the outcome of the debate is unclear, it will impact the Future Internet. Therefore, even now, QoS architectures are assessed with respect to their neutrality.

Current networks are over-provisioned which helps certain multimedia applications to obtain good quality without any additional traffic management on top of best-effort. When service quality starts to deteriorate a network operator faces a known dilemma: whether to invest in the infrastructure or to deploy a QoS architecture. The real problem is that each proposed QoS architecture, including the most mature, i.e., IntServ and DiffServ, has some flaws. IntServ's problems with scalability are described extensively in the literature, e.g., in [26]. Although considered as a leading proposal, DiffServ is criticized mainly for its increased granularity and complexity. As both architectures may be considered orthogonal, they represent a trade-off between scalability and possible QoS guarantees. Although DiffServ-capable routers are commonly available, operators rarely use this functionality, and even if so, only locally. Therefore, it is necessary to find a new architecture, one that could really be used in the Future Internet.

Common QoS architectures, including IntServ and DiffServ, provide means for the network operators to differentiate the service without any limitations. It is possible to discriminate traffic based on virtually anything the operator decides, such as the application type, source or destination addresses, traffic volume, etc. It is also possible to implement deep packet inspection mechanisms and police the traffic based on its mother application or content. However, since most of the differentiation actions violate net neutrality, choosing such a powerful and complex solution is neither useful nor cheap. The real goal, therefore, is to find a solution which could be used with the IP protocol, and would be simple, efficient, scalable, and in conformity with network neutrality rules.

Flow-Aware Networking as a QoS architecture fits perfectly into these boundaries. We present the main differences between classic approaches to QoS assurance and Flow-Aware Networking. We also explain why FAN seamlessly blends into the net neutrality concept while introducing QoS awareness.

Figure 3.3 shows a concept diagram of various approaches to assuring QoS in IP networks. Originally, the Internet was designed to be simple and efficient. However, mainly due to its simplicity, the traffic can be carried only in a best-effort way (Fig. 3.3a). This means that we do not control the quality of service, relying solely on over-provisioning of the link resources.

Figures 3.3b and c present two different methods of achieving QoS. The standard approach (Fig. 3.3b) focuses on dividing the traffic into classes and treating different classes separately. The term ‘class of service’ is understood differently in various proposals, yet the idea always revolves around a separate treatment of different transmissions. Firstly, a flow must be identified by the classifier block and assigned to a certain class. The classification process is explicit, because nodes are pre-informed on how to recognize and treat a particular transmission.

Flow-Aware Networks (Fig. 3.3c), on the other hand, operate quite differently. First of all, the flow identification process is implicit and its goal is not to divide flows into different classes, but only to create an instance on which the service differentiation will be performed. Then, all the flows that are currently in progress, i.e., are present on the Protected Flow List (PFL), are forwarded unconditionally, and all the new flows are subject to admission control. Admission control in FAN is measurement-based which implies that the accept/reject decisions are made based only on the current link congestion status.

The main advantage of FAN, with respect to the net neutrality issue, is that it provides service differentiation, taking into account only the traffic characteristics of the ongoing transmissions. Therefore, it does not discriminate certain applications or end-users explicitly. Moreover, instead of providing differentiated treatment, FAN introduces fairness, which even enhances current IP network equality.

Table 3.4 summarizes the differences between various approaches to QoS guarantees. The current best-effort Internet, as shown over the last decade, has

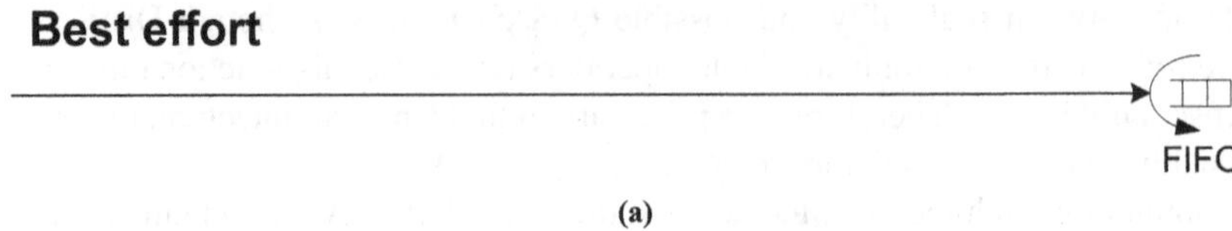

(a)

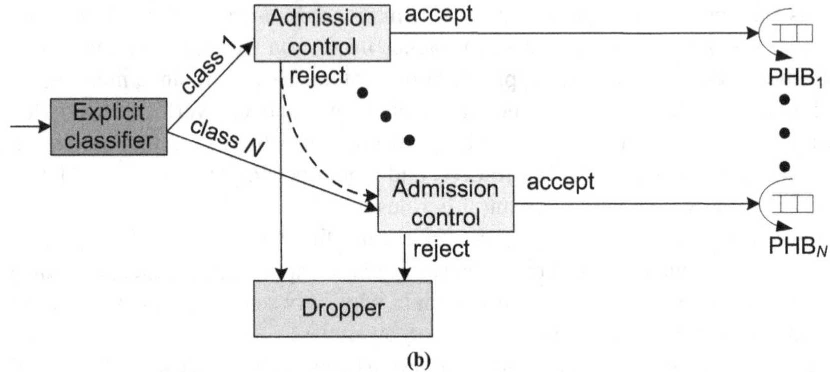

(b)

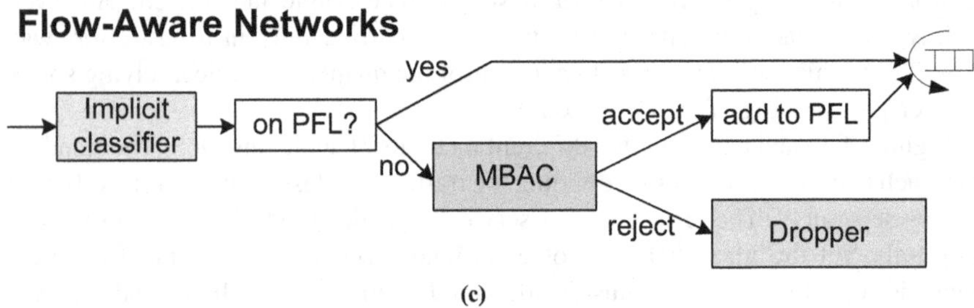

(c)

Fig. 3.3 Different approaches to QoS: (**a**) best-effort, (**b**) standard, class-based QoS architectures, (**c**) Flow-Aware Networks

Table 3.4 Comparison of QoS architectures

	Service differentiation	Salability	Net neutrality conformity
Best-effort	None	High	Yes
IntServ	Explicit	Very low	No
DiffServ	Explicit	Medium	No
FAN	Implicit	High	Yes

no problems with scalability and is seen as the only possible solution for the future by some net neutrality proponents. Unfortunately, best-effort does not support service differentiation of any kind which is its obvious drawback. IntServ and DiffServ were chosen as the most common representatives for standard class-based QoS architectures. For the price of introducing explicit service differentiation, these architectures degrade network scalability, significantly increase its complexity, and become net neutrality unfriendly. Flow-Aware Networks, on the other hand, retain high scalability, while introducing implicit service differentiation techniques. Additionally, the FAN QoS methods do not interfere with the view of the neutral Internet. FAN, as opposed to IntServ and DiffServ, does not allow an explicit differentiation by the ISPs. This is a very important advantage of this technology. Of course, ISPs may try to change a router's software and provide a traffic classification which allows for packet queuing and servicing according to their rules. However, such behavior is opposed to FAN principles, and so it is more difficult to introduce than in, say, DiffServ, which natively supports explicit differentiated treatment.

3.7 The Future of Net Neutrality

Although the debate has been active for a number of years now, it has not reached stalemate. New proposals related to the debate are emerging more than ever. In [24], the authors present Network Access Neutrality Observatory (NANO), a system which detects network neutrality violations. They claim that NANO can detect violations very effectively. Such initiatives put pressure on the network operators, as they can no longer hope to hide their malpractices and discriminations. Moreover, people have more tools to check if their operator applies any traffic policies to their transmissions.

There is also a sign that operators have begun to care about network neutrality, or at least to fear the consequences. In August 2010, Google and Verizon publicly announced their joint policy proposal for an open Internet. These companies see their proposal as a compromise. The plan is to preserve the open Internet, while allowing network operators the flexibility and freedom to effectively manage their networks. A broadband Internet access provider would be prohibited from preventing users from:

1. sending and receiving lawful content of their choice,
2. running lawful applications and using lawful services of their choice,
3. connecting their choice of legal devices that do not harm the network or service, facilitate theft of service, or harm other users of the service.

This framework proposal resulted in nothing concrete. However, it showed the rest of the community that network neutrality should be considered seriously.

On 23 April, 2014 the FCC was reported to be considering a new resolution—one that is opposite to their previous views. They want to permit network operators to differentiate broadband lanes. At roughly the same time, European Parliament voted to restrict operators' ability to charge for better traffic service. Therefore, current EU status is pro net neutrality, contrary to what is being debated in the US.

The debate follows different trails around the world and the most probable resolutions will also be different. However, as explained in this chapter, FAN is a QoS technique which works with all current views, including both American and European. Therefore, regardless of the final outcome, FAN will not violate regulations, which makes it a very sound proposal.

3.8 Check Your Knowledge

1. What is the main reason why network neutrality is not a law?
2. Which parties are generally for and which are against network neutrality?
3. Is quality of service impossible with network neutrality?
4. Why do network operators not want network neutrality?
5. How do network operators explain that network neutrality is not needed?

References

1. A. Bany Mohammed, J. Altmann, A funding and governing model for achieving sustainable growth of computing e-infrastructures. Ann. Telecommun. **65**(11-12), 739–756 (2010). [Online]. Available: http://dx.doi.org/10.1007/s12243-010-0188-9
2. U.F.C. Commission, Preserving the Free and Open Internet, http://hraunfoss.fcc.gov/edocs_public/attachmatch/FFCC-10-201A1_Rcd.pdf, December 2010, Commision Report
3. P. Coucheney, P. Maille, B. Tuffin, Impact of competition between isps on the net neutrality debate. IEEE Trans. Netw. Serv. Manag. **PP**(99), 1–9 (2013)
4. J. Crowcroft, Net neutrality: the technical side of the debate: a white paper. ACM SIGCOMM Comput. Commun. Rev. **37**(1), 49–56 (2007)
5. G. D'Acquisto, M. Naldi, How much can content providers afford to pay for network charges? in *2012 Sixth UKSim/AMSS European Symposium on Computer Modeling and Simulation (EMS)*, pp. 257–262, 2012
6. K. Deeb, S.P.O. Sr., M.E. Weiner, A survey on network neutrality; a new form of discrimination based on network profiling. Int. J. Networking Virtual Organ. **6**(4), 426–436 (2009)
7. N. Economides, J. Tag, Net Neutrality on the Internet: A Two-sided Market Analysis, NET Institute, Working Papers 07–14, Sep. 2007. [Online]. Available: http://ideas.repec.org/p/net/wpaper/0714.html
8. P. Ganley, B. Allgrove, Net neutrality: A user's guide. Comput. Law Secur. Rev. **22**(6), 454–463 (2006)
9. G. Goth, The global net neutrality debate: back to square one? IEEE Internet Comput. **14**(4), 7–9 (2010)
10. S. Greenstein, Four nightmares for net neutrality. Micro IEEE **26**, 12–13 (2006)
11. L. Guijarro, V. Pla, J.R. Vidal, J. Bauset, Search engine and content providers: neutrality, competition and integration. Trans. Emerg. Telecommun. Technol. (2014). [Online]. Available: http://dx.doi.org/10.1002/ett.2827
12. G. Held, Net neutrality may be a necessity. Int. J. Netw. Manag. **17**(1), 1–1 (2007)
13. A. Joch, Debating net neutrality. Commun. ACM **52**(10), 14–15 (2009)
14. S. Jordan, Traffic management and net neutrality in wireless networks. IEEE Trans. Netw. Serv. Manag. **8**(4), 297–309 (2011)
15. B. Kim, A comparison of network neutrality debates between US and South Korea, in *Proc. 11th international conference on Advanced Communication Technology, ICACT 2009* (IEEE Press, Piscataway, NJ, USA, 2009), pp. 1785–1790
16. M. Kitsing, Network neutrality in europe, in *Proceedings of the 5th International Conference on Theory and Practice of Electronic Governance*, ser. ICEGOV '11 (ACM, New York, NY, USA, 2011), pp. 313–316. [Online]. Available: http://doi.acm.org/10.1145/2072069.2072126

17. P. Larouche, Law and technology: The network neutrality debate hits Europe. Commun. ACM **52**(5), 22–24 (2009)
18. A. Odlyzko, The delusions of net neutrality, August 2008. Available at: http://www.dtc.umn.edu/~odlyzko/, downloaded on 2010-11-02
19. P. Ohm, When network neutrality met privacy. Commun. ACM **53**(4), 30–32 (2010)
20. B.M. Owen, The Net Neutrality Debate: Twenty Five Years After United States v. AT&T and 120 Years After the Act to Regulate Commerce, *Stanford Law and Economics Olin Working Paper No. 336*
21. K. Rafique, C. Yuan, M. Saeed, Net neutrality pradox: Regulator's dilemma, in *7th International Conference on Wireless Communications, Networking and Mobile Computing (WiCOM) 2011*, pp. 1–5, 2011
22. F.B. Schneider, Network neutrality versus internet trustworthiness? IEEE Secur. Priv. **6**(4), 3–4 (2008)
23. A. Tareen, Next generation broadband access networks evolving market structure and implications of network neutrality regulation, in *2011 IEEE International Conference on Cloud Computing and Intelligence Systems (CCIS)*, pp. 280–284, 2011
24. M.B. Tariq, M. Motiwala, N. Feamster, M. Ammar, Detecting network neutrality violations with causal inference, in *Proc. 5th International Conference on Emerging Networking Experiments and Technologies, CoNEXT 2009*, New York, NY, USA, pp. 289–300, December 2009
25. T. Trinh, L. Gyarmati, How to price internet access for disloyal users under uncertainty. Ann. Telecommun. **65**(3-4), 171–188 (2010). [Online]. Available: http://dx.doi.org/10.1007/s12243-009-0133-y
26. B. van Schewick, D. Farber, *Technical, Commercial and Regulatory Challenges of QoS: An Internet Service Model Perspective* (Morgan Kaufmann Publishers, San Francisco, CA, USA, 2008)
27. B. van Schewick, D. Farber, Point/counterpoint network neutrality nuances. Commun. ACM **52**(2), 31–37 (2009)

Congestion Control in Flow-Aware Networks 4

The Internet "browser"... is the piece of software that puts a message on your computer screen informing you that the Internet is currently busy and you should try again later.

— Dave Barry

4.1 Motivation for Congestion Control in FAN

In FAN, when the outgoing link is congested, new flows cannot be accepted by MBAC. A congestion state may be observed for a long time, which may not be acceptable for streaming flows implementing tasks such as real-time transmissions, for example VoIP (Voice over IP). It should be noted that according to [9], the setup time (post-selection delay) for local calls should be less than 6 s, while for international calls it should not exceed 11 s. The main motivation for the introduction of congestion control mechanisms in the MBAC block of XP routers is to reduce the access time to the congested link for new streaming flows.

Seven congestion control mechanisms have been proposed for FAN thus far. The main assumption of the EFM (Enhanced Flushing Mechanism), EFMP (Enhanced Flushing Mechanism with Priority), RAEF (Remove Active Elastic Flows), RBAEF (Remove and Block Active Elastic Flows), RPAEF (Remove and Prioritize in access Active Elastic Flows) and RAMAF (Remove and Accept Most Active Flows) is to periodically remove identifiers of selected elastic flows from PFL. This way, the congestion is eliminated for a moment and new flows may be accepted. The concept of the SCCM (Simple Congestion Control Mechanism) is different. In this solution, we do not remove any identifiers but steer the level of min_FR instead. In the following sections, we describe the congestion mechanisms in detail and present the simulation analysis that confirms their usefulness. We also present other solutions which improve transmission efficiency in congestion.

J. Domżał et al., *Guide to Flow-Aware Networking*, Computer Communications and Networks, https://doi.org/10.1007/978-3-030-57153-5_4

4.2 Enhanced Flushing Mechanism

The EFM, presented in [2] and [3], is the first congestion control mechanism proposed for FAN to solve the problem of too long acceptance delays of new streaming flows in the MBAC block. The operation of the EFM is presented in Fig. 4.1. During congestion the identifiers of all elastic flows are periodically removed from the PFL in the EFM. It makes it possible to eliminate congestion for one measurement interval of the *FR* parameter. In this congestion-less period, new flows (as well as those removed before) are accepted in the MBAC. If we clean the PFL quickly enough, new streaming flows are accepted in an acceptable period.

The pseudo-code for realizing the EFM functionality in FAN is presented in Fig. 4.2.

The *pfl_flushing_timer* is a parameter defining the minimum time between two runs of the EFM. If a packet of a new flow arrives at the admission control block in congestion and the period since the last flushing action is greater or equal to the value of the *pfl_flushing_timer*, the EFM is activated (lines 1–3). The For loop is executed for each flow, and this identifier is written to the PFL (line 5). The ID of each elastic flow is then removed from the PFL (lines 7–8). A flow is selected as

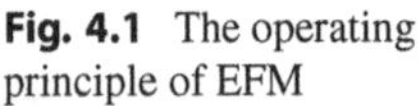

Fig. 4.1 The operating principle of EFM

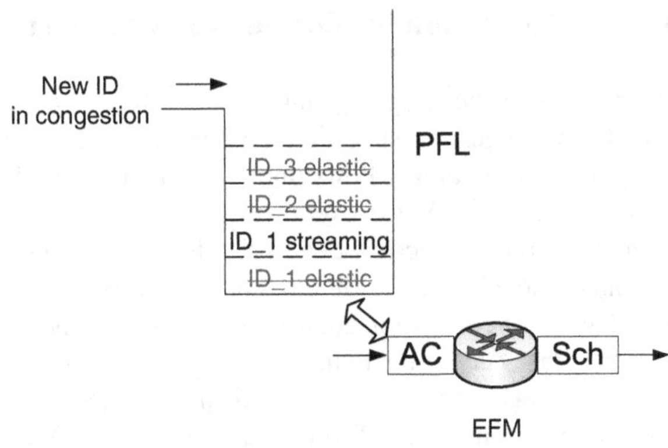


```
1   on a new flow packet arrival in congestion
2   current_time = Scheduler :: instance().clock()
3   if current_time − flushing_start ≥ pfl_flushing_timer then
4   begin
5       for (i = 1; i ≤ pfl_size; i++) do
6       begin
7           if flow_bytes(i) ≥ MTU then
8           remove ID(i) from PFL
9       end
10      flushing_start = Scheduler :: instance().clock()
11  end
```

Fig. 4.2 Pseudo-code for realizing the EFM functionality in FAN

elastic if the number of bytes of its traffic in a queue is greater than or equal to MTU. At the end of each cleaning action, the value of the pointer, which indicates the time of the last flushing action, is set to the current time (line 10).

The implementation of the EFM in the XP router is relatively simple and does not significantly increase the complexity and processing resources.

4.2.1 Simulation of the EFM

Using the following simulation experiments, we show how the EFM may improve network performance in the congestion state. We present results for FAN with the PFQ architecture only. Results for other FAN architectures are similar.

250 simulation runs were made in various conditions to show the time of acceptance of a new streaming flow (*waiting_time*) in the AC block in a FAN link. We analyzed a FAN link with 20 streaming flows and the number of elastic flows ranging from 200 to 600. The first streaming flow began its transmission at 50 s and the remaining streaming flows began their transmission one by one. The duration of each simulation run was set to 250 s, which allowed us to observe the acceptance delay of flows. The simulation topology and other simulation parameters used were as in Sect. 2.6.4. Mean values of *waiting_time* as a function of the number of elastic flows active in the background for FAN with PFQ are presented in Fig. 4.3.

We can see that the values of the parameter are constant for each *pfl_flushing_timer* value. It means that a new streaming flow is accepted in the AC block at the same time for particular values of the *pfl_flushing_timer* parameter, independently of the number of elastic flows waiting to send traffic. Without using the flushing mechanism the *waiting_time* values (tens of seconds) are significantly greater than those when the flushing mechanism (EFM) is implemented. The

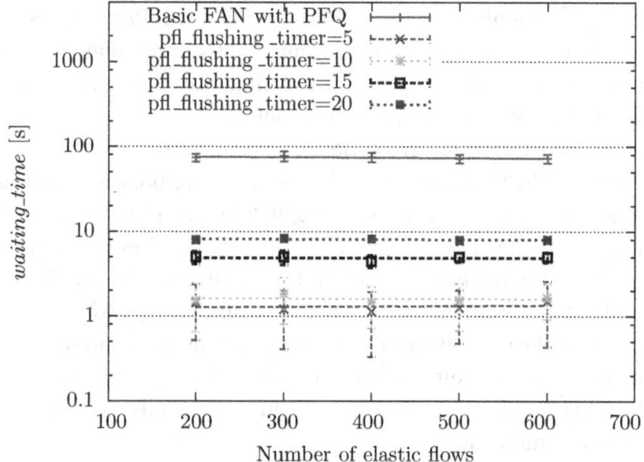

Fig. 4.3 The mean *waiting_time* in FAN with PFQ and EFM

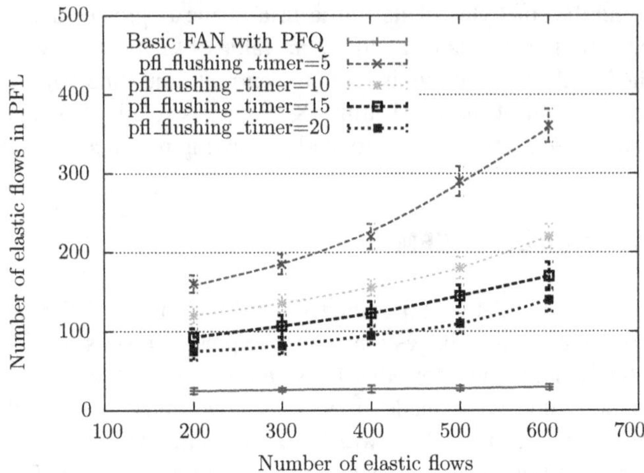

Fig. 4.4 The mean number of elastic flows in PFL in FAN with PFQ and EFM

waiting_time values increase with increasing values of the *pfl_flushing_timer* parameter in the examined range. It is clear that the best results were obtained when the *pfl_flushing_timer* was set to 5 s. Simulation results show that in this case a new flow was always accepted within 2 s from the time when it started sending traffic. In the cases when the *pfl_flushing_timer* was set to 10 or 15 s a new flow was accepted a few seconds later, although the results are still acceptable for local voice calls [9]. When the *pfl_flushing_timer* was set to 20 s, the results show that a new streaming flow was accepted after approximately 8 s, which is not acceptable for local calls but sufficiently low for international calls [9].

After almost every cleaning action the number of elastic flows accepted again is greater than in the basic FAN (where it is about 25 flows). In this simulation experiment, the mean number of elastic flows in FAN with PFQ was estimated. The simulation duration was set to 500 s, which enabled us to calculate the values of the analyzed parameter in the steady state for a sufficiently long time. The remaining simulation parameters were set as in the previous case.

The values of the mean number of elastic flows as a function of the number of elastic flows active in background for FAN with PFQ are presented in Fig. 4.4.

The mean number of elastic flows accepted in the router after any flushing action increases with the increasing number of elastic flows waiting to start or continue transmission in the background. In FAN with PFQ the number of accepted flows after flushing is significantly higher than in the basic FAN, where the mean number of accepted elastic flows is almost independent of the number of all elastic flows waiting to transmit their packets. This is a strong drawback of the EFM and shows that this solution may not be scalable, especially for low values of the *pfl_flushing_timer* parameter.

4.3 Enhanced Flushing Mechanism with Priority

This section presents the congestion control mechanism known as EFMP (EFM with Priority) [6]. It is a combination of the EFM with admission control policies proposed for MFAN and PAFL (Priority Access Flow List). The packet service in EFMP with the 'oldest-flow' policy is presented in Fig. 4.5.

The pseudo-code for realizing the EFMP functionality with the 'oldest-flow' policy is presented in Fig. 4.6.

When a packet of a new flow arrives at the admission control block in congestion, it starts the EFMP procedure. The *For* loop is executed for each flow from the PFL (line 7). It is necessary to find the active time of the flow (line 9) and check whether it is elastic (line 10). The procedure to find the oldest flow (lines 12–15) is run next.

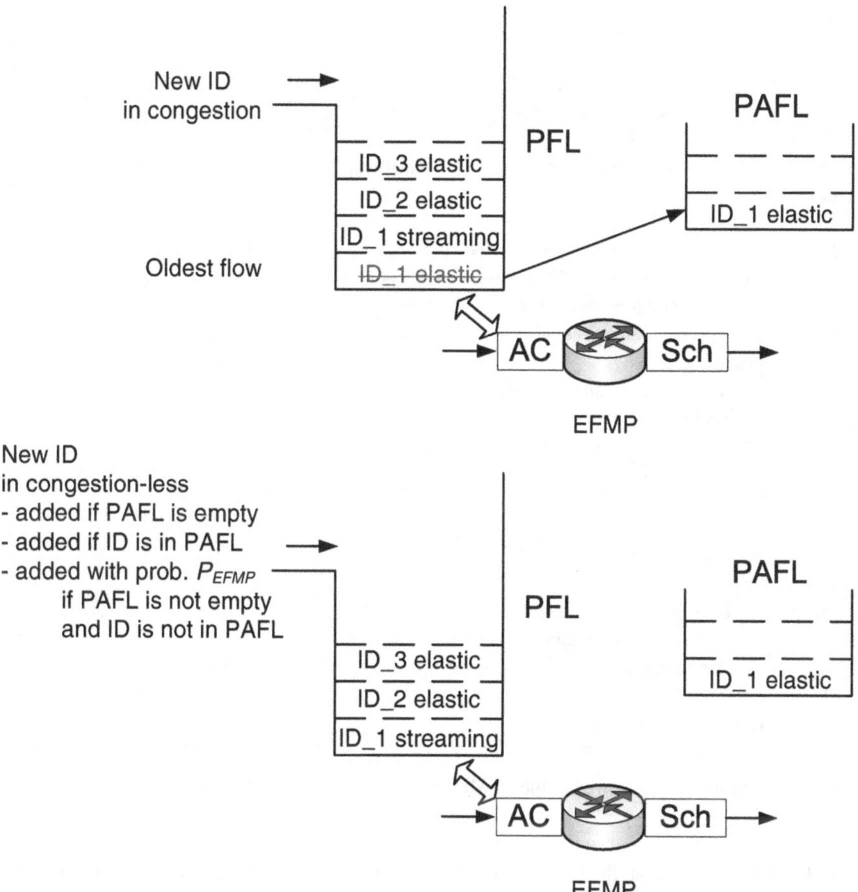

Fig. 4.5 Packet service in Flow-Aware Networks with EFMP with the 'oldest-flow' policy

```
1  on a new flow packet arrival in congestion
2  while link is congested do
3  begin
4      current_time = Scheduler :: instance().clock() then
5      if current_time − last_EFMP_action > priority_access then
6      begin
7          for (i = 1; i ≤ pfl_size; i++) do
8          begin
9              active_time(i) = current_time − first_operation_time(i)
10             if flow_bytes(i) ≥ MTU then
11             begin
12                 if oldest_flow_time < active_time(i) then
13                 begin
14                     oldest_flow_time = active_time(i)
15                     oldest_flow_id = i
16                 end
17             end
18         end
19         remove FID(oldest_flow_id) from PFL
20         add FID(oldest_flow_id) to PAFL
21         PAFL_occup = 1
22         last_EFMP_action = Scheduler :: instance().clock()
23     end
24 end
25 ######### admission decision #########
26 on arriving packet P of flow i in congestion −less state after EFMP run
27 current_time = Scheduler :: instance().clock()
28 if current_time − last_EFMP_action > priority_access then
29 begin
30     if PAFL_occup = 1 then
31     begin
32         clean PAFL content
33         PAFL_occup = 0
34     end
35 end
36 if PAFL is not empty then
37 begin
38     if i is in PAFL then
39         proceed with packet P
40     else proceed with P with acceptance probability P_EFMP
41 end
42 else proceed with P
```

Fig. 4.6 Pseudo-code for realizing the EFMP functionality in FAN

The FID of the oldest flow is removed from the PFL (line 19) and added to the PAFL (line 20). Moreover, the parameter *PAFL_occup* is set to 1 which means that the PAFL is not empty (line 21). The procedure is repeated until the outgoing link is not congested (lines 2 and 24).

If there are any identifiers in the PAFL in a congestion-less state (*PAFL_occup=1*), the flows whose FIDs are not in the PAFL are accepted with a low P_{EFMP} probability (experimentally calculated as 0.03) (line 40). On the other hand, the flows whose FIDs are in the PAFL are accepted without limitations, with the highest possible priority (lines 38–39). If the PAFL is empty, the packets of flows whose FIDs are in the PFL are always accepted and the other packets are served if there is no congestion in the outgoing link (line 42).

The PAFL content is cleaned in a congestion-less state after the time given by the *priority_access* parameter (in our analysis, this value was set to 1 s—twice the *FR* measurement interval) since the last cleaning action on the PFL (lines 28–35). Based on our observations, it can be assumed that the value of double the *FR* measurement interval guarantees that the majority of streaming flows are accepted by the admission control block. On the other hand, during this period almost no new elastic flows are accepted.

The implementation of the EFMP in the cross-protect router is more complex than the EFM. In EFM, we have to find all elastic flows (one loop) and remove their identifiers from PFL. In EFMP, we have to find the oldest or the most active flow (one loop), remove its ID from PFL and write it to PAFL. Such operations are repeated until the link becomes uncongested. This increases complexity because loops may be executed many times. Moreover, we have to check if *priority_access* time ends and according to this make acceptance decisions in the congestion-less state in different ways. We can see that the cross-protect router with EFMP has to execute more operations in comparison to EFM; however, it should not be a problem for currently used devices, which usually have sufficient memory and efficient processors.

4.3.1 Simulation of the EFMP

In this section, we present the results of the simulation analysis of the EFMP with both the 'oldest-flow' and 'most-active-flow' policies originally proposed for MFAN. In comparison to the EFM, in the first policy only the oldest flow is removed from PFL instead of all elastic flows as the case in the EFM. In the 'most-active-flow' policy, the flow which has the highest number of bytes in the queue is removed. The results, presented in Figs. 4.7 and 4.8, show that the solution gives acceptable values of all analyzed aspects in both admission control policies. The EFMP ensures fast acceptance of new streaming flows and good transmission properties of elastic flows, and it is scalable.

It should be noted that in this mechanism the *pfl_flushing_timer* means the difference between the end of *priority_access* and the beginning of the next EFMP run. The acceptance delay of streaming flows and the number of elastic flows accepted again in the PFL increase significantly with the increasing value of the *pfl_flushing_timer* parameter. On the other hand, when the value of this parameter is lower than 1 s, the EFMP mechanism is unstable.

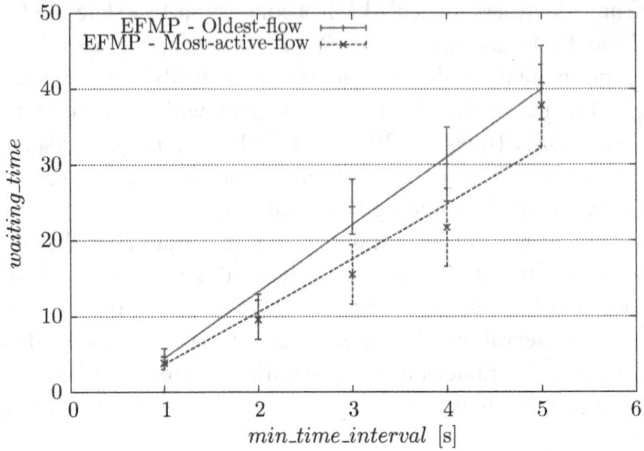

Fig. 4.7 Acceptance delay of streaming flows in FAN with EFMP or in MFAN

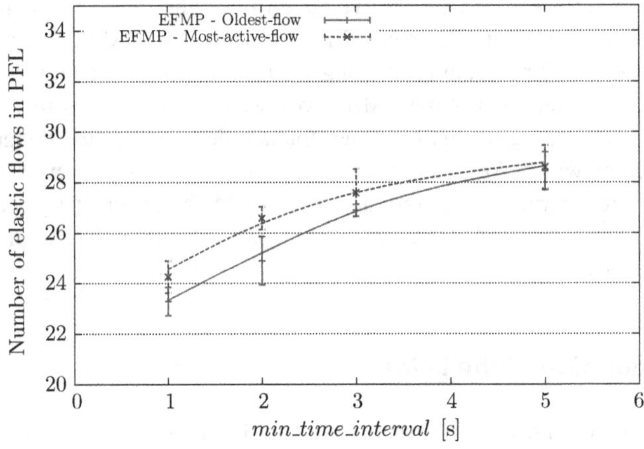

Fig. 4.8 Number of elastic flows accepted in PFL after flushing in FAN with EFMP or in MFAN

In the next simulation experiment, we checked how the values of *waiting_time* and the number of elastic flows admitted to the PFL change as a function of the active elastic flows in the background. The number of active elastic flows varied from 200 to 600. The *pfl_flushing_timer* was set to 1 s. The duration of each simulation run was set to 250 s. The other simulation parameters were set as in the previous cases. The results are presented in Figs. 4.9 and 4.10.

Acceptance delay values of streaming flows and the number of accepted elastic flows on the PFL are almost constant in each case. It is consistent with the predictions, and confirms that the EFMP is scalable and ensure quality of service for both traffic types in FAN independently of the traffic load in the network.

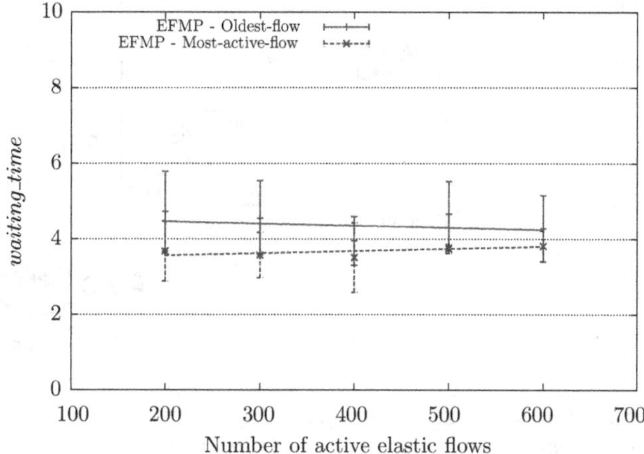

Fig. 4.9 Acceptance delay of streaming flows in FAN with EFMP or in MFAN

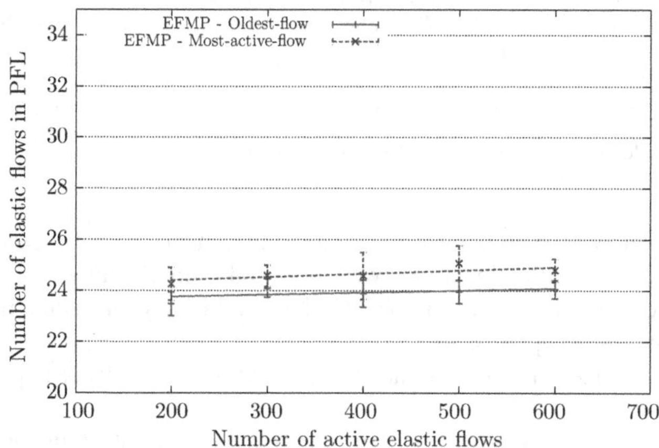

Fig. 4.10 Number of elastic flows accepted in PFL after flushing in FAN with EFMP or in MFAN

4.4 Remove Active Elastic Flows

RAEF (*Remove Active Elastic Flows*) is the second proposed mechanism for solving the problem of too long acceptance delays of new streaming flows in the AC block [2]. In this algorithm, the identifiers of all elastic flows active for at least a specified period (*active_time*) are removed from the PFL each time the congestion is noticed by a packet of a new flow (see Fig. 4.11). Flows whose identifiers were removed from the PFL are not blocked in the AC block and can resume the transmission promptly, as in the EFM. The disadvantages of this algorithm are the same as in the EFM. It is possible that the identifiers of such flows will not be added to the PFL

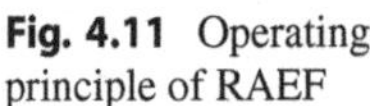

Fig. 4.11 Operating principle of RAEF

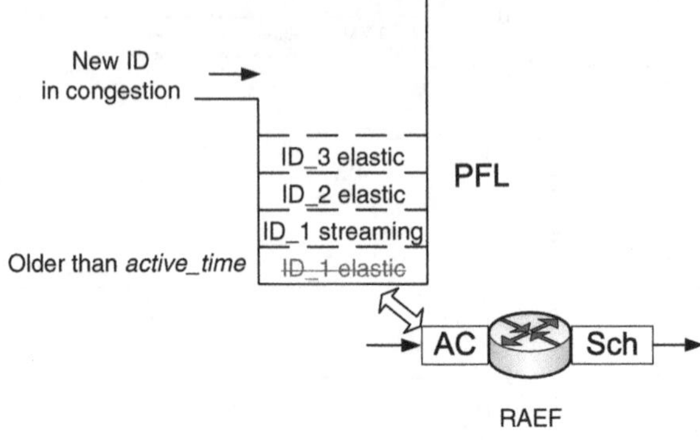


```
1  on a new flow packet arrival in congestion
2  current_time = Scheduler :: instance().clock()
3  for (i = 1; i ≤ pfl_size; i++) do
4  begin
5      active_time(i) = current_time − first_operation_time(i)
6      if flow_bytes(i) ≥ MTU && active_time(i) ≥ active_time then
7          remove ID(i) from PFL
8  end
```

Fig. 4.12 Pseudo-code for realizing the RAEF functionality in FAN

again immediately or even in a short time and the transmission of their traffic may lengthen. The flows whose identifiers were removed from the PFL, have to compete with other flows for acceptance in the AC block and it may take some time before such flows will be accepted again.

The pseudo-code for realizing the RAEF functionality in FAN is presented in Fig. 4.12.

If a packet of a new flow arrives at the admission control block the procedure of the RAEF mechanism is activated. The *For* loop is executed for each flow whose identifier is written to the PFL (line 3). If elastic flow i has been transmitting its traffic for at least $active\_time$, its flow ID is deleted from the PFL (lines 5–7). A flow is selected as elastic if its number of bytes in the queue is greater or equal to the MTU.

If a next packet of flow i arrives at the admission control block it may be accepted in a congestion-less state. Then its $first\_operation\_time$ is set to the $current\_time$ value. On the other hand, in congestion, it is dropped.

The implementation of the RAEF mechanism in the cross-protect router is simple and does not significantly increase the complexity and power processing.

4.4.1 Simulation of the RAEF

Results of the following simulation experiments show the usefulness of the RAEF mechanism and its ability to improve network performance in the congestion state.

The *waiting_time* values were analyzed as a function of the number of elastic flows active in the background in this simulation experiment. 250 simulation runs were made in various conditions with the number of elastic flows waiting to transmit their traffic ranging from 200 to 600. The duration of each simulation run was set to 250 s, allowing us to observe the acceptance delay of new streaming flows. Other simulation parameters were set as in the previous simulation experiments. The mean values of *waiting_time* as a function of the number of elastic flows active in background for FAN with PFQ are presented in Fig. 4.13.

The results show that in the examined range the *waiting_time* values are constant independently of the number of elastic flows waiting to send traffic. As we can see, the *waiting_time* values increase with the increasing values of the *active_time* parameter. The results are similar to those obtained in the experiment provided for the EFM, and significantly better than those presented for the basic FAN without any flushing mechanism. The best results were obtained when the *active_time* was set to 5 s. In this case, a new flow was always accepted within 2 s from the time when it started sending traffic, as in the EFM. The values of the *active_time* parameter equal to 10 or 15 s are acceptable for local voice calls and the value of 20 s ensures a sufficiently low acceptance delay of new streaming flows for international calls.

The reason for the long transmission time of elastic flows for low values of *active_time* is the same as for FAN with EFM. After almost every cleaning action the number of elastic flows accepted again is greater than in the basic FAN. In this simulation experiment, the mean number of elastic flows in FAN with PFQ was analyzed. The simulation duration was set to 500 s, which allowed us to analyze

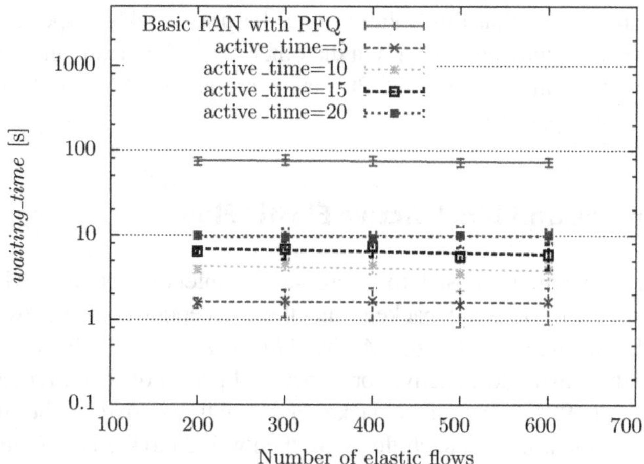

Fig. 4.13 Mean *waiting_time* in FAN with PFQ and RAEF

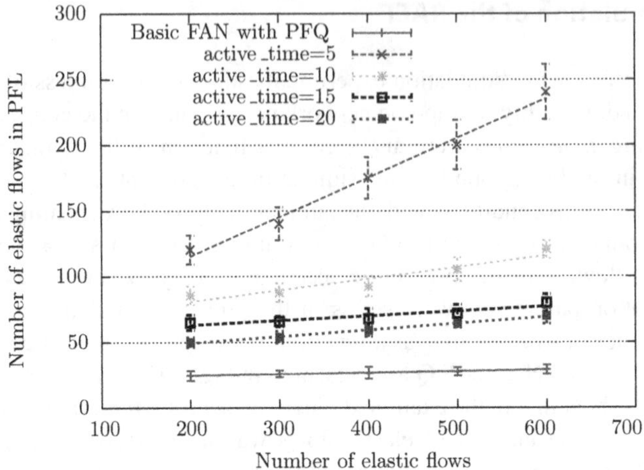

Fig. 4.14 Mean number of elastic flows in PFL in FAN with PFQ and RAEF

values of the estimated parameter in the steady state for a sufficiently long time. The other simulation parameters were set as in the previous case.

The values of the mean number of elastic flows as a function of the number of elastic flows active in the background for FAN with PFQ are presented in Fig. 4.14.

The results are better than for FAN with the EFM. While the mean number of elastic flows accepted in the router after any flushing action increases with the increasing number of elastic flows waiting to begin or continue transmission in the background, their values are significantly lower than in FAN with EFM. Unfortunately, the results are significantly worse than in the basic FAN, where the mean number of accepted elastic flows is almost independent of the number of all elastic flows waiting to transmit their packets. This is a disadvantage of the RAEF mechanism and shows that this solution may be not scalable, especially for low values of the *active_time* parameter. On the other hand, the mean number of elastic flows after any cleaning action of the PFL is lower than in FAN with EFM, making this solution more appropriate.

4.5 Remove and Block Active Elastic Flows

The next mechanism, proposed to decrease the interval between when a new streaming flow starts to send packets and their acceptance in the AC block, is called RBAEF (*Remove and Block Active Elastic Flows*) [2]. In this algorithm, identifiers of the elastic flows active for a specified period of time (*active_time*) are removed from the PFL every time a packet of a new flow arrives at the AC block in congestion. The identifiers of such flows are then written to the BFL (*Blocked Flow List*) for a short, fixed period (see Fig. 4.15). If a packet arriving at the admission

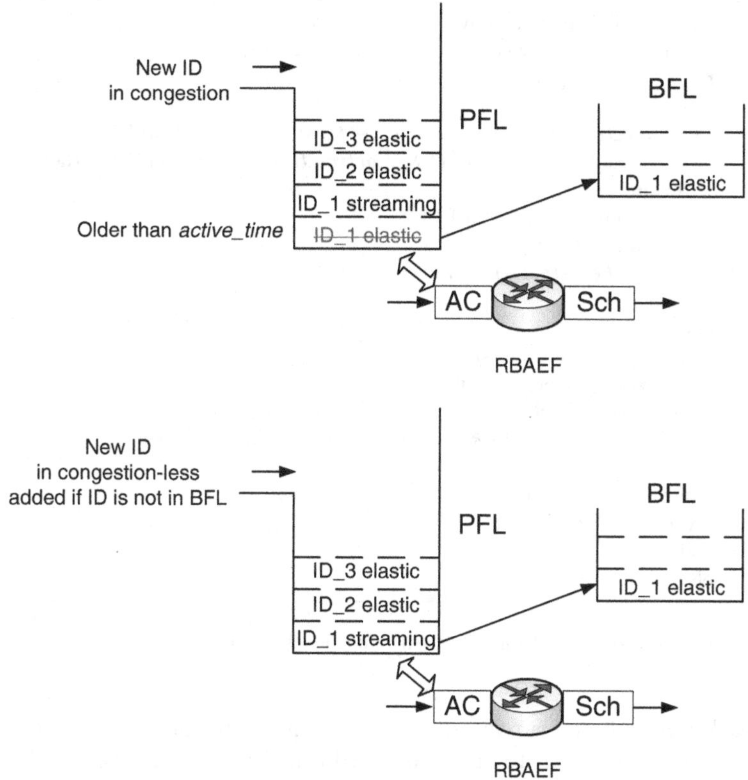

Fig. 4.15 Operating principle of RBAEF

control block belongs to the flow whose identifier is in the BFL, the packet is always dropped. Therefore, the flows removed from the PFL can continue transmission only after their tag has been removed from the BFL. The flows whose identifiers were removed from the BFL, can continue transmission, but again, they have to compete with other flows for link resources and it may take some time before such flows will be accepted again.

The pseudo-code for realizing the RBAEF functionality in FAN is presented in Fig. 4.16.

If a packet of a new flow arrives at the admission control block the procedure of the RBAEF mechanism starts. The For loop is executed for each flow whose identifier is written to the PFL (line 3). If elastic flow i is active for at least the time value written to the $active\_time$ parameter, its flow ID is removed from the PFL and added to the BFL (lines 6–9). A flow is selected as elastic if the number of bytes of its traffic is greater than or equal to the MTU. At the end of each RBAEF action, the $blocked\_start$ value of flow i is set to the current time (line 10).

```
1   on a new flow packet arrival in congestion
2   current_time = Scheduler :: instance().clock()
3   for (i = 1; i ≤ pfl_size; i++) do
4   begin
5       active_time(i) = current_time − first_operation_time(i)
6       if flow_bytes(i) ≥ MTU && active_time(i) ≥ active_time then
7       begin
8           remove ID(i) from PFL
9           add ID(i) to BFL
10          blocked_start(i) = current_time
11      end
12  end
13  ######### admission decision #########
14  on arriving packet P of flow i
15  current_time = Scheduler :: instance().clock()
16  if current_time − blocked_start(i) > blocked_period then
17  begin
18  remove ID(i) from BFL
19  proceed with packet P
20  end
21  else drop P
```

Fig. 4.16 Pseudo-code for realizing the RBAEF functionality in FAN

If packet p of flow i arrives at the admission control block within less time than the *blocked_period* it must be dropped (line 21). On the other hand, its ID is removed from the BFL and packet p is processed further (lines 16–19).

The implementation of the RBAEF mechanism in the cross-protect router is more complicated than in the RAEF mechanism, although it does not increase the complexity and processing resources significantly.

4.5.1 Simulation of the RBAEF

The following two simulation experiments show how the RBAEF mechanism may be able to improve network performance in congestion. The mechanism is proposed as an answer to the drawbacks of EFM and RAEF.

The mean *waiting_time* of streaming flows was estimated in various conditions of 250 simulation runs. The *blocked_period* parameter was set to 1 s. This value was chosen experimentally. For greater values of this parameter, there were no advantages in the acceptance delay of new streaming flows and the mean transmission time of elastic flows was longer. On the other hand, lower values of *blocked_period* are not appropriate because the flows removed from the PFL are accepted again too quickly, significantly increasing the number of accepted elastic flows after a flushing action. The other simulation parameters were set as in the simulation for the EFM.

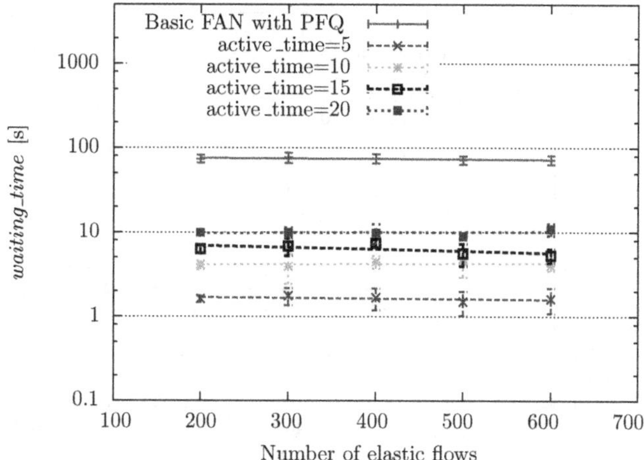

Fig. 4.17 Mean *waiting_time* in FAN with PFQ and RBAEF

Mean values of *waiting_time* as a function of the number of elastic flows active in the background for FAN with PFQ are presented in Fig. 4.17.

The results show that in the examined range the *waiting_time* values are constant independently of the number of elastic flows waiting to send traffic. The *waiting_time* values increase with increasing values of the *active_time* parameter in the examined range. The results for FAN with RBAEF are similar to those obtained for FAN with EFM. The best results are observed for *active_time* set to 5 s. The simulation results show that in this case a new flow was always accepted within 2 s, as in FAN with EFM. Similarly, when the *active_time* was set to 10 or 15 s new flows were accepted a few seconds later, but they were still in the acceptable range for local voice calls. When the *active_time* was set to 20 s, new streaming flows were accepted after approximately 9 s, which is acceptable for international calls.

The long transmission time of elastic flows for low values of the *active_time* parameter is caused among other things by a too high number of elastic flows accepted after flushing. In this simulation experiment, the mean number of elastic flows in FAN with PFQ was analyzed. The simulation duration was set to 500 s and other simulation parameters were set as in the previous case.

The values of the mean number of elastic flows as a function of the number of elastic flows active in background for FAN with PFQ are presented in Fig. 4.18.

The mean number of elastic flows accepted in the router after any flushing action increases with the increasing number of elastic flows waiting to begin or continue transmission in the background. In FAN with PFQ the best results are observed for *active_time* equal to 15 or 20 s. For lower values of this parameter, the mean transmission time of elastic flows increases faster. Moreover, the values obtained are comparable with those observed for the basic FAN link and increase relatively slowly. This is an advantage of the RBAEF mechanism and shows that this solution may be scalable for all analyzed values of the *active_time* parameter.

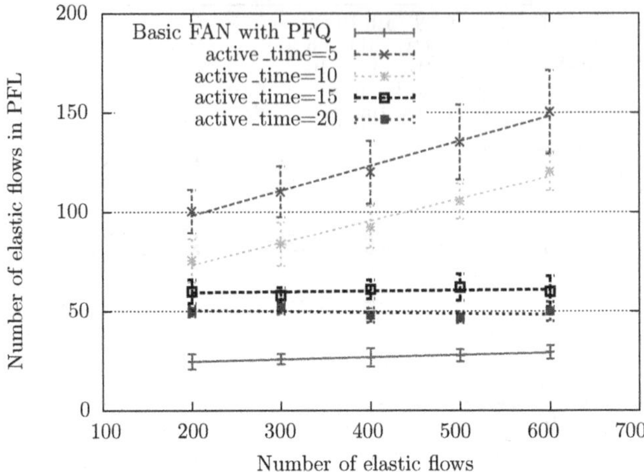

Fig. 4.18 Mean number of elastic flows in PFL in FAN with PFQ and RBAEF

4.6 Remove and Prioritize in Access Active Elastic Flows

The next mechanism presented in this chapter aiming to decrease the acceptance delay of a new streaming flow in the AC block is RPAEF (*Remove and Prioritize in access Active Elastic Flows*) [4]. In this solution, identifiers of elastic flows active for at least the *active_time* period are removed from the PFL every time when a new flow is waiting to begin transmission in congestion. The identifiers of the removed flows are then written to the PAFL (*Priority Access Flow List*) for a short *priority_access* time period (see Fig. 4.19). If a packet arriving at the admission control block in a congestion-less state belongs to a flow whose identifier is in the PAFL, the packet is always accepted. On the other hand, the packets of flows whose identifiers are not in the PAFL are accepted with low probability P_{RPAEF}. The P_{RPAEF} probability is set to 1 if there is no ID in the PAFL. The idea of this solution is to ensure a short acceptance delay of new streaming flows and a short inactivity time of elastic flows whose identifiers are removed from the PFL. Moreover, the mechanism makes it possible to reduce the total number of all flows accepted after a cleaning action of the PFL content. This is an important advantage of this algorithm. It ensures that the accepted elastic flows have an opportunity to transmit their traffic with very short, harmless breaks and with an acceptable rate.

The pseudo-code for realizing the RPAEF functionality in FAN is presented in Fig. 4.20.

If a packet of a new flow arrives at the admission control block in congestion, the procedure of the RPAEF mechanism starts. The *For* loop is executed for each flow whose identifier is written to the PFL (line 3). If elastic flow i is active for at least the time value written to the *active_time* parameter, its flow ID is removed from the PFL and added to the PAFL (lines 5–9). A flow is selected as elastic if its

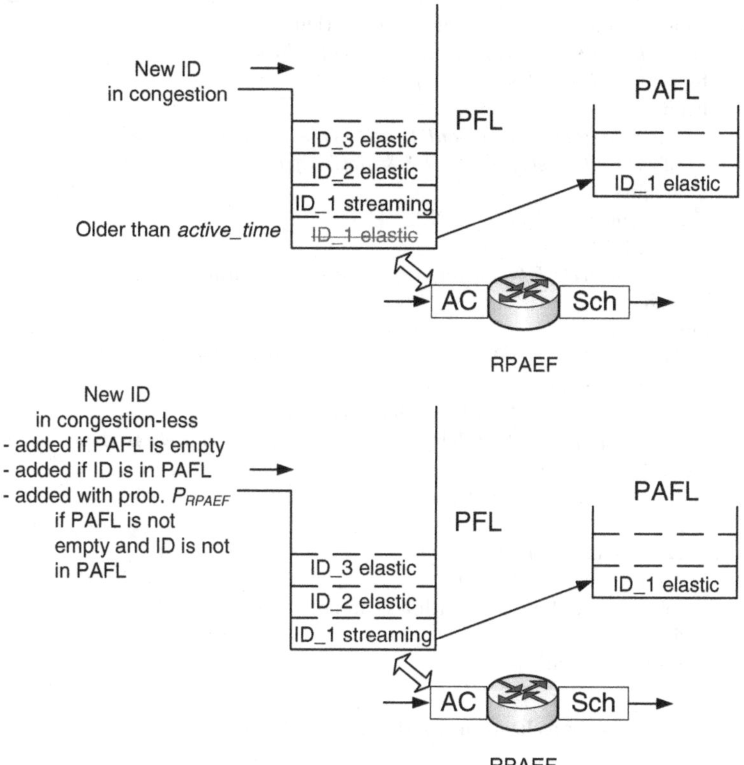

Fig. 4.19 Operating principle of RPAEF

number of bytes in the queue is greater than or equal to the MTU. At the end of each RPAEF action, the value of $last\_RPAEF\_action$ is set to the current time (line 10).

If packet p of flow i arrives at the admission control block after a time given by the $priority\_access$ parameter from the last cleaning action on the PFL, the content of the PAFL is cleaned and packet p may be accepted in a congestion-less state (lines 15–16 and line 24). If the PAFL is not empty, packet p is accepted if its flow ID is in the PAFL (lines 20–21). On the other hand, when the PAFL is not empty and the flow ID is not in the PAFL, the packet p may be accepted with a low P_{RPAEF} probability (line 22).

The implementation of the RPAEF mechanism in the cross-protect router is more complex than EFM or RAEF and equivalent to RBAEF, although it does not increase the complexity and processing resources significantly.

```
on a new flow packet arrival in congestion
current_time = Scheduler :: instance().clock()
for (i = 1; i ≤ pfl_size; i++) do
begin
    active_time(i) = current_time − first_operation_time(i)
    if flow_bytes(i) ≥ MTU && active_time(i) ≥ active_time then
    begin
        remove ID(i) from PFL
        add ID(i) to PAFL
        last_RPAEF_action = Scheduler :: instance().clock()
    end
end
######### admission decision #########
on arriving packet P of flow i
current_time = Scheduler :: instance().clock()
if current_time − last_RPAEF_action > priority_access then
clean PAFL content
if PAFL is not empty then
begin
    if i is in the PAFL then
        proceed with packet P
    else proceed with P with acceptance probability P_RPAEF
end
else proceed with P
```

Fig. 4.20 Pseudo-code for realizing the RPAEF functionality in FAN

4.6.1 Simulation of the RPAEF

The RPAEF mechanism has the same goals as RBAEF, i.e., to decrease the number of elastic flows accepted after a flushing action and to ensure the mean transmission time of elastic flows is at an acceptable level. While the concepts behind RPAEF and RBAEF are similar, they work completely differently. In RPAEF, the IDs of flows rejected after flushing are written to the PAFL. If in the congestion-less state the ID of an incoming packet is in the PAFL or the PAFL is empty, the flow is accepted with a probability equal to one. On the other hand, if the flow ID is not in the PAFL, the flow is accepted with a low probability. It makes it possible to reduce the number of elastic flows accepted after flushing and an almost continuous transmission of each flow accepted in the router. The following two simulation experiments show how the RPAEF mechanism may improve network performance in congestion.

The *waiting_time* parameter for FAN with PFQ is analyzed in this simulation experiment. The mean acceptance delay of new streaming flows (*waiting_time*) in the AC block in a FAN link was analyzed in this experiment by 250 simulation runs made in various conditions. The duration of each simulation run was set to 250 s, which allowed us to observe acceptance delays of new streaming flows. The P_{RPAEF} probability was set to 0.03. This value was chosen experimentally. Other

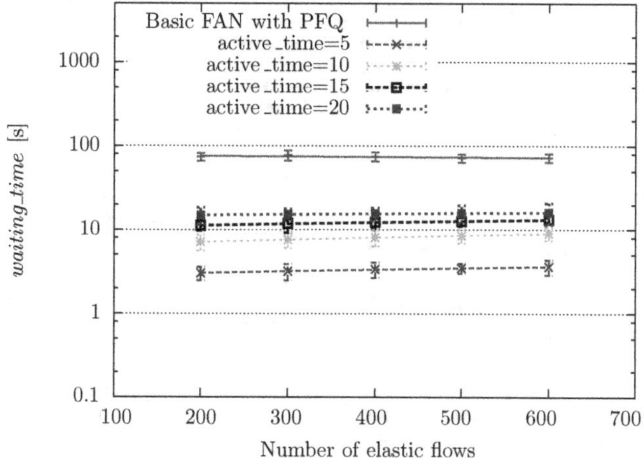

Fig. 4.21 Mean *waiting_time* in FAN with PFQ and RPAEF

simulation parameters were set as in the previous simulation experiment. The mean values of *waiting_time* as a function of the number of elastic flows active in the background for FAN with PFQ are presented in Fig. 4.21.

The values of the *waiting_time* parameter are constant for each *active_time* value in the examined range. It means that, as in all previously described mechanisms, new streaming flows are accepted in the AC block independently of the number of elastic flows waiting to send traffic. The *waiting_time* values increase with increasing values of the *active_time* parameter in the examined range, but they are significantly lower than in the basic FAN. The best results were obtained when the *active_time* was set to 5 s. The *active_time* equal to 10 s is also acceptable for local calls, while the values of 15 and 20 s ensure sufficiently low *waiting_time* values for international VoIP connections.

In the next simulation experiment, the mean number of elastic flows in FAN with PFQ accepted after any flushing action was analyzed. The simulation duration was set to 500 s, which allowed us to estimate the analyzed parameter in the steady state for a sufficiently long time. Other simulation parameters were set as in the previous case.

The values of the mean number of elastic flows as a function of the number of elastic flows active in the background are presented in Fig. 4.22.

As we can see, the number of accepted elastic flows after flushing is lower than for EFM, RAEF and RBAEF. Moreover, the transmission of accepted elastic flows is broken periodically for very short periods. The algorithm appears to be stable and scalable. It should be noted that the mean break in transmission of elastic flows after flushing is 0.41 ± 0.05 s in FAN with PFQ. 99.5% of the removed elastic flows are accepted again in less time than the value of the *priority_access* parameter. This advantage of the RPAEF mechanism justifies its use in FAN.

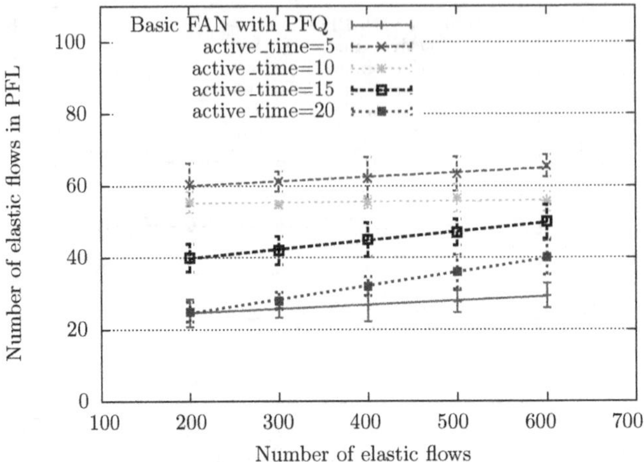

Fig. 4.22 Mean number of elastic flows in PFL in FAN with PFQ and RPAEF

4.7 Remove and Accept Most Active Flows

In this section, we present the mechanism known as RAMAF (Remove and Accept Most Active Flows) [5]. RAMAF periodically removes IDs of a number of most active flows from PFL. This number is set dynamically based on queue occupancy. Next, in a congestion-less state, the removed IDs are added to PFL again. It enables dynamic changes of values of the *FR* parameter around the minimum acceptable value, and consequently gives opportunities to new flows to begin their transmissions. The packet service in RAMAF is presented in Fig. 4.23. The pseudo-code for realizing the RAMAF functionality is presented in Fig. 4.24.

The RAMAF mechanism is invoked when a packet of a new flow arrives at the admission control block of the XP router. Regardless of the state of congestion of the outgoing link, RAMAF checks for the time that PFL was last “cleared”. If it is greater than the value of the *clear_el_time* parameter (lines 2–4), IDs of each flow which began transmission prior to the value of *clear_el_time* parameter (lines 5–18) are removed. *control_param* helps to ensure that IDs of new elastic flows are removed from PFL only once after PFL is flushed (lines 4 and 13).

Next, in congestion, RAMAF periodically writes the number of queued bytes of elastic flows to the table tab (lines 20–26). Then, the maximum value in table *tab* is found (line 27). Next, the number N of flows to be removed from PFL is computed as the difference between the number of flows which have queued packets and the coefficient $100/min\_fair\_rate$ minus 1 (line 28). The estimated value of the coefficient means the number of flows which may be served with the guaranteed fair rate. Next, the function $draw$ (line 29) is run. It draws N flows, which have max_bytes bytes in the queue from table tab, removes their IDs from PFL, and

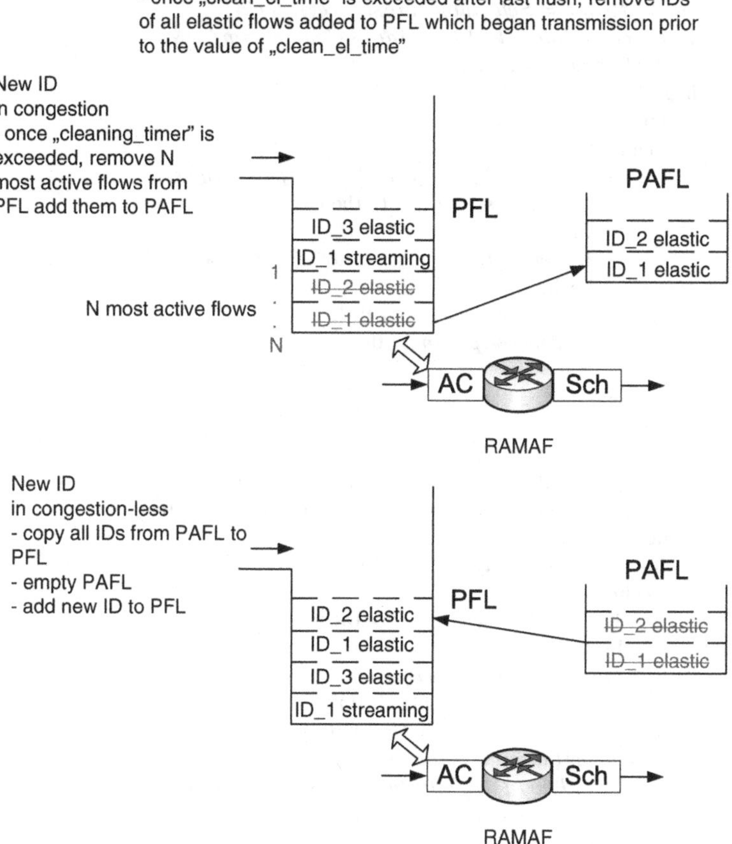

Fig. 4.23 Packet service in FAN with the RAMAF mechanism

puts them into PAFL (Priority Access Flow List). At the end, the incoming packet p is discarded (line 35).

In the congestion-less state, all IDs from PAFL are copied into PFL (line 39) and then removed from PAFL (line 40). At the end, the incoming packet p is accepted and sent for queuing (line 42).

The RAMAF mechanism works dynamically. We only assume the maximum time of acceptance of streaming flows and the rest is performed automatically. This is a very important advantage over the other proposals. Moreover, the RAMAF mechanism is the first proposal among the existing congestion control solutions that assumes all removed flows are always accepted again after a clearing action of PFL. It allows for short breaks in transmission and provides satisfactory transmission parameters for each elastic flow. Other congestion control mechanisms assume that the removed flows are accepted again with a high probability, or even order them to

```
on a new flow packet  p arrival
current_time = Scheduler :: instance().clock()
if current_time − last_clearing > clear_el_time &&
control_param = 1 then
begin
    for (i = 1; i ≤ pfl_size; i++) do
    begin
        active_time(i) = current_time − first_time(i)
        if flow_bytes(i) ≥ MTU then
        begin
            if active_time(i) <= clear_el_time then
            begin
                remove ID( i) from PFL
                control_param = 0
            end
        end
    end
end
######### in congestion state #########
if current_time − last_clearing > clearing_timer then
begin
    for (i = 1; i ≤ pfl_size; i++) do
    begin
        if flow_bytes(i) ≥ MTU then
        begin
        tab[i] = flow_bytes(i)
        max_bytes = find_max(tab)
        N = q_l − (100/min_fair_rate − 1)
        draw(tab, max_bytes, removed_flows)
        last_clearing = Scheduler :: instance().clock()
        control_param = 1
        end
    end
end
discard packet  P
######### in congestion  −less state #########
for (i = 1; i ≤ pafl_size; i++) do
begin
    copy ID( i) from PAFL to PFL
    remove ID( i) from PAFL
end
proceed with packet  P
```

Fig. 4.24 Pseudo-code for realizing the RAMAF functionality in FAN

compete with new flows for acceptance in a router without any privilege. RAMAF assumes that outages in the transmission of elastic flows are short-lived, and all new elastic flows added after a flushing action are removed from PFL after a short time.

4.7.1 Simulation of the RAMAF

In this section, we present the simulation analysis of the RAMAF mechanism. The results demonstrate the viability of the proposed solution and confirm its advantages.

In the specification of the RAMAF mechanism, we assumed that the number of removed flows from PFL (N) should be calculated from the following equation:

$$N = q\_l - (100/min\_fair\_rate - 1) \tag{4.1}$$

where q_l is the number of flows, which have at least one packet in the queue. It means that in our experiments, after a clearing action, 19 IDs are left in PFL. This means that after the next *FR* estimation, the outgoing link usually became congestion-less, and new flows were able to begin their transmission. We also assumed that the value of the $clear\_el\_time$ parameter was set to 1.5 s, implying that the new elastic flows accepted after a clearing action were removed from PFL after 1.5 s from the time when the link became congestion-less. This value was chosen experimentally and ensured that all new elastic flows were removed from PFL in a sufficiently short time. Other simulation parameters were set as in the previous experiment.

250 simulation runs were provided in the same conditions as in the previous experiments to show the time of acceptance of a new streaming flow (*waiting_time*) in the AC block in a FAN link. The mean values of *waiting_time* in function of the number of elastic flows active in background for FAN with PFQ are presented in Fig. 4.25.

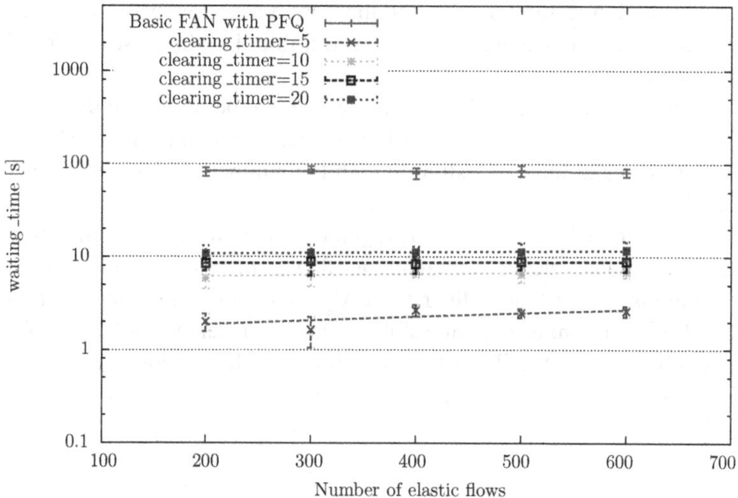

Fig. 4.25 Mean *waiting_time* in FAN with PFQ and RAMAF

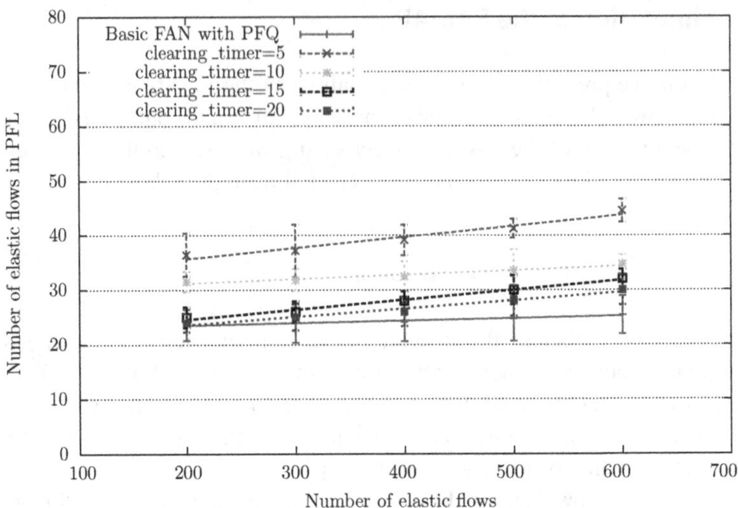

Fig. 4.26 Mean number of elastic flows in PFL in FAN with PFQ and RAMAF

As we can see, the values of the observed parameter are almost constant for each *clearing_timer* value. It means that a new streaming flow is accepted in the AC block at the same time for particular values of the *clearing_timer* parameter, independently of the number of elastic flows waiting to send traffic. Without using the RAMAF the mean acceptance delay of streaming flows is much greater. The *waiting_time* values increase with increasing values of the *clearing_timer* parameter in the examined range. The best results were obtained when the *clearing_timer* was set to 5 s. Simulation results show that in this case a new flow was always accepted within 4 s from the time when it began to send traffic. In other cases the results are unacceptable [9].

The results presented in Fig. 4.26 show that the number of elastic flows accepted again after the cleaning action of the PFL is greater than in the basic FAN (where it is about 25 flows) and increases slightly with the number of elastic flows active in background.

It should be noted that for *clearing_timer* equal to 5 s (which ensures an acceptable acceptance delay of streaming flows) the number of elastic flows accepted again is greater than in the basic FAN. However, this value is significantly lower than for other congestion control mechanisms presented for FAN so far. This is a strong advantage of the RAMAF and shows that this solution ensures the best transmission performance of elastic flows and is scalable.

4.8 Simple Congestion Control Mechanism

The last mechanism presented in this book that aims to decrease acceptance delays of new streaming flows in the AC block is SCCM (*Simple Congestion Control Mechanism*) [1]. In this solution, we do not remove any identifiers from PFL. Instead, we steer the value of the min_FR parameter. This parameter is periodically set to zero, which eliminates congestion for a moment. During this time, new flows are accepted in MBAC. When the min_FR is set again to the original value, congestion is observed in the link. Next, we remove the IDs of all elastic flows accepted in MBAC after the SCCM run.

The pseudo-code for implementing this proposal is presented in Fig. 4.27.

The main assumption of the mechanism is to eliminate congestion periodically for a short time and then to eliminate the IDs of elastic flows accepted during that time. The goal is realized by periodically reducing the min_fair_rate value to 0 (line 27). The period is set by the $reduce\_timer$ value (line 25). After reducing the min_FR value, new flows are accepted during half of the measurement interval of the FR value (lines 3–6). This period is long enough to accept all flows waiting for transmission. After the period given by the $clean\_el\_time$ parameter from the final reduction of the min_FR, identifiers of all elastic flows accepted during this interval are deleted from PFL (lines 9–23). The value of the $clean\_el\_time$ parameter should be estimated experimentally to eliminate all undesirable elastic flows. In the experiments provided in this section, it was assumed that $clean\_el\_time$ was equal to three times of the FR measurement interval. Lines 34–35 ensure that the procedure works in the congestion state only.

The implementation of SCCM in the cross-protect router is more complex than EFM or RAEF, but less complex than the other congestion control mechanisms proposed for FAN. Moreover, this mechanism does not increase the complexity and processing resources significantly and ensures better transmission parameters of elastic flows. It is possible because transmission of elastic flows is not interrupted.

4.8.1 Simulation of the SCCM

A simulation analysis of the SCCM is presented in this section. The results confirm the efficiency and scalability of the solution analyzed.

250 simulation runs were executed in the same conditions as in the previous experiments to observe acceptance delays of new streaming flows (*waiting_time*) in the AC block in a FAN link. Mean values of *waiting_time* as a function of the number of elastic flows active in background for FAN with PFQ are presented in Fig. 4.28.

As we can see, the values of the observed parameter are almost constant for each *reduce_timer* value. It means, as in RAMAF, that a new streaming flow is accepted in the AC block at the same time for particular values of the *reduce_timer* parameter, independently of the number of elastic flows waiting to send traffic. The

```
on a new flow packet  P arrival
current_time = Scheduler :: instance().clock()
if current_time − last_reduce > 0.5 ∗ FR_int then
begin
    min_FR = org_min_FR
    control_param2 = 0
end
if current_time − last_reduce > clean_el_time &&
control_param1 = 1 then
begin
    for  (i = 1; i ≤ pfl_size; i++) do
    begin
        active_time(i) = current_time − first_time(i)
        if flow_bytes(i) ≥ MTU then
        begin
            if active_time(i) <= clean_el_time then
            begin
            remove ID( i) from PFL
            control_param1 = 0;
            end
        end
    end
end
######### in congestion state #########
if current_time − last_reduce > reduce_timer then
begin
    min_FR = 0
    last_reduce = Scheduler :: instance().clock()
    control_param1 = 1
    control_param2 = 1
end
else  discard packet  P
######### in congestion  −less state #########
last_reduce = Scheduler :: instance().clock()
proceed with packet  P
```

Fig. 4.27 Pseudo-code for realizing the SCCM functionality in FAN

waiting_time values increase with increasing values of the *reduce_timer* parameter in the examined range. The best results were obtained when the *reduce_timer* was set to 5 s; however, the acceptable values were also observed for the *reduce_timer* value of 10 s. Simulation results show that in this case a new flow was always accepted within 4 s from the time when it began sending traffic and in the second case within 6 s. In other cases the results are unacceptable [9].

The results presented in Fig. 4.29 show that the number of elastic flows accepted again after a cleaning action of the PFL is almost the same as in the basic FAN

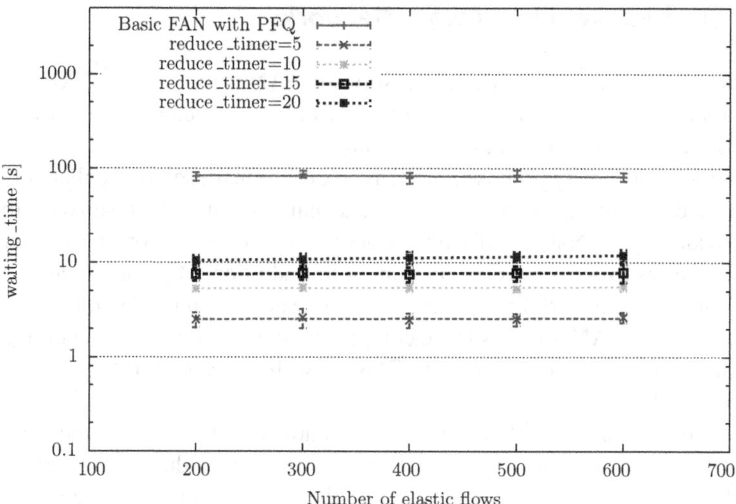

Fig. 4.28 Mean *waiting_time* in FAN with PFQ and SCCM

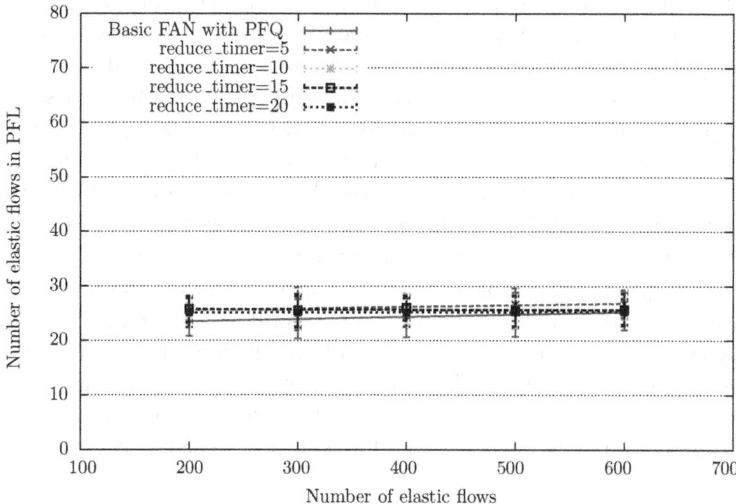

Fig. 4.29 Mean number of elastic flows in PFL in FAN with PFQ and SCCM

(where it is about 25 flows) and is constant independently of the number of elastic flows active in background. Moreover, the results are similar for each value of the *reduce_timer* parameter. These results confirm that this mechanism ensures the best performance of transmission of elastic traffic among all analyzed congestion control mechanisms proposed for FAN.

4.9 Multi-Layer Flow-Aware Networks

The other option for dealing with congestions in FAN is to use the MFAN concept, which assumes the use of additional resources at the optical layer for traffic that cannot be accepted in FAN links at the IP layer.

MFAN was originally proposed in [8] as an evolutionary solution enhancing FAN performance in multi-layer environments. The main assumption of MFAN is that the QoS provided by FAN at the IP layer is good enough for network performance in a congestion-less state. However, in congestion additional operations are needed. MFAN can use the underlying optical layer where an optical lightpath is set up. The structure of the MFAN router is more complex than the original XP router. It is able to transmit traffic at the IP layer using FAN, as well as sending traffic using optical resources as illustrated in Fig. 4.30.

The map of available optical resources is known by the MFAN nodes and if a new lambda is needed they may use it. As a result, flows that have been rejected by the IP-layer in FAN may be redirected to the optical path. Once the new optical connection is set up, flows transmitted through it are stored in the PFLλ list. The PFLλ list has exactly the same functionality as the standard PFL list for IP-layer FAN routers. Each MFAN node has to maintain more than one PFL list. This makes the algorithm more complex, but in congestion more traffic may be served. Several lambdas may be used at the optical layer to transmit redirected traffic.

Three policies to select which flows are the most suitable for transmission using the optical layer have been defined for MFAN [8]. In the first policy, known as 'newest-flow' policy, new flows waiting to transmit their traffic in congestion are redirected to the optical layer. In this case, MFAN tests whether the optical resources can accept more traffic and, if so, the new packet is transmitted through the optical layer. In order to determine whether there are resources in the optical layer, MFAN checks if the queue occupation is lower or greater than the threshold known as *OQTh*. In the second policy, known as 'most-active-flow', when a packet of a new flow arrives at the XP router in congestion, a flow which has the most bytes in the queue is redirected to the optical layer and the new flow is accepted at the primary FAN queue. The third approach, the 'oldest-flow' policy, works similarly to the 'most-active-flow' policy; however, the flow which has been active the longest is

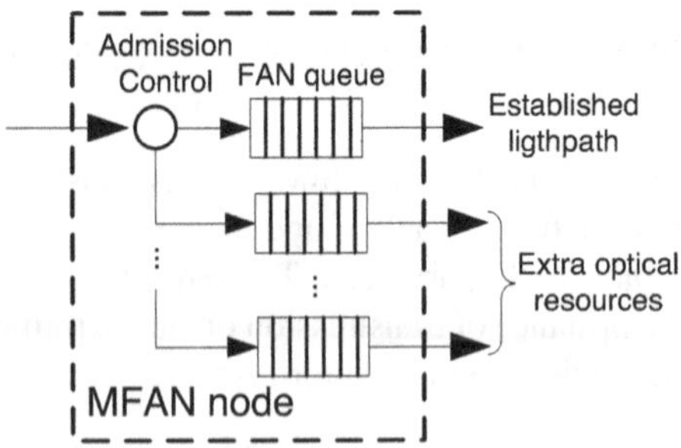

Fig. 4.30 Multi-layer Flow-Aware Networking (MFAN) node architecture (source: [6])

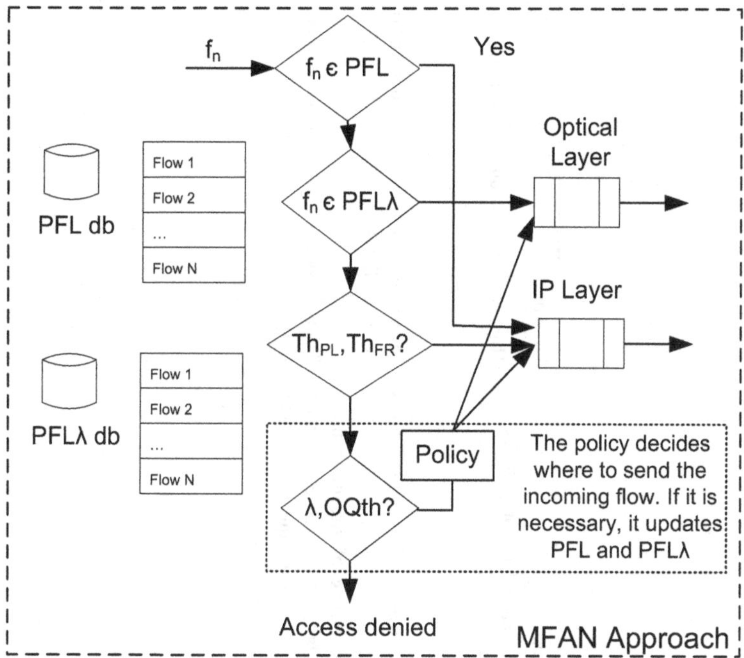

Fig. 4.31 Packet service in Multilayer Flow-Aware Networks (source: [6])

selected for redirecting. Figure 4.31 summarizes the complete admission control in MFAN nodes, including the policies.

4.9.1 Simulation of MFAN

The results of simulating MFAN with the two most promising admission control policies (oldest-flow and most-active-flow) are presented in the first two rows of Table 4.1 and compared with results obtained in the same conditions for EFM and EFMP. The simulation experiments were provided in the same topology and in the same conditions as presented in previous experiments (for EFM or EFMP). However, for MFAN, an additional optical link between routers was implemented. In the analyzed case, transmission in the optical link was implemented as a best effort service (with FIFO queue). Flows were rerouted in congestion if the buffer occupancy of the optical link did not exceed 80%. Otherwise, new flows were rejected.

For each analyzed case, new streaming flows were accepted after a short, acceptable time. Moreover, in MFAN and EFMP the number of elastic flows accepted after a run of the congestion control mechanism was sufficiently low, providing good transmission possibilities for elastic flows. Unfortunately, in MFAN, it was impossible to assure a fair rate on the 5 Mbit/s level in the backup optical link.

Table 4.1 The properties of admission control policies

Architecture or mechanism	*waiting_time* [s]	Admitted flows	Advantages	Drawbacks
MFAN (1 s. Oldest-flow)	3.36 ± 0.76	26.05 ± 0.48	Short acceptance delay of all flows, low number of accepted flows	High cost, lack of fair rate assurance
MFAN (1 s. Most-active-flow)	2.93 ± 0.90	25.35 ± 0.76		
EFM (5 s)	1.43 ± 0.91	160.43 ± 10.91	Quick acceptance of streaming flows, low cost	Instability of fair rate, high number of accepted flows
EFM (1 s. Oldest-flow)	4.73 ± 1.06	23.48 ± 0.56	Quick acceptance of streaming flows, low cost, fair rate assurance, low number of accepted flows, quick acceptance of removed flows	Transmission of elastic flows is not continuous
EFMP (1 s. Most-active-flow)	3.68 ± 0.80	24.26 ± 0.64		

For MFAN and EFMP we needed to run the mechanism more frequently than for the EFM. This is because in MFAN and EFMP we select the number of flows to be rerouted or removed from PFL. As we can see, MFAN ensures quality of service for both traffic types. However, it must be noted that it requires additional resources in the physical layer, which increases the cost of transmission.

4.10 Congestion Control in Wireless Environments

The congestion control mechanisms presented in this chapter have been analyzed in a wired FAN. This section presents a pioneering analysis of FAN in a heterogeneous environment, with wired and wireless links, which was originally published in [5]. The aims of this part of the book are twofold. Firstly, we analyze the effectiveness of TCP transmission in a heterogeneous wired-wireless FAN. It is important to note that the methods of guaranteeing quality of service for wireless networks differ greatly from those proposed for wired networks. In wireline networks, TCP usually assumes that all losses of ACKs are caused by congestion. In wireless networks, TCP has to react to packet loss in a different way because the loss may also be caused by wireless link errors. Improving the performance of TCP in wireless IP communications has been an active research area. In this section, we analyze a hybrid wired-wireless network operated with different versions of the TCP protocol. The aim is to observe the effectiveness of transmission when an end-user is connected by a wireless link and to find the best solution for transmission in heterogeneous Flow-Aware Networks with QoS guarantees.

We start by presenting a brief overview of selected TCP versions, which are further analyzed using extensive simulations. The aim is to find the best solution for implementing the wired-wireless transmission in FAN, to be used in Future Internet. TCP versions usually differ in how they react to packet loss in a network. In wired networks, packet losses are usually caused by congestion, while in wireless networks it is also necessary to consider losses caused by wireless link errors.

TCP NewReno is a well-known scheme used for transmission in data networks. NewReno is a modification of TCP Reno such that a fast recovery algorithm is not activated by each lost packet. NewReno copes with multiple losses from a single window. It assumes that the fast recovery algorithm may be terminated when all losses, indicated from one window, are recovered. One of the main drawbacks of NewReno is its inability to distinguish the cause of a packet loss. Thus, the implementation of a more effective fast recovery algorithm is not possible.

TCP Sack (TCP Selective Acknowledgment Options) uses the same congestion control mechanisms as TCP Reno to steer the congestion window size. The difference between the two versions is observed when many packets belonging to the same window are lost. By using additional options in a packet header, the receiver may inform the sender which segments are correctly received and which need to be retransmitted. Based on this information, the sender may immediately send the lost packets again. TCP Sack has similar drawbacks as those of TCP NewReno.

TCP Tahoe uses a congestion avoidance algorithm which implements an additive-increase-multiplicative-decrease (AIMD) scheme and slow-start. It does not use the fast recovery algorithm. When Tahoe detects a congestion, it reduces the congestion window to the maximum segment size, and activates the slow-start phase.

In TCP Westwood, the bandwidth estimator is used at the sender side. The transmission rate is estimated based on the rate of received acknowledgements. The size of the congestion window is calculated dynamically according to the number of lost packets. This version of TCP also does not consider what causes packet losses.

TCP Vegas was proposed in 1994, before TCP NewReno and TCP Sack. It differs from the above TCP versions in that the congestion is detected based on increasing Round Trip Time values of the packets in a connection. It assumes that, during congestion, real bandwidth is lower than the estimated value, and based on this information, the window size is increased or decreased. TCP Vegas tries to use the available capacity without causing congestions. However, the causes of the congestion are not analyzed once again.

The TCP versions presented above are well known and have been described in many papers. The final TCP version analyzed here is TCP NewJersey [11, 12]. It is a relatively new TCP version, which enables an appropriate response to the cause of congestion. TCP Jersey, which is a predecessor to TCP NewJersey, adopts the slow start algorithm, congestion avoidance, and fast recovery from Reno, but replaces fast retransmission with explicit retransmission and introduces a rate control procedure based on ABE (available bandwidth estimation). If the ACK of a packet arrives at the sender without the CW (Congestion Warning) mark, it proceeds as NewReno. The rate control procedure is invoked by the ACK or third DUPACK marked with the CW bit. It adjusts the widow size for further transmission. It is assumed that a packet drop is caused by random error when the sender receives the third DUPACK without the CW mark. In this case, the fast retransmit procedure is called without adjusting the window size. The combination of ABE and CW improves TCP's ability to differentiate sources of packet losses. In TCP NewJersey, the performance in heterogeneous networks is improved by modifying the inaccurate bandwidth estimation caused by t ACK burstiness. Moreover, the transmission rate is stabilized by minimizing the volatility of the flow load.

TCP NewJersey works in a different way in FAN links. We do not mark any packets. Our observations show that there are almost no packet losses in congested basic FAN links (without any congestion control mechanism). In such a case, it is not important whether we mark packets. On the other hand, many packet losses occur in the FAN link with a congestion control mechanism. When we remove flow IDs from PFL, flow packets cannot be queued and are lost. However, such losses cannot be treated as congestion-induced but rather like errors in links. Therefore, we should not decrease rates of flows for packets lost due to the congestion control mechanism properties. TCP NewJersey ensures that all packets lost in a FAN link are retransmitted without adjusting the window size. The same situation is observed for the SCCM where we do not remove IDs from PFL. In this case, the transmission of elastic flows accepted before the SCCM run should not be slowed down.

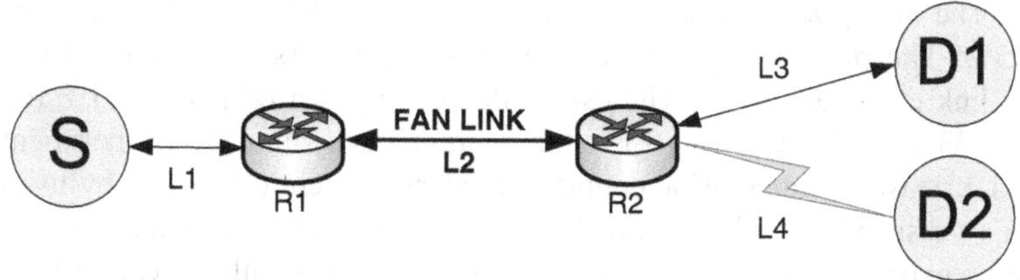

Fig. 4.32 Simulation topology

4.10.1 Simulation Analysis of Wired-Wireless FAN Topology

In this section, we present the results of carefully selected simulation experiments of FAN with different versions of the TCP protocol. The aim is to show the impact of particular TCP versions on transmission in FAN with end users connected by wireless links. Moreover, we analyzed the viability of the RAMAF mechanism in wired-wireless FAN. We chose the RAMAF mechanism because it is the most promising solution where we remove IDs of elastic flows in congestion. We used the topology shown in Fig. 4.32. We have observed the goodput (the number of packets received by end users) during the transmission from the source to the destination node D2.

The source node S was connected to the FAN router R1 via link L1 (with 1 Gbit/s capacity). FAN routers (R1, R2) were connected via link L2 (with 100 Mbit/s capacity). The R2 router was connected to the destination node D1 via link L3 (with 1 Gbit/s capacity) and to the destination node D2 by a wireless link L4 (with 5 Mbit/s capacity).

We analyzed cases with 400 elastic flows (ftp connections) and 20 streaming flows (VoIP connections via Skype) transmitting their traffic from the source to the destination node D1. The FAN link was heavily loaded from the beginning of the simulation experiments in both directions. The traffic pattern followed the Pareto distribution, and thus the volume of traffic to be sent by the elastic flows could be calculated accordingly. An exponential distribution for generating time intervals between starting points of transmissions of elastic flows and for generating the start times of streaming flows was adopted. The packet size for elastic flows was set to 1000 bytes, while that for streaming flows was set to 100 bytes. The transmission rate of streaming flows was set to 80 kbit/s. The elastic traffic was treated as background traffic and used to saturate the links analyzed. We also added one elastic flow which began its transmission when the simulation started and was sending its traffic during the whole simulation to the destination node D2. For this flow, we observed goodput. The duration of each simulation run was set to 300 s, which allowed us to observe the acceptance delays of streaming flows (*waiting_time*) in the R1 router. Buffers in the XP routers were sized to 1000 packets, a reasonable value for FAN links, and the *MTU* was set to 1500 bytes. The measurement interval for the *PL* parameter was set to 50 ms while the *FR* values were estimated every

500 ms. The *max_PL* parameter was set to 70% and the *min_FR* parameter was set to 5%. The *flow_time_out* parameter was set to 20 s. We assumed that the random link error rate at the wireless bottleneck link varied from 0.01% (0.0001 in Figs. 4.33 and 4.34) to 10% (0.1 in the figures). Each simulation experiment was repeated at least 10 times. 95% confidence intervals were calculated by using the Student's t-distribution. The assumed value of the warm-up parameter used in the simulation experiments was 20 s, which ensured that the results of each simulation run represented the steady-state.

The efficiency of the wireless link (goodput/wireless link capacity) versus the packet loss rate for the basic FAN is presented in Fig. 4.33.

We can see that for low values of the wireless packet loss, the results are similar for all TCP versions. It is also shown that for the first two values of the wireless packet loss (0.0001 or 0.001), the values of the efficiency are constant for each case. The observed values begin to decrease when wireless packet loss is equal to 0.01. For the last analyzed value of the wireless packet loss parameter (0.1), the efficiency of transmission in the wireless link is by far the worst in each case. The results meet our expectations. However, it is worth noting that the efficiency of the observed link when wireless packet loss was set to 0.1 for the TCP NewJersey version is about double that for the other analyzed cases. In TCP NewJersey, the window size is not decreased if packets are lost due to wireless link errors when the buffer occupancy threshold is not exceeded. In the other TCP versions, the window size is changed each time a packet is lost. This is a very strong advantage of the NewJersey proposal. The results show that this version of TCP may be the best choice for transmission in wireless links with a high number of errors.

We also checked the efficiency of the RAMAF mechanism in the analyzed case. We had to determine the value of the *clearing_timer* parameter, which decided how

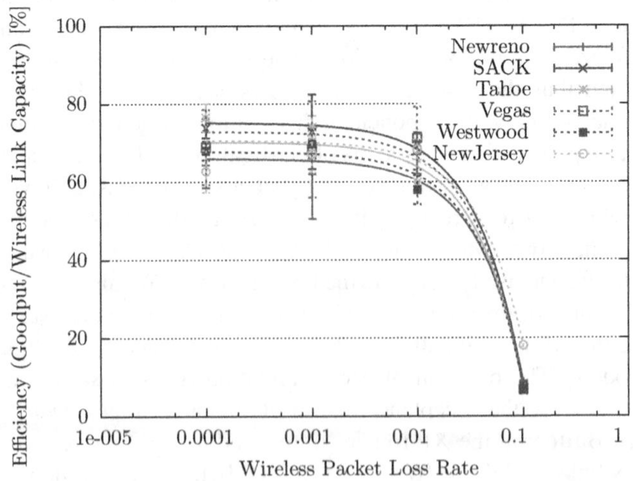

Fig. 4.33 TCP efficiency in basic FAN

often the IDs of the most active elastic flows had to be removed from PFL. We assumed that the sum of the interval between two *FR* estimations multiplied by two (there were cases when congestion was not eliminated after the first update), the value of the *clearing_timer* and the interval between the time instant when the link became congestion-less and when the first packet of a new streaming flow arrived at the XP router had to be less than 6 s. Based on this estimation, the value of the *clearing_timer* parameter was set to 3 s. We also assumed that the value of the *clear_el_time* parameter was set to 1.5 s, implying that new elastic flows accepted after a clearing action were removed from PFL after 1.5 s from the time when the link became congestion-less. This value was chosen experimentally and ensured that all new elastic flows were removed from PFL in a sufficiently short time. Other simulation parameters were set as in the previous experiment.

Results presented in Table 4.2 show that values of the *waiting_time* are sufficiently low for each TCP version, if we implement the RAMAF mechanism. Results presented in Fig. 4.34 show that the implementation of the RAMAF mechanism degrades the transmission of elastic flows. However, the results are acceptable.

It should also be noted that the results are similar for all TCP versions (TCP Vegas looks to be slightly better than other cases) when the wireless packet loss rate is low. TCP NewJersey achieves the best efficiency when the wireless packet loss rate is high. We conclude that for wireless links without packet loss, any TCP version may be used, while in links susceptible to packet loss the best choice would be TCP NewJersey. Moreover, we see ways of improving TCP NewJersey in FAN under the control of the RAMAF mechanism.

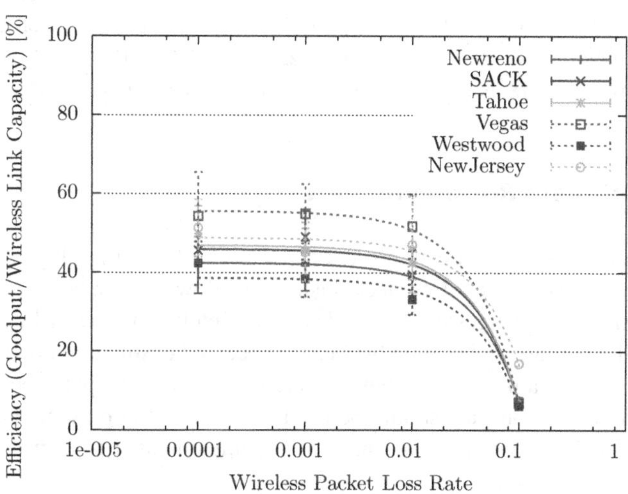

Fig. 4.34 TCP efficiency in FAN with the RAMAF mechanism

Table 4.2 The properties TCP versions in FAN with wireless link

TCP vers.	Pkt loss rate	Efficiency [%]	*waiting_time* [s]	Efficiency [%]	*waiting_time* [s]
		Basic FAN		RAMAF	
Newreno	0.0001	64.44 ± 5.99	138.83 ± 39.81	41.82 ± 7.21	3.17 ± 1.01
	0.001	61.97 ± 11.41	130.97 ± 38.78	41.82 ± 6.39	2.82 ± 0.96
	0.01	62.10 ± 4.90	131.76 ± 50.97	39.82 ± 6.06	3.12 ± 1.12
	0.1	8.70 ± 0.39	120.37 ± 46.66	7.62 ± 0.78	3.12 ± 1.11
Sack	0.0001	73.85 ± 2.55	73.31 ± 20.72	45.69 ± 4.16	2.57 ± 0.64
	0.001	72.90 ± 9.54	70.86 ± 32.92	49.11 ± 5.99	3.17 ± 1.11
	0.01	69.99 ± 2.60	71.07 ± 28.96	39.51 ± 6.02	4.32 ± 1.07
	0.1	7.51 ± 1.14	62.66 ± 14.27	7.23 ± 0.94	2.82 ± 1.03
Tahoe	0.0001	76.50 ± 3.54	62.86 ± 13.13	49.87 ± 7.12	3.22 ± 1.00
	0.001	74.08 ± 2.92	72.36 ± 35.47	45.41 ± 5.86	2.77 ± 0.96
	0.01	59.85 ± 1.89	76.46 ± 16.95	42.51 ± 4.11	2.47 ± 0.66
	0.1	6.86 ± 1.14	86.06 ± 18.99	7.40 ± 0.74	2.57 ± 0.64
Vegas	0.0001	68.91 ± 9.67	80.02 ± 17.06	54.33 ± 11.10	2.51 ± 0.54
	0.001	68.34 ± 12.36	68.46 ± 17.95	54.94 ± 7.48	2.10 ± 0.15
	0.01	71.21 ± 8.05	74.97 ± 20.42	51.81 ± 8.13	2.11 ± 0.15
	0.1	6.86 ± 0.72	72.37 ± 30.69	7.11 ± 0.53	2.36 ± 0.68
Westwood	0.0001	68.03 ± 2.38	94.45 ± 26.83	42.40 ± 5.50	3.65 ± 1.11
	0.001	69.79 ± 3.69	96.90 ± 23.75	38.54 ± 4.78	3.80 ± 1.07
	0.01	57.97 ± 3.75	96.35 ± 15.43	33.22 ± 3.92	4.00 ± 1.63
	0.1	6.86 ± 1.18	114.90 ± 17.30	6.24 ± 0.87	3.90 ± 1.25
NewJersey	0.0001	62.74 ± 5.41	93.22 ± 27.29	51.33 ± 7.22	2.66 ± 0.98
	0.001	67.21 ± 4.76	84.72 ± 20.87	45.29 ± 7.49	2.86 ± 0.83
	0.01	68.32 ± 2.56	86.62 ± 22.67	47.10 ± 12.22	2.31 ± 0.68
	0.1	18.08 ± 0.52	80.37 ± 18.33	16.91 ± 0.66	2.31 ± 0.18

4.11 Multi-Path Routing for FAN

The main aim of this section is to present a new algorithm for intelligent routing in FAN. Without congestion control mechanisms, new flows cannot begin transmission if the outgoing link is congested. While there is no intelligence according to routing protocols in FAN routers, the route between source and destination nodes is always chosen through the same path. However, there may exist many paths between such nodes and in congestion they should be used. The algorithm presented here meets the requirements presented above and may be implemented to improve network performance in congestion.

The pseudo-code of the algorithm is presented in Fig. 4.35.

A new flow may be accepted at the admission control block in a congestion-less state. Then, based on the current routing table its identifier (ID) is added to PFL with the identifier of the outgoing interface and the incoming packet is sent for queuing (lines 4–8). If the ID of the flow represented by the arriving packet is in PFL, then

```
1  on a packet P of new flow F arrival in the congestion −less state
2  if routing table has changed then
3      update all IDs in PFL
4  if ID(F) is not in PFL then
5  begin
6      add ID(F) to PFL
7      based on routing table add ID(out int) to ID(F) in PFL
8      send packet P for queuing
9  end
10 else
11 begin
12     find in PFL the ID of outgoing interface for P
13     send packet P for queuing
14 end
15 ######### in congestion state #########
16 on a packet P of new flow F arrival in the congestion state
17 if routing table has changed then
18     update all IDs in PFL
19 if ID(F) is in PFL then
20 begin
21     find in PFL the ID of outgoing interface for P
22     send packet P for queuing
23 end
24 else
25 begin
26     find new temporal routing table
27     if new routing table has been found then
28     begin
29         based on new routing table add ID(out int) to ID(F) in PFL
30         send packet P for queuing
31     end
32 end
```

Fig. 4.35 Pseudo-code for realizing the intelligent routing in FAN

the outgoing interface is found in PFL and the packet is sent for queuing (lines 12–13).

In congestion, the situation is more complex. If the ID of flow represented by the incoming packet is in PFL, then the operation taken in the XP router is similar to that described in the previous case. The outgoing interface is found in PFL and the packet is sent to the scheduler block (lines 19–22). On the other hand, a new temporal routing table must be determined. It has to be assumed that all congested links are treated as failed links at this time (line 26). The process of finding the temporal routing table may take some time. It depends on the routing protocol. For example, in OSPF it may take up to tens of seconds. However, this process may be activated before the link becomes congested. The use of hysteresis may be a good solution to this problem. Moreover, temporal routing tables may be written to the router memory and used in the future in a fast way. If a new routing table is determined, it can be used to add the ID of the incoming flow to PFL with the ID of the outgoing interface, while the arriving packet is sent for queuing (lines 29–30). It is important to note that after any topology change in a network (e.g., due to a link or node failure), the registrations in PFL have to be updated (lines 2–3 and 17–18).

The algorithm is based on the load balancing assumption, although the additional operations are needed. The key point is that outgoing interfaces in XP routers are selected based on registrations in PFL (in contrast to the current approach where outgoing interfaces are fixed based on the routing table). The new algorithm is a smart solution which does not increase operation complexity in XP routers significantly and improves transmission performance in FAN.

4.11.1 Comparison of Intelligent Routing for FAN with Existing Solutions

The concept of an intelligent routing for Flow-Aware Networks is similar to load balancing. However, the approach uses a new method for choosing routes for packets which represent flows. Many reports in literature have analyzed similar problems. This section discusses and compares three solutions against our proposal.

Load balancing is a popular method of improving network performance. It is implemented in almost every routing protocol. When we have several paths to the destination node with equal cost, traffic is divided equally and sent through these paths. Several more advanced solutions also exist, e.g., in EIGRP, where load balancing is enabled by using paths of unequal cost [7]. However, to the best of our knowledge, no load balancing mechanisms exist which make it possible to dynamically change path costs, e.g., based on traffic load in network links.

Valiant's load balancing was introduced in [13]. It assumes that the outgoing interface may be randomly selected from all non-congested ports. However, this solution works only in fully-connected logical mesh networks. The proposal presented in this section does not assume such a limitation and as such it is more universal.

Traffic engineering in MPLS, described in more detail in [10], assumes that paths for particular flows are determined using a link-state database which contains flooded topology and resource information. In this context, traffic engineering in MPLS is similar to the mechanism described in this section. However, our proposal eliminates one important drawback of this solution. In intelligent routing for FAN, signaling protocols such as RSVP or LDP and packet labels are not needed, which improves network performance. Moreover, this advantage improves the scalability of the mechanism analyzed in this section.

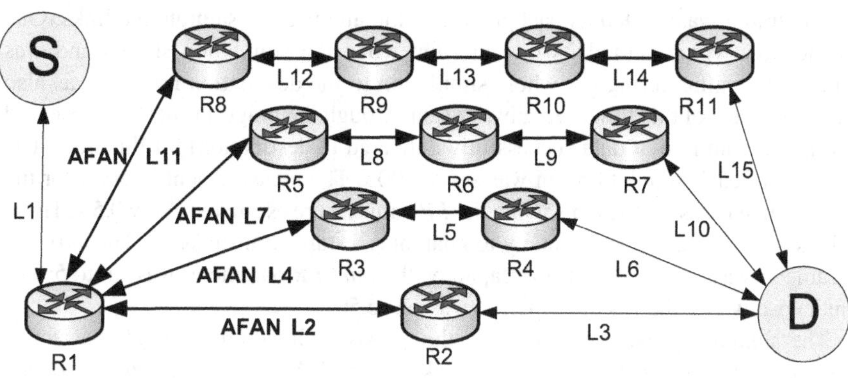

Fig. 4.36 Simulation topology

4.11.2 Simulation Analysis

In this section, results of carefully selected simulation experiments run in the ns-2 simulator are presented. The aim is to show how the new algorithm for intelligent routing in FAN improves network performance in congestion. Moreover, the advantages and disadvantages of the RAMAF and the SCCM are presented with several simulation experiments.

120 simulation runs were provided for four network topologies. The most advanced topology is presented in Fig. 4.36, referred to as topology no. 4 from now on. In topology no. 3 links L11–L15 are not present. Consequently, in topology no. 2 links L1–L6 are present and in topology no. 1 only one path between the source (*S*) and destination (*D*) nodes is implemented (through L1, L2 and L3 links). The aim of the experiments for each topology was to show how the volume of total traffic changes if the number of routes between nodes *S* and *D* increases after the implementation of the intelligent routing algorithm in FAN.

It was assumed that the capacity of each FAN link was set to 100 Mbit/s. The capacity of other links was set to 1 Gbit/s. The simulations were repeated at least 10 times for each experiment. 95% confidence intervals were calculated using the Student's t-distribution.

The traffic pattern with Pareto distribution for calculating the volume of traffic to be sent by each of the 200 elastic flows from node *S* to *D* (the volume of data to be sent was set to 150 Mbit and the shape parameter was set to 1.5) was provided. We used exponential distribution for generating the time intervals between start points of the transmissions of elastic flows (the mean value of the inter-arrival time was set to 0.2 s). Exponential distribution was also used for generating time intervals between start points of the transmissions of 20 streaming flows (the mean inter-arrival time was set to 1 s). The packet size for the elastic flows was set to 1000 bytes, while that for the streaming flows was set to 100 bytes. The transmission rate of streaming flows was set to 80 kbit/s (as in a typical Skype VoIP connection).

Elastic traffic was treated as background traffic and used to saturate the links. One elastic flow which started its transmission when the simulation started and was sending its traffic during the whole simulation to the destination node D was also added. Packets of this flow were always sent through the longest route. We observed goodput (mean rate of data successfully delivered to destination) for this flow. The duration of each simulation run was set to 300 s. The measurement interval for the PL parameter was set to 50 ms while the FR values were estimated every 0.5 s. These values were chosen experimentally to guarantee a stable transmission. The max_PL parameter was set to 70% of link capacity, the min_FR parameter was set to 5% of link capacity and the warm-up period was set to 50 s.

The simulations were provided for the AFAN architecture. min_th was set to 4000 packets and max_th to 9000 packets. For RAMAF, the $cleaning\_timer$ (minimum time between any flushing of PFL action) was set to 5 s. For SCCM, the $reduce\_timer$ was set to 5 s.

The results of the simulation experiments are presented in Table 4.3 and in Figs. 4.37 and 4.38. The simulation experiments provided in each topology show that the RAMAF and the SCCM result in a significant reduction of acceptance delay of streaming flows. The results are at an acceptable level (less than 6 s) in each case while in basic AFAN (without congestion control mechanisms) the streaming flows were accepted after tens of seconds (see Table 4.3).

Table 4.3 The values of mean acceptance delay in the analyzed topologies

n routes in topology	Accept. time [s] (Basic AFAN)	Accept. time [s] (RAMAF)	Accept. time [s] (SCCM)
1	114.22 ± 25.02	0.63 ± 0.63	1.70 ± 0.22
2	82.37 ± 18.00	0.91 ± 0.73	1.03 ± 0.63
3	85.81 ± 11.90	0.47 ± 0.47	0.65 ± 0.49
4	77.00 ± 11.78	0.31 ± 0.29	0.94 ± 0.66

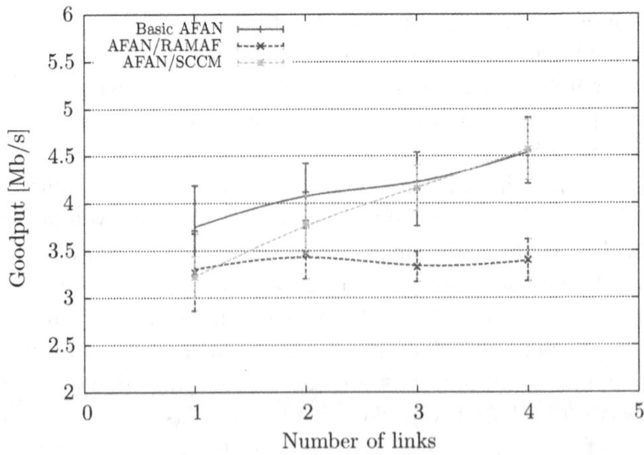

Fig. 4.37 TCP efficiency in the analyzed topologies

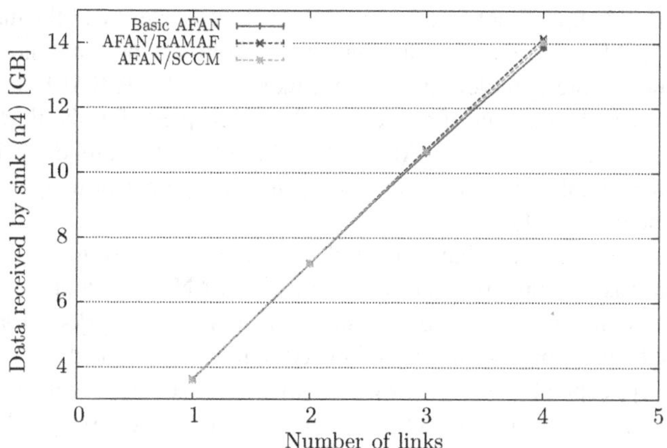

Fig. 4.38 TCP efficiency in the analyzed topologies

In Fig. 4.37, we can see that goodput in AFAN with RAMAF is worse than in basic AFAN. This is a result of periodical cleaning of the PFL content, and in consequence breaks in transmission of elastic flows. Moreover, the value of goodput is almost the same in AFAN with RAMAF independently of topology. This is because RAMAF cleans the content of the PFL of each link in the topology and, as a result, the flow has to slow down from time to time when the AFAN link on its route becomes congested. In basic AFAN the goodput increases with the number of routes to the destination. A similar situation is observed for SCCM where IDs of elastic flows are not removed from the PFL. The flow slows down when congestion is periodically eliminated and new flows are accepted. However, its transmission is never broken and when we have more routes to the destination node the difference between the SCCM and basic AFAN is reduced.

The most interesting results are presented in Fig. 4.38. We can see that the number of routes to the destination node increases linearly, the volume of total transmitted traffic in a network also increases linearly. It is consistent with our expectations because the amount of data received by the sink should increase in proportion to the number of links. This confirms that the intelligent routing algorithm for Flow-Aware Networks works as it was assumed. It improves the usage of available resources in a network and significantly improves performance in a network. This conclusion is true for basic AFAN as well as for AFAN with RAMAF or SCCM.

4.12 Conclusion

Seven congestion control mechanisms have been proposed for FAN to solve the problem of long acceptance delays of streaming flows. Most of them assume periodical cleaning of the PFL content in congestion. The SCCM steers the level of

min_FR to enable the acceptance of new flows. The complexity of the mechanisms is different. EFM is the simplest mechanism, although it provides no protection to elastic flows. More complex mechanism, including EFMP, RAEF, RBAEF and RPAEF, minimize the number of new elastic flows accepted after the flushing of the PFL content. However, only RAMAF and SCCM reduce the number of new elastic flows to an acceptable level. They improve transmission performance realized by already accepted elastic flows.

MFAN is an effective mechanism which uses additional resources at the optical layer. An analysis of transmission in wired-wireless FAN shows that the NewJersey TCP protocol is recommended for transmission in such networks. Moreover, the RAMAF mechanism may be successfully used in this environment.

The new concept of routing allows us to minimize the negative aspects of congestion. Traffic is distributed among available uncongested paths which makes it possible to send a higher volume of traffic in congestion.

4.13 Check Your Knowledge

1. How many congestion control mechanisms based on cleaning of the PFL content have been proposed for FAN?
2. What is the main motivation for implementing a congestion control mechanism in FAN?
3. The SCCM is based on steering the level of (1) min_FR or (2) FR?
4. What is the basic TCP version for wireless FAN?
5. How many PFLλ lists does MFAN use in the optical layer?
6. Which is the least complex congestion control mechanism for FAN?
7. How many IDs should remain in PFL after flushing in RAMAF when the link capacity is 1 Gbit/s and $min\_FR = 10$ Mbit/s?
8. List MFAN policies.
9. What is the maximum acceptance time of streaming flows according to [9]?
10. Why is transmission of elastic traffic usually deteriorated by using congestion control mechanisms in FAN?
11. How is congestion eliminated in FAN by using multi-path routing?
12. Which parameter is added to PFL in multi-path routing?

References

1. J. Domzal, Intelligent routing in congested approximate flow-aware networks, in *IEEE Global Communications Conference (GLOBECOM)* (2012), pp. 1751–1756
2. J. Domzal, N. Ansari, A. Jajszczyk, New congestion control mechanisms for flow-aware networks, in *Proceedings of the IEEE International Conference on Communications ICC 2008*, Beijing (2008)
3. J. Domzal, N. Ansari, A. Jajszczyk, The flushing mechanism for MBAC in flow-aware networks, in *Proceedings of the 4th EURO-NGI Conference on Next Generation Internet Networks, NGI 2008*, Krakow (2008), pp. 77–83

4. J. Domzal, N. Ansari, A. Jajszczyk, Reliable transmission in flow-aware networks, in *Proceedings of the IEEE Global Communications Conference GLOBECOM 2009*, Honolulu (2009), pp. 1 –6
5. J. Domzal, N. Ansari, A. Jajszczyk, Congestion control in wireless flow-aware networks, in *IEEE ICC 2011*, Kyoto (2011)
6. J. Domżał, R. Wójcik, V. López, J. Aracil, A. Jajszczyk, EFMP—a new congestion control mechanism for flow-aware networks. Trans. Emerg. Telecommun. Technol. **25**(11), 1137–1148 (2014)
7. Load balancing data center services. Cisco Systems (2004)
8. V. Lopez, C. Cardenas, J.A. Hernandez, J. Aracil, M. Gagnaire, Extension of the Flow-Aware Networking (FAN) architecture to the IP over WDM environment, in *Proceedings of the 4th International Telecommunication Networking Workshop on QoS in Multiservice IP Networks*, Venice (2008)
9. Network grade of service parameters and target values for circuit-switched services in the evolving ISDN, ITU-T Recommendation E.721 (1999)
10. E. Osborne, A. Simha, *Traffic Engineering with MPLS* (Pearson Education, London, 2002)
11. K. Xu, Y. Tian, N. Ansari, TCP-jersey for wireless IP communications. IEEE J. Sel. Areas Commun. **22**, 747–756 (2004)
12. K. Xu, Y. Tian, N. Ansari, Improving TCP performance in integrated wireless communications networks. Comput. Netw. **47**, 219–237 (2005)
13. R. Zhang-Shen, N. McKeown, Designing a predictable internet backbone network, in *HotNets*, San Diego (2004)

References

Fairness in FAN

5

Auditur et altera pars. (The other side shall be heard as well.)

— Lucius Annaeus Seneca, Medea

Fairness may be perceived in many ways. For example, best effort transmission is fair because each packet has the same chance of being transmitted. In FAN, each flow is assigned the same rate, which is also fair. However, in current networks we need more sophisticated fairness. Multi-flow applications (e.g., P2P) may overload access networks and result in bandwidth per flow being very low. Such P2P flows may consume almost all bandwidth and the quality of transmission of the remaining traffic may be drastically deteriorated. This brief discussion shows that fairness per flow may not be the best solution. In this chapter, we demonstrate a new approach to assuring fairness in Flow-Aware Networking. We show and evaluate two approaches to improve fairness in FAN. One, already known from the literature, which is based on altering the admission control routine. The other, presented in this chapter, with a redesigned scheduling mechanism. Evaluation shows that a new concept of fairness provides utterly fair resource distribution regardless of the behaviour of users. The results were first published in [5].

The design of Flow-Aware Networking meant to impose fairness upon the network. However, fairness is perceived in the scope of flows. Since a single user can generate many flows, it is easy to game the system by dividing a connection (ideally one flow) into many smaller flows. Fairness among flows may not be acceptable in a network. A user who generates many flows may consume a significant part of bandwidth in the outgoing link. As a result, it may not be possible for other users to begin transmission for a long time or their flows may be granted a small part of the link capacity. In this chapter, we present the per-user fair packet scheduling mechanism (PUFPS), which ensures fairness among users. If only a user has traffic to send she receives the bandwidth at least equal to the link capacity divided by the

J. Domżał et al., *Guide to Flow-Aware Networking*, Computer Communications and Networks, https://doi.org/10.1007/978-3-030-57153-5_5

number of active users. The mechanism does not increase complexity of router's operation and is fully automatic.

5.1 Per-User Fairness for Flow-Aware Networking

The first attempt to provide the per-user fairness was presented in [3]. In that proposal, the functionality of the admission control block in the cross-protect router is changed. The mentioned solution assumes that the weighted fair queuing (WFQ) algorithm is implemented in the MBAC to ensure fair access to resources for network users. In basic FAN, flows are served in a fair manner. However, a user can generate many flows which may occupy the link for a long time. As a result, new flows may have not been accepted and a user can consume more bandwidth than others. The per-user fairness algorithm assumes that the number of flows being served at a moment is similar for each user. This eliminates the problems mentioned above maintaining fairness among flows and users and giving precedence for streaming flows.

To reduce disproportion in the number of active flows generated by users, the implementation of the limiting mechanism was suggested. Two versions of the limiting mechanism have been proposed for FAN, so far [2, 4]. The main goal of them is to limit the number of flows accepted in an XP router when an outgoing link becomes congestion-less. It was noticed that in a highly loaded network too many flows are accepted in the admission control block of the XP router when congestion is eliminated. The limiting mechanism ensures that this number is minimized to ensure proper transmission parameters of active flows. The per-user fairness mechanism uses the limiting approach to ensure fair access to the resources for each user. In this solution, it is assumed that during the FR measurement interval maximum N flows of each user can be accepted in the router. N is a fixed number set by a network operator. This solution is quite simple and easy to implement. The pseudo-code of the per-user fairness algorithm is presented in Fig. 5.1. The identifiers of a user (i) and a flow (j) are extracted from the packet's P header when it arrives at the router (lines 1–3 in Fig. 5.1). If j is not in the PFL, the user counter ($i\_counter$) is not greater than the fixed value N, and the outgoing link is not congested, the packet can be accepted (lines 4–11). In such a case j is added to the PFL, i is added (if not added before) to the active user list (AUL), and $i\_counter$ is increased by one. Moreover, the incoming packet is enqueued in the priority queue (PQ_i) (line 10). If j is in the PFL, the incoming packet is enqueued in the priority queue (if $ByteCount\_j$ does not exceed the fixed quantum) or in the elastic queue (line 16 or 18). Each time the new FR value is estimated, the counters for all users are set to zero (lines 20–23).

The results presented in [3] confirm that the mechanism works properly. It has been shown that the fairness among users is achieved, even in highly-loaded links. However, it is hard to set N properly. If it is too low, the acceptance delay of flows may become unacceptable. On the other hand, when N is too high, the acceptance of too many flows may result in poor transmission parameters of active flows.

```
on arrival of packet  P
i = ExtractUser( P)
j = ExtractFlow( P)
if (j ∉ PFL and i_counter ≤ N and link is not congested)
begin
    if (i ∉ AUL)
        add i to AUL
    add j to PFL
    i_counter += 1
    Enqueue( PQ_i, P)
end
if (j ∈ PFL )
begin
    ByteCount_j += Size( P)
    if (ByteCount_j ≤ Q) then
        Enqueue( PQ_i, P)
    else
        Enqueue( EQ_i, P)
end
############ for each FR estimation ###########
for (i=1; i ≤ AUL_size; i++){
    i_counter = 0
}
```

Fig. 5.1 Per-user fairness algorithm

5.2 Per-User Fair Packet Scheduling Mechanism

The per-user fair packet scheduling mechanism assumes that traffic of each network user is served in a fair manner, but the limiting mechanism is not used. Instead, the scheduling of packets of flows is modified; however the streaming flows are still served with high priority. The mechanism is illustrated in Fig. 5.2. The pseudo-code of packet queuing in PUFPS is presented in Fig. 5.3, while the pseudo-code of packet dequeuing in PUFPS is presented in Fig. 5.4. The queuing and dequeuing algorithms are based on the PDRR concept [1]; however in PUFPS fairness is assured among users. The mechanism assumes that one FIFO queue is dedicated for each active user (who generates flows) in the router. Moreover, each user has own queues (one for priority packets of all user's flows and one for packets of each user's elastic flow) which allows to realize the PDRR concept among her flows.

When a new packet P arrives at the router, the identifiers of user (i) and flow (j) are extracted from the packet header (lines 1–3 in Fig. 5.3). If j is not in the PFL and the outgoing link is not congested, the packet can be accepted. In such a case j is added to the PFL and i is added to the priority queue list (PQL) (lines 4–7). PQL is the list of identifiers of users who have packets in priority queues. Next, user's and flow's enqueued byte counters ($ByteCount$) are updated by the packet size and the packet is enqueued in the user's priority queue (lines 8–11). On the other hand, if j

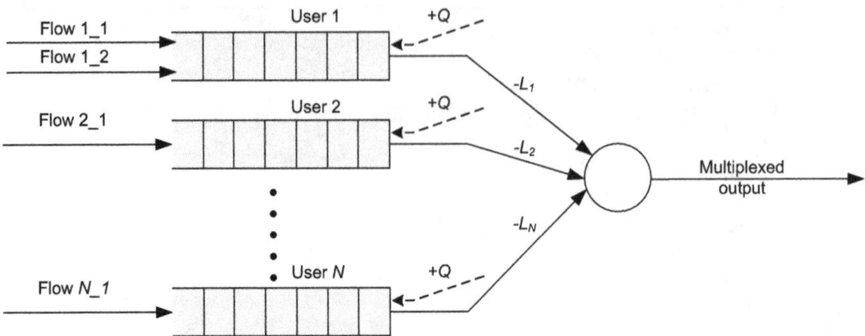

Fig. 5.2 Packet scheduling in PUFPS

```
1   on arrival of packet P
2   i = ExtractUser( P)
3   j = ExtractFlow( P)
4   if (j ∉ PFL and link is not congested)
5   begin
6       add j to PFL
7       add i to PQL
8       ByteCount_i + = Size( P)
9       ByteCount_j = Size( P)
10      Enqueue( PQ_i, P)
11  end
12  if (j ∈ PFL )
13  begin
14      ByteCount_i + = Size( P)
15      ByteCount_j + = Size( P)
16      if (ByteCount_j ≤ Q) then
17      begin
18          Enqueue( PQ_i, P)
19          if (i ∉ PQL) then
20              add i to PQL
21      end
22      else
23          Enqueue( EQ_i, P)
24  end
```

Fig. 5.3 PUFPS packet arrival operations

is in the PFL, user's and flow's counters are also updated (lines 14–15) but the queue for the incoming packet is selected based on the number of flow's bytes currently being enqueued. If *ByteCount* of the flow exceeds quantum Q then packet P is sent to the proper elastic queue (line 23). On the other hand, packet P is enqueued in the user's priority queue.

The process for selecting a packet to send is more complex. Users are selected based on the content of AUL and served based on the DRR regime. First the discount

```
1   while PQL not empty do
2   begin
3       get head of AUL, say user i
4       DC_i + = Q
5       while (DC_i > 0) and (PQ_i not empty) do
6       begin
7           PacketSize = Size(Head(PQ _i))
8           if (PacketSize ≤ DC_i) then
9           begin
10              Send(Dequeue(PQ_i))
11              DC_i − = PacketSize
12          end
13          else
14              break ; (*skip while loop *)
15          if (PQ_i is empty)
16              remove i from PQL
17      end
18      RemoveActiveList( i)
19      if Queue_i is not empty then
20          add i to AUL
21  end
22  if AUL is not empty then
23  begin
24      get head of AUL, say user i
25      DC_i + = Q_i
26      while (DC_i > 0) and (EQ_i not empty) do
27      begin
28          PacketSize = Size(Head(EQ _i))
29          if (PacketSize ≤ DC_i) then
30          begin
31              Send(Dequeue(EQ_i))
32              DC_i − = PacketSize
33          end
34          else
35              break ; (*skip while loop *)
36      end
37      RemoveActiveList( i)
38      if Queue_i is not empty then
39          add i to AUL
40  end
```

Fig. 5.4 PUFPS packet departure operations

counter (*DC*) for the first user on the AUL is increased by *Q* (lines 3–4 in Fig. 5.4). Priority packets of user *i* are served until the discount counter for this user is greater than the priority packet to be sent (lines 5–17). The *while* loop is broken when the discount counter is too low or the user's priority queue is empty (in this case, also the user's ID is removed from PQL (line 16)). When the *while* loop ends, the user's

ID is removed from the AUL and added again at the end of this list (lines 18–20). It ensures fair round-robin regime. When there are no identifiers in the PQL and the AUL is not empty, packets from elastic queues can be sent. Similarly to the service of the priority packets, first the discount counter (DC) for the first user on the AUL is increased by Q (lines 24–25). Packets of user i are served until her elastic queue is not empty and the deficit discount is greater than zero (lines 26–36). If any of these conditions is not assured, the user's ID is shifted to the end of the AUL (lines 37–39) and packets of another user can be sent.

5.3 Evaluation

To show the performance of the new fairness mechanism, we used the ns-2 simulator with the FAN module. We simulated one overloaded 100 Mbit/s FAN link. In each scenario, there were users who generate various numbers of flows. The idea was to demonstrate how one can exploit the network by dividing their transmission into a number of smaller flows. Therefore, in each case, we compared the achieved performance under the following four paradigms:

- classical IP-based packet forwarding (denoted as IP),
- standard FAN architecture (denoted as FAN),
- FAN architecture with limitation-based fairness mechanism (denoted as FAN LIMIT),
- FAN architecture with the new fairness mechanism (denoted as FAN PER USER).

The presented comparison allowed us to expose a significant weakness of FAN and a robust method to amend it. The goal was to evaluate the fairness that each mechanism provides. We have defined fairness as the standard deviation of goodput achieved by users. The smaller value the better fairness is achieved.

The simulated topology is presented in Fig. 5.5. There is a number of users connected to the XP router, who are connected with the FAN bottleneck link to the server. Every user link has the bandwidth of 100 Mbit/s and the propagation delay of 1 ms. In each interface, a FIFO queue with the buffer size of 1000 packets is installed. Each user tries to send some amount of data to the server. To enhance unfair bandwidth usage, we have defined two different scenarios, which are described below.

Each simulation captures 250 s of the network operation. All the simulations were repeated at least 10 times with different seeds for random number generator to obtain statistically credible results. The 95% confidence intervals were calculated following the Student's t-distribution. In each case, we disregarded the results until the FAN link became congested, i.e., until the fair rate dropped below the desired 5% threshold. In simulations where FAN was used, the following configuration was applied: Minimum Fair Rate: 5% of the bottleneck link's capacity, Fair Rate Measurement Interval: 0.5 s. In case of FAN with the limiting mechanism, the limitation was set to 1 user flow per measurement interval.

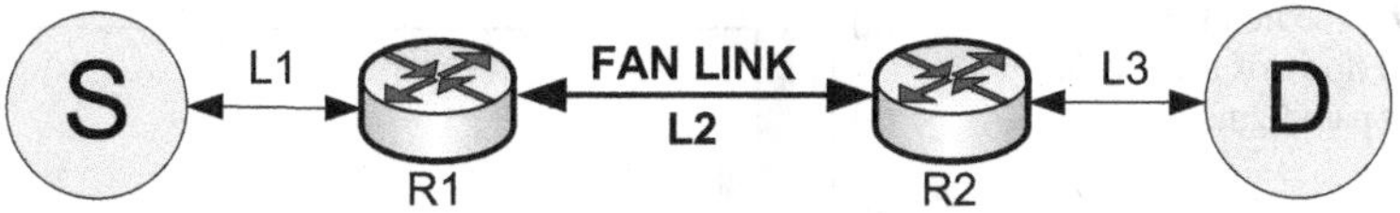

Fig. 5.5 Evaluated topology

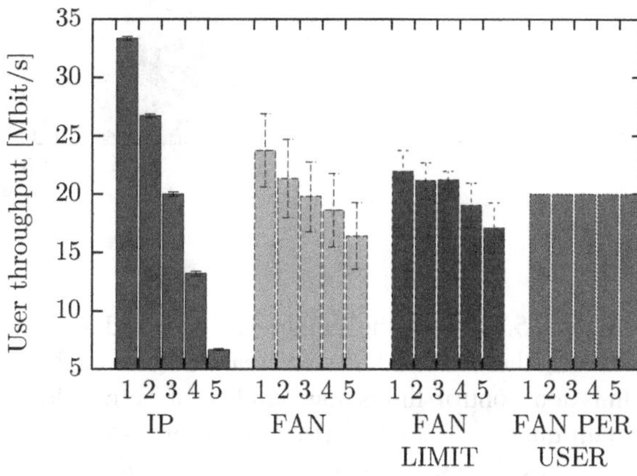

Fig. 5.6 The achieved throughput of users 1–5 and four paradigms

5.3.1 Scenario 1

In this scenario, a 100 Mbit/s bottleneck link is shared by five users. Each user wants to send 4 GB of data through the link and, therefore, divides it into flows. Each user has the same 100 Mbit/s access link available. Users 1 through 5 generate 60, 48, 36, 24 and 12 flows, respectively. The packet size was set to 1500 bytes. Each user starts transmission from the beginning of the simulation and intervals between beginnings of transmissions of the TCP flows were generated with exponential distribution with mean value of 0.2 s.

Figure 5.6 shows the average throughput each user achieves during the simulation. Standard IP packet forwarding, which is based on a FIFO queue, is the most strict. The achieved throughput is strictly proportional to the number of generated flows. This is due to the fact that the rate of each flow is controlled by the TCP protocol. Because we disregard the impact of various access rates and round trip times, the performance of each TCP controlled flow is identical. Note that in general, TCP does not impose fairness per flow, as was shown e.g., in [6].

FAN, even in its simplest form provides some sort of fairness. That is why the throughputs achieved by particular users are more averaged. FAN with the limitation mechanism provides a bit more fair division, however, this solution yields better results when the number of users is greater. Finally, the PUFPS mechanism assures exactly the same bandwidth for each user regardless of the number of flows the user generates.

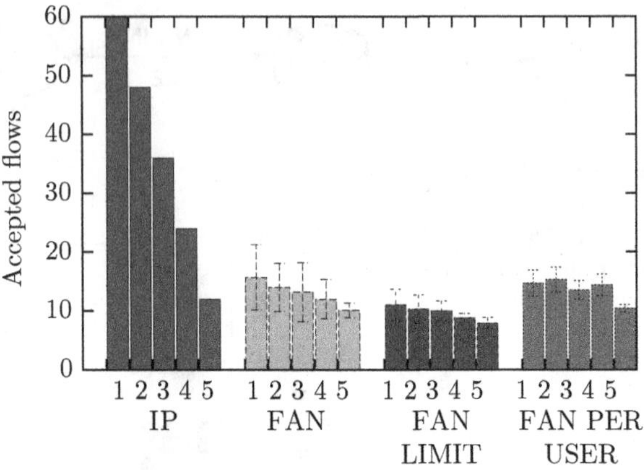

Fig. 5.7 The number of accepted flows of users 1–5 and four paradigms

Figure 5.7 shows the number of accepted flows for each user. In classic IP networks, there is no admission control, therefore, all the flows are accepted. FAN's admission control limits the number of active flows to such level that assures certain quality of service. However, even in FAN, the number of accepted flows differs, based on the number of flows that a user originally creates. This is also the reason why the obtained throughputs differ. PUFPS also shows small inequity in the number of accepted flows, however, this does not have any impact on the obtained throughput.

5.3.2 Scenario 2

In this scenario there were 15 users divided equally into 3 groups: G1, G2 and G3. Users in G1 divided their traffic into 10 streams, in G2 into 2 streams and in G1 into 1 stream. We have simulated 7 cases, in which every stream was composed of 1, 2, 3, 4, 5, 10 and 20 flows. Therefore, in the last case, users in G1 created $10 \times 20 = 200$, in G2 $2 \times 20 = 40$ and in G3 $1 \times 20 = 20$ simultaneous flows, respectively. The packet size was set to 1500 B and flow size was generated with uniform distribution between 200 and 400 MB. Each user starts transmission from the beginning of simulation with the mean interval equal to 0.05 s for users in group 1, 0.1 s for users in group 2 and 0.5 s for users in group 3. Intervals correspond to the distribution of flows between groups so that the product of the interval length and the number of streams remained constant. This way, users do not gain resource access advantage from generating their flows earlier than the rest.

Figure 5.8 shows the achieved throughputs of groups of users with low (a) medium (b) and large (c) number of flows per stream. In all cases, standard IP and FAN networks behaved almost exactly the same, i.e., the obtained throughput relied heavily on the number of accepted flows. In case of the IP networks, all the flows were accepted. In case of standard FAN, due to admission control, only a portion of the flows were accepted, however, their composition was proportional to the number

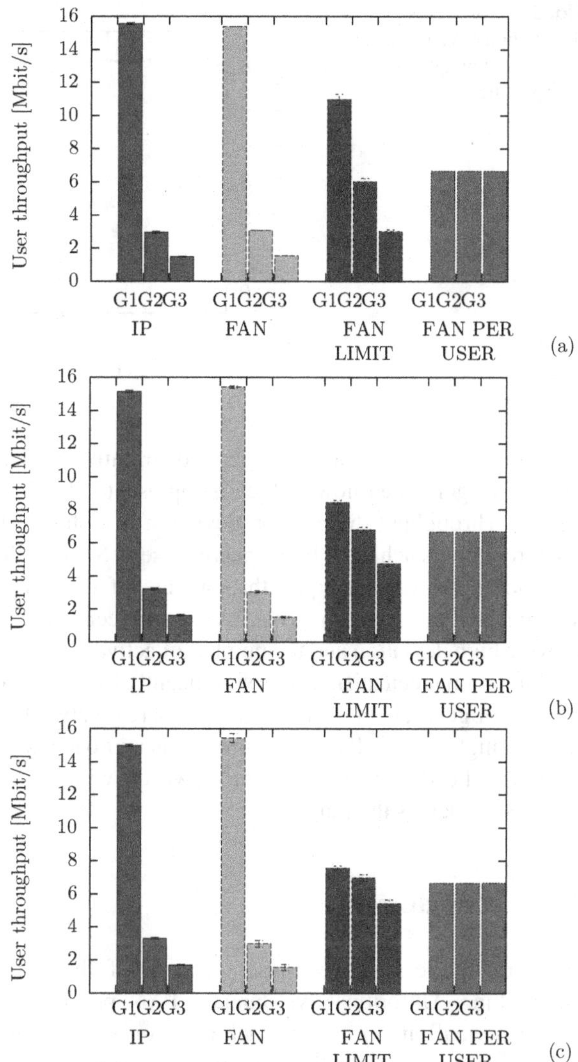

Fig. 5.8 The achieved throughput of groups 1–3 and four paradigms. Flow quantity multiplicator: 1 (**a**), 10 (**b**), 20 (**c**)

of flows offered by each group. Hence, the observed throughput is similar to the standard IP networks.

FAN with the limitation mechanism attempts to provide fairness. Here, in one measurement interval, only a limited number of flows can be accepted from each user which restricts the flow number inequity. The effect is more visible when the number of flows is greater and in case (c), the obtained throughputs are almost equal. The PUFPS mechanism, on the other hand, provides superior results regardless of the total load and the number of generated flows. This is a considerable advantage of this approach.

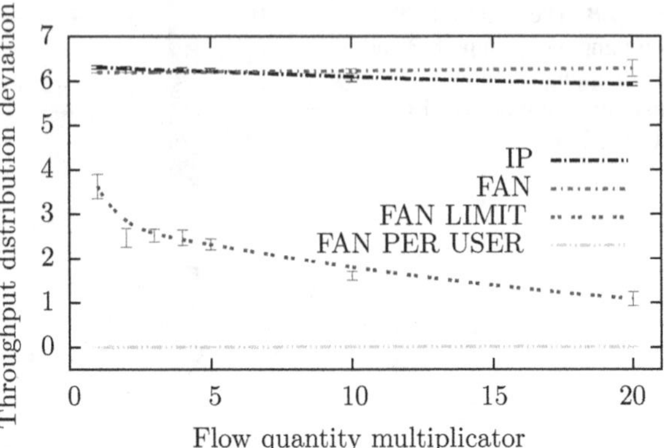

Fig. 5.9 Throughput distribution deviation with respect to flow quantity and four paradigms

In Fig. 5.9 we present a throughput distribution deviation with respect to the total number of generated flows which is represented by different numbers of flows per stream. Throughput distribution deviation is a standard deviation calculated from the throughputs achieved by respective users. Smaller deviation indicates that users achieved more or less equal throughputs. If throughputs differ from each other significantly, the deviation grows. As can be seen in the Figure, standard IP and FAN provide high deviation and the number of active flows does not affect that. FAN with the limitation mechanism offers significantly lower deviation, which improves as the number of generated flows increases. In a real network, where the number of active flows is high, especially in core links, this approach is enough to statistically assure fairness. The PUFPS mechanism, however, with its near zero deviation provides best results across the range.

5.4 Conclusion

Assuring fairness between users is one of the core concepts of Flow-Aware Networking. Unfortunately, standard FAN provides fairness among flows only. Under normal circumstances such a notion works. However, given that each user is free to create multiple flows, gaming the architecture for greater throughput is not only possible, but very easy. In FAN, it is better to divide each transmission into multiple flows. In this situation fairness among users is not achieved.

We showed and compared two approaches to solve the problem. Particularly, the one based on a redesigned scheduling mechanism yields superior results. Evaluation shows that regardless of the amount of traffic, the solution provides perfect equality among users. It is no longer beneficial to divide the transmission into many flows.

For the network operator, this is very important. Firstly, users are offered the assurance of fairness. Secondly, users are not inclined to create unnecessary flows which contributes to FAN's scalability.

5.5 Check Your Knowledge

1. Which type of fairness was originally proposed for FAN?
2. What is the main assumption of the per-user fairness concept?
3. What is the main assumption of the Per-User Fair Packet Scheduling Mechanism?

Acknowledgement The authors would like to thank Piotr Gawłowicz for his support, valuable comments and suggestions on improving the quality of this chapter.

References

1. J. Domzal, R. Wojcik, A. Jajszczyk, Implicit service differentiation using deficit round robin, in *Proceedings of the 19th International Teletraffic Congress, ITC 2005*, Beijing (2005)
2. J. Domzal, R. Wojcik, A. Jajszczyk, Reliable transmission in flow-aware networks, in *Proceedings of the IEEE Global Communications Conference GLOBECOM 2009*, Honolulu (2009), pp. 1 –6
3. J. Domzal, R. Wojcik, A. Jajszczyk, Per user fairness in flow-aware networks, in *Proceeding of the IEEE International Conference on Communications ICC 2012*, Ottawa (2012)
4. R. Wojcik, J. Domzal, A. Jajszczyk, Fair rate degradation in flow-aware networks, in *Proceedings of the IEEE International Conference on Communications ICC 2010* (2010), pp. 1 –5
5. R. Wojcik, J. Domzal, P. Gawlowicz, A new concept of fairness in flow-aware networking. Int. J. Commun. Syst. **30**(18), e3362 (2017) [Online]. https://onlinelibrary.wiley.com/doi/abs/10.1002/dac.3362
6. L. Xue, S. Kumar, C. Cui, S.-J. Park, A study of fairness among heterogeneous TCP variants over 10 Gbps high-speed optical networks. Opt. Switch. Netw. **13**(0), 124–134 (2014)

FAN in Case of Failure

6

If it fails, admit it frankly and try another. But above all, try something.

—Franklin D. Roosevelt

In the basic FAN architecture, the ID of a flow can only be removed from the PFL if it has been inactive for a certain period. This means that the transmission of all flows accepted in the AC block cannot be broken in a failure-less state. In this chapter, we analyze traffic performance in FAN in the event of a link failure. The main assumption is that streaming flows should be quickly accepted in a link and immediately redirected to a backup link when a failure occurs.

In FAN, when a failure occurs, flows must be redirected to a backup link. If this backup link is not congested, the flows from the failed link are quickly accepted on a new route. However, when the new path is congested, the redirected flows have to wait for acceptance. In basic FAN, this may take up to tens of seconds. This time may be limited to a few seconds for streaming flows by using a congestion control mechanism, as presented in [6]. Unfortunately, in both cases the redirection time is too long, because streaming flows should be transmitted without any breaks. Two solutions have been proposed for this problem. The first, known as GPFL (Global Protected Flow List), is analyzed in [7]. The second proposal, presented in [8], demonstrates a multi-layer recovery strategy whose operation is based on the EHOT (Enhanced Hold-Off Timer) algorithm.

6.1 Global Protected Flow List

The GPFL enables continuous transmission of packets of streaming flows, even when the traffic is rerouted after a link or node failure. Each router in a network has one GPFL which covers IDs of streaming flows written in all PFLs maintained by the router. We have to remember that a router has as many PFLs as outgoing

J. Domżał et al., *Guide to Flow-Aware Networking*, Computer Communications and Networks, https://doi.org/10.1007/978-3-030-57153-5_6

links it serves. The idea of using the GPFL is that streaming flows whose identifiers are written to it, are always accepted in FAN routers independently of the chosen route. The GPFL collects the IDs of all streaming flows active in the router, and if redirection in the router is needed, the streaming flows are always immediately accepted in the backup outgoing link and their IDs written to the PFL of this outgoing link.

The pseudo-code for realizing the GPFL concept in FAN is provided in Fig. 6.1. If a packet of a flow arrives at the admission control block and its ID is in the PFL of the outgoing link it means that its ID was previously added to the GPFL. Then, if the flow is of the streaming type, its priority is set to 1 in the GPFL (lines 1–5). For elastic flows the priority is set to 0 (line 6). On the other hand, if this flow was not previously accepted in the router and the link is congested, its ID may be added to the PFL only if this ID is in the GPFL and its priority is set to 1 (lines 9–19). In a congestion-less state, the ID of a new flow is added to the GPFL (if it is not there), and to the PFL, and the packets may be sent (lines 20–29).

```
1    on a packet p of flow F arrival
2    if ID(F) is in the PFL then
3    begin
4        if F is streaming then
5            set F_prior = 1 in the GPFL
6        else set F_prior = 0 in the GPFL
7        send p for queuing
8    end
9    else (not in the PFL)
10   begin
11       If link is congested then
12       begin
13           if ID(F) is in GPFL and F_prior = 1 then
14           begin
15               add ID (F) to PFL
16               send p for queuing
17           end
18           else drop p
19       end
20       else (link not congested)
21       begin
22           if ID(F) is not in GPFL then
23           begin
24               add ID (F) to GPFL
25               add ID (F) to PFL
26               send p for queuing
27           end
28       end
29   end
```

Fig. 6.1 Pseudo-code for realizing the GPFL concept in FAN

When a failure occurs and the backup link is not congested, too many flows redirected from the failed link may be accepted. To solve this problem, we propose the use of the limiting mechanism (LM). The main aim of the proposed algorithm is to ensure that in the period between any two consecutive measurements of the *FR* parameter, it is possible to add up to *N* identifiers to the PFL of the considered outgoing link. The *N* parameter is estimated from the following formula:

$$\begin{cases} N = 100/(min\_FR \times i) & \text{if } i > 0 \\ N = \infty & \text{if } i = 0 \end{cases} \tag{6.1}$$

where $i \in \mathbb{N}$ is the parameter which was changed in our simulation experiments to estimate the correct value of *N*. If *i* is set to 1 and *min_FR* is set to 5%, it means that up to 20 flows can be accepted in the router during one measurement period of *FR*. We analyzed four cases, with *i* set to 1, 2, 3 or 4.

When the LM is implemented in routers with GPFL, it has to be slightly modified. It should count elastic flows only and enable the acceptance of all streaming flows. Therefore, the $addmitted\_flows\_number$ variable should be increased only if the flow priority is set to zero.

6.1.1 Simulation Analysis of FAN with RPAEF, LM and GPFL

In this section we present the results of carefully selected simulation experiments carried out in the ns-2 simulator to show the usefulness of GPFL. Along with GPFL, we checked the functionality of the FAN router with the LM and the RPAEF congestion control mechanisms. The simulation topology is presented in Fig. 6.2.

For simplicity, in this simulation experiment we used one source node and two destination nodes. The *S* node is the source node of streaming and elastic flows, while the nodes *D*1 and *D*2 are destination nodes of traffic sent from the *S* node. It was assumed that bottleneck links L1 and L2 are FAN links, each with the capacity of 100 Mbit/s. The buffer was sized to 1000 packets and *MTU* was set to 1500 bytes. The capacity of the remaining links with the FIFO queue was set to 1 Gbit/s.

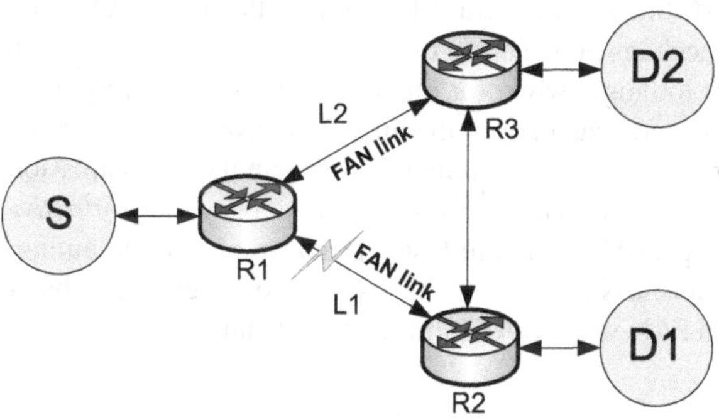

Fig. 6.2 The simulation topology

The shortest path routing was implemented in this network, which means that under normal conditions the traffic to node D1 is sent through nodes R1 and R2 while the traffic to node D2 is sent through nodes R1 and R3. By using this topology we assumed that link L2 was treated as a backup link with background traffic for packets usually sent through link L1. The effects of failures of link L1 at a chosen time instant were analyzed and presented in the experiments described below.

Hundred and sixty simulation runs were performed. The number of elastic flows was set to 200 for each destination node. The analysis was provided for two values of the *active_time* parameter (5 and 10 s). The simulation duration was set to 500 s and at 200 s the link L1 was set down. We used the traffic pattern with Pareto distribution for calculating the volume of traffic to be sent by elastic flows. Additionally, we used exponential distribution for generating the time intervals between the start times of the transmissions of elastic flows as well as for streaming flows. All 40 streaming flows were destined to D1. The elastic traffic was treated as background traffic and used to saturate the analyzed links. We chose to analyze the VoIP connections realizing the Skype service. The packet size was set to 100 bytes and the transmission rate was set to 80 kbit/s for each streaming flow. We analyzed the acceptance delay of each streaming flow in the AC block of router R1 for both outgoing links (L1 before failure and L2 after failure). The measurement interval for the PL parameter was set to 50 ms while the FR values were estimated every 500 ms. The *max_PL* and *min_FR* values were set to 70 and 5% of the link capacity, respectively, and the *pfl_flow_timeout* parameter was set to 20 s. Ninety Five percentage confidence intervals were calculated using the Student's t-distribution.

The results are presented in Figs. 6.3 and 6.4. The values of *waiting_time* decrease slightly with increasing values of i in the examined range in link L1. The TCP flows whose packets are discarded have to slow their transmission rate. If i increases, fewer flows may be accepted during a *fair_rate* computation interval. It means that with increasing values of i more TCP flows are not accepted in the AC block, decreasing their transmission windows. As a result, the streaming flows (UDP flows) can be accepted faster. As was expected, the streaming flows are accepted immediately in the FAN link of the backup route (see Fig. 6.3, two lines overlapping one another).

We can see that it is possible to reduce the number of elastic flows accepted in the AC block to the value observed for the basic FAN links (without congestion control mechanisms). This is observed for $i = 2$. For $i = 1$ the number of accepted flows is too high, while for higher values of i, it is too low and not all rejected flows are accepted again after flushing. Moreover, for values of 5 and 10 s of the *active_time* parameter, the streaming flows begin their transmission in a short, acceptable time.

Summarizing the results, we can say that for *active_time* = 5 or 10 s, $i = 2$, it is possible to assure fast acceptance of new streaming flows, good performance of transmission of elastic flows, and good network behavior after a link or node failure in FAN with RPAEF, limiting mechanism and GPFL.

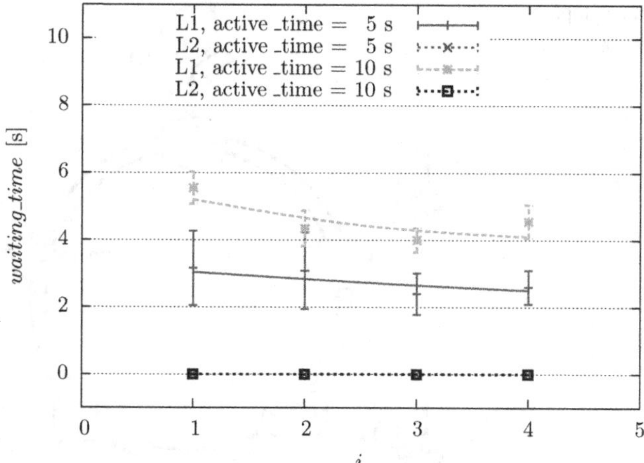

Fig. 6.3 Mean *waiting_time* in a FAN link with RPAEF, limiting mechanism and GPFL

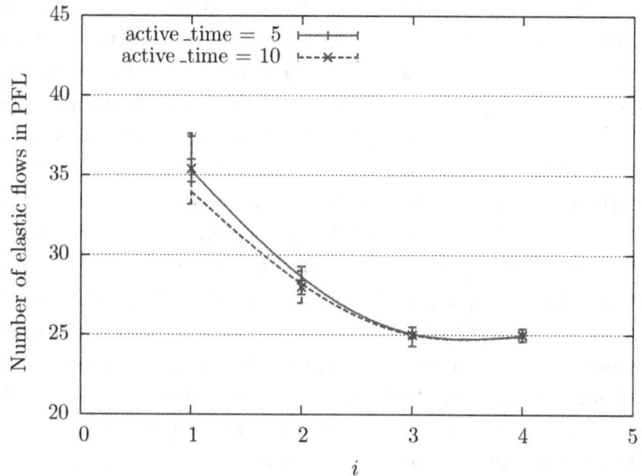

Fig. 6.4 Mean number of elastic flows in PFL in FAN with RPAEF, limiting mechanism and GPFL

6.2 Flow-Aware Resilient Ring

In this section, we present the concept of Flow-Aware Resilient Ring (FARR) proposed in [4] and further analyzed in [3]. We also show that congestion control mechanisms proposed for FAN and GPFL may be successfully used in FARR.

Resilient Packet Ring (RPR) is a well-known, stable standard, although it still needs improvements. Traffic classification in RPR is not unambiguously specified. It is not clear how to distinguish packets and assign them to the appropriate traffic

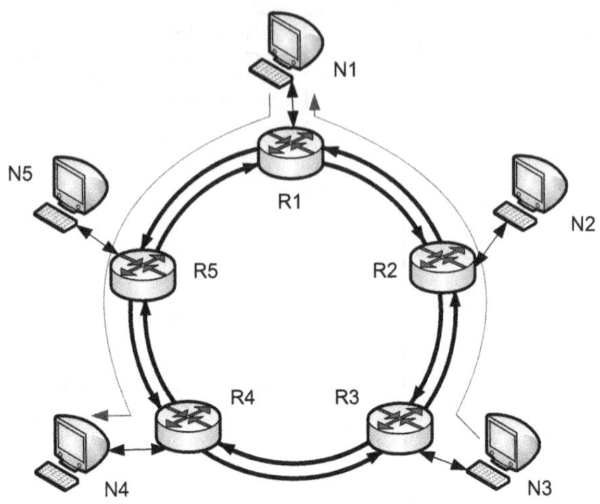

Fig. 6.5 Reference topology of a FARR network

class. One possible solution is to use the DS field in the header of the IP packet. In IPv4 it is the ToS (*Type of Service*) field while in the IPv6 it is the TC (*Traffic Class*) field. To avoid marking the wrong packets, it may be useful to adopt the traffic classification concept from FAN. One of the most important advantages of RPR is its reliability [1]. Protection and topology discovery mechanisms ensure fast traffic redirection in less than 50 ms.

FARR combines advantages of both the architectures described above. In FARR we assume the ring topology. The neighbor nodes are connected using two single one-way links (in the opposite directions). The routers are cross-protected. As packets are destination stripped, spatial reuse is allowed. The traffic is sent as flows (elastic or streaming) without any packet marking and signaling. Only the topology discovery protocol is implemented to ensure the correct behavior of protection mechanisms (steering or wrapping). The streaming flows are sent with priority, and fairness among elastic flows is guaranteed by implementing the scheduling algorithm. Flow classification is implicit, as in FAN.

An example of the FARR network composed of five nodes is presented in Fig. 6.5.

6.2.1 Global Protected Flow List in FARR

To improve network performance following a failure in FARR networks, the GPFL may be used. It should be implemented in each router in the ring. The global list contains the IDs of flows accepted on both links (in the inner and outer rings) connected to the router. Moreover, GPFL also includes information whether a flow is streaming or elastic. This condition is checked each time when a packet arrives at the router based on the number of bytes queued at a time. If a packet of a new flow arrives in the congestion-less state its ID is added to the PFL and GPFL. On

```
1   on arriving packet p to the router in congestion
2   if P is a source packet then
3       set DS=0 of packet P
4   if flow_ID(P) is in the PFL of outgoing link then
5       accept packet P
6   else
7   begin
8       if flow_ID(P) is in the GPFL or DS=1 of packet P then
9       begin
10          add flow_ID(P) to the PFL of outgoing link
11          if DS=0 of packet P then
12          begin
13              set DS=1 of packet P
14              accept packet P
15          end
16      end
17      else discard packet P
18  end
```

Fig. 6.6 Pseudo-code for realizing the GPFL concept in FARR

the other hand, if a packet of a new flow arrives in the congestion state it is accepted if its ID is in the GPFL and it is a streaming flow. It means that streaming flows in a router realizing the steering protection are redirected immediately.

The pseudo-code for realizing the GPFL functionality in FARR is presented in Fig. 6.6. We propose the use of the DS field in a packet header to mark the first packets of redirected streaming flows. We set DS=0 in the header of each packet incoming from a source node (lines 2–3). If a router sees that DS=1 then it knows that it is the first packet of a redirected streaming flow and accepts the packet (lines 8–10). The DS field of a packet is set to 1 if this is the first packet of a redirected streaming flow (if the packet is accepted based on the GPFL criterion) (lines 11–13).

6.2.2 Simulation Analysis of FARR with RPAEF, LM and GPFL

First, we present the simulation analysis of FARR with RPAEF and LM. The simulation experiment is illustrated in Fig. 6.7. We conducted 20 simulation experiments (10 with steering and 10 with wrapping, which are the protection mechanisms in FARR). The duration of each simulation run was set to 500 s to observe acceptance delays of streaming flows in each router on their routes. We assumed that each node sends a constant number of elastic flows (200) and at 200 s the links between routers R1 and R2 fail. Moreover, we decided that node N3 sends 200 elastic flows to node N5. It means that inner links between routers R3 and R5 were congested. The elastic flows in the outer ring were sent as follows: from N1 to N4, from N2 to N5, from N3 to N1, from N4 to N2, and from N5 to N3. This meant that elastic traffic was sent

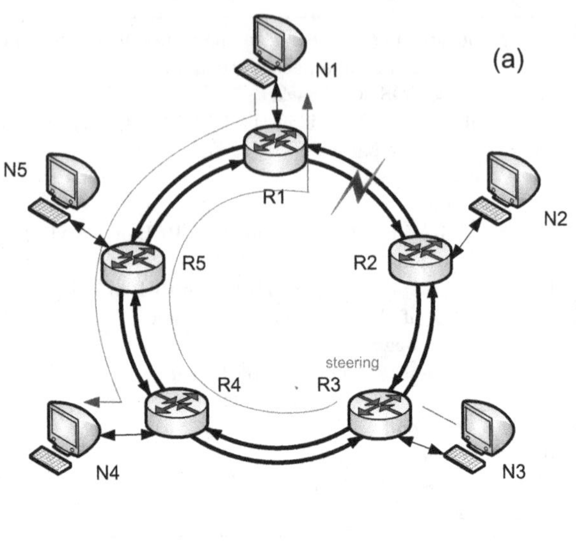

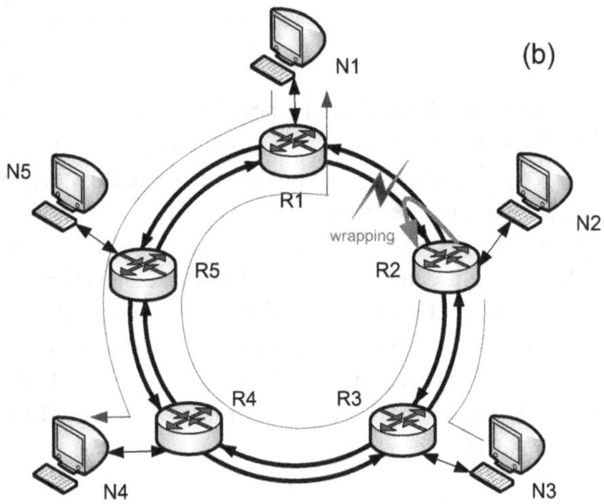

Fig. 6.7 FARR network: (**a**) failure repaired by the steering mechanism, (**b**) failure repaired by the wrapping mechanism

through the outer ring and each link in this ring was congested from the beginning of the simulation experiment. We decided to provide the traffic pattern with the Pareto distribution for calculating the volume of traffic to be sent by the elastic flows (ftp connections). We used exponential distribution for generating the time intervals between the start times of the transmissions of the elastic flows as well as for the streaming flows. Twenty streaming flows were sent by node N3 to N1 and another 20 streaming flows were sent from node N1 to N4. In both cases traffic was sent through the outer link based on the information from the topology discovery protocol. We analyzed VoIP connections using the Skype service. The packet size was set to 100 bytes and the transmission rate was set to 80 kbit/s for each streaming

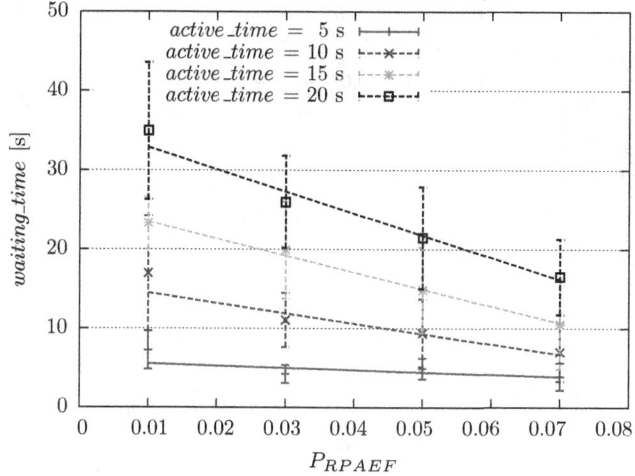

Fig. 6.8 Acceptance delay of streaming flows in FARR with RPAEF

flow. The elastic traffic was treated as background traffic and used to saturate the analyzed links. It was assumed that the capacity of links between routers was set to 100 Mbit/s and the PFQ algorithm was implemented. The capacity of access links (with FIFO queues) was set to 1 Gbit/s. The buffers in FARR routers were sized to 1000 packets, which is a reasonable value for FAN links, and *MTU* was set to 1500 bytes. The measurement interval for the *PL* parameter was set to 50 ms while the *FR* values were estimated every 500 ms. The *max_PL* and the *min_FR* values were set to 70 and 5% of the link capacity, respectively, and the *pfl_flow_timeout* parameter was set to 20 s, which is the time after which the ID of an inactive flow is removed from the PFL. Each experiment was repeated 10 times in the same conditions to ensure statistical credibility. Ninety five percentage confidence intervals were calculated using the Student's t-distribution.

Two cases were considered: the failure was repaired by the steering (Fig. 6.7a) or wrapping (Fig. 6.7b) mechanism. We can see that the wrapping mechanism lengthens the route following failure in comparison to the steering mechanism. It increases the acceptance delay of redirected flows. We assumed that the steering mechanism is better and the results of simulation experiments are presented for the network shown in Fig. 6.7a.

The analysis was provided for different values of the *active_time* parameter (5, 10, 15, and 20 s) and P_{RPAEF} parameter (0.01, 0.03, 0.05 and 0.07). The results presented in Fig. 6.8 show the acceptance delay of streaming flows sent by node N3 in router R2 (before failure). We can see that the values of the *waiting_time* parameter decrease with the increasing values of the P_{RPAEF} values. Moreover, the values of the observed parameter also increase with increasing values of the *active_time* parameter, that is, when the IDs of elastic flows are removed from the

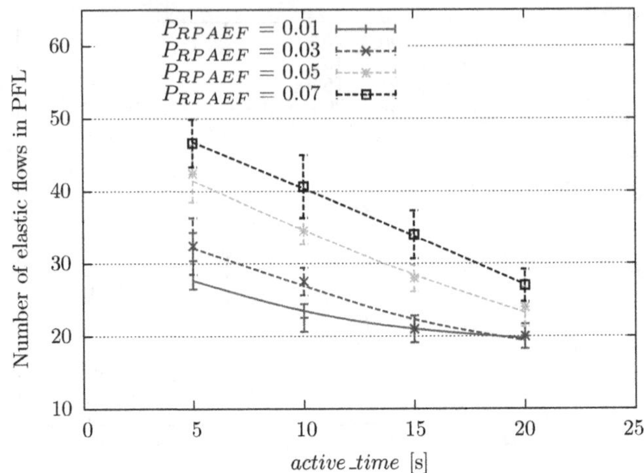

Fig. 6.9 Number of elastic flows accepted in the PFL in FARR with RPAEF

Table 6.1 The *waiting_time* values on a backup route of streaming flows

waiting_time/i	R3	R4	R5
-/-	231.20±47.74	231.30±47.70	236.82±46.13
5/2	201.50±1.04	202.05±1.14	203.95±2.05
10/2	202.25±2.37	205.05±6.58	209.95±10.96

PFL less frequently. It should be noted that according to [9], acceptable values (less than 6 s) are observed only for *active_time* = 5 s and $P_{RPAEF} \geq 0.03$.

Results presented in Fig. 6.9 show the mean number of elastic flows accepted in router R2 (before failure). We can see that the values of the observed parameter decrease with increasing values of the *active_time* parameter and increase with increasing values of the P_{RPAEF} parameter. The analyzed values are best for $P_{RPAEF} = 0.01$ and slightly worse for $P_{RPAEF} = 0.03$.

Results presented in Table 6.1 show the mean acceptance delay of redirected streaming flows after failure (at 200 s) in each router on their new route. We can see that if we do not use RPAEF and the limiting mechanisms (the first row in the table) the break in transmission is clearly too long. If we implement RPAEF and the limiting mechanisms (with $P_{RPAEF} = 0.03$ and $i = 2$) the outages in transmission of streaming flows are reduced to a few seconds. While these values may be acceptable from the user point of view, the desirable solution should not cause any breaks at all.

Next, we conducted 10 simulation runs in the same conditions as in the previous experiment but with the GPFL implemented. The simulation results show that the redirected streaming flows (under the control of the steering mechanism) were accepted immediately in each router on their new route and the performance of the network was achieved on an invariable level.

6.3 Multi-Layer Recovery Strategy in FAN

In this section, we present a multi-layer recovery strategy in FAN/WDM (Flow-Aware Networking/Wavelength Division Multiplexing) architecture. The EHOT (Enhanced Hold-Off Timer) algorithm is used to control network operation after link or node failure. This solution, first proposed in [5], is an improved version of a well-known HOT (Hold-Off Timer) algorithm [2] which ensures better coordination between layers. The analysis presented in this section shows that it is possible to achieve sufficiently low (less than 50 ms) recovery times in FAN working over an intelligent optical layer. WDM ensures fast failure detection and restoration of network links. In [10] it is shown that the protection or restoration actions in WDM networks take a few milliseconds in most cases. After this time the broken transmission may be continued.

The algorithm first attempts to repair the failure at the optical layer. If this is impossible, traffic has to be redirected in the IP layer, e.g., using the fast reroute mechanism. We can conclude from this that FAN with EHOT in multi-layer architecture inherits the advantages of fast reroute by adding the option of network recovery. The EHOT algorithm is presented in Fig. 6.10. The IP layer can detect failures in different ways, either on their own or from upper or lower layers. In

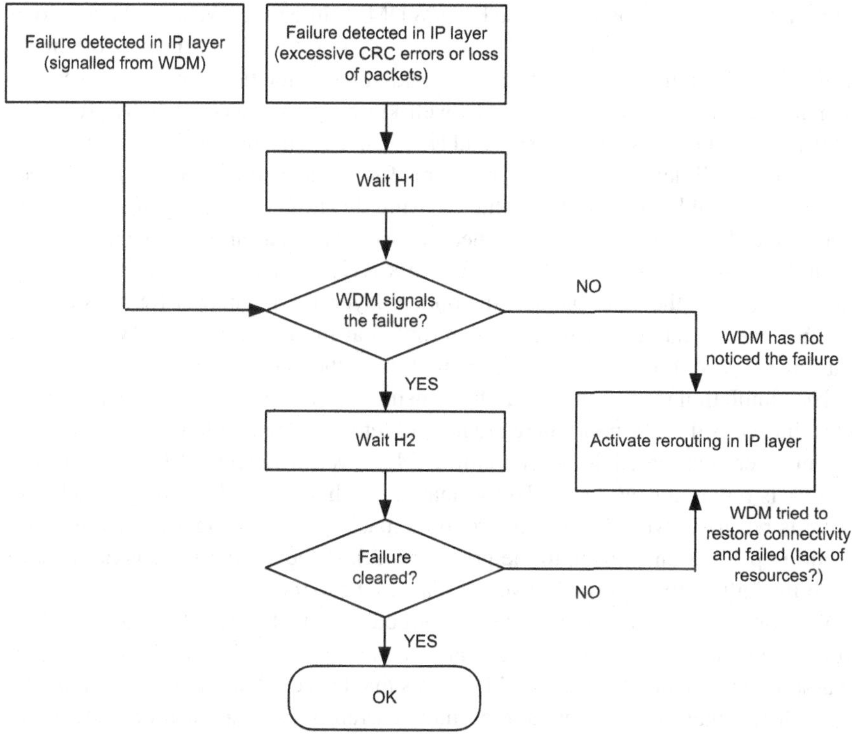

Fig. 6.10 Enhanced hold-off timer (EHOT) approach

particular, it is able to distinguish whether the information is from the optical layer. This is used by the EHOT algorithm, which is based on dividing the entire Hold-Off Timer into two parts: H1 (short) and H2 (long). The first part (H1) is activated when the IP layer detects a failure and gives the optical layer a chance to decide if it is possible to recover connectivity at this level. If the answer is positive the H2 timer is activated and the recovery mechanism in the lower layer begins. The restoration procedure in the optical layer includes fault localization and recovery mechanisms (i.e., dedicated path protection or restoration). If the optical layer is unable to solve the failure (due to a lack of available resources) during the H2 period, then the rerouting algorithm in the IP layer is launched. This also happens if there is no positive answer from the optical layer during the H1 time. The main assumption of the algorithm is that WDM is required to signal both signal degradation and signal failure to its client layer while the IP layer is able to accept such signals. The operation of the algorithm is simple, and it is easy to predict whether it makes it possible to reduce recovery time in comparison to the HOT algorithm when the failure occurs in the IP layer.

6.3.1 Simulation Analysis of FAN with EHOT in Case of Failure

In this section we present the results of the simulation experiments with and without the EHOT mechanism in the FAN/WDM architecture. We used the topology presented in Fig. 6.11 and analyzed the time needed to reconfigure the network in the event of link L2 failure. The traffic pattern and other simulation parameters were set as in Sect. 6.1.1. Moreover, based on the well-known parameters (partially presented in [10]) for EHOT we set H1 to 5 ms and H2 to 20 ms. This means that after noticing the failure, the IP layer waited for up to 5 ms for the decision from the optical layer whether it was able to repair the failure. During this time the routing algorithm was deactivated. If the optical layer returned positive information, it received 20 ms to repair the failure (we assumed that the failure was repaired in a random time between 5 and 10 ms). On the other hand, if the optical layer did not answer for 5 ms (or the response was negative) the traffic was rerouted at the network layer. We assumed that link L2 was protected by an additional link in the optical layer.

The simulation results show that the transmission in link L2 is broken for a very short time (less than 10 ms). There are no problems with redirected traffic and a too-high number of accepted flows after failure. Moreover, without the EHOT algorithm, the link is repaired even faster. Unfortunately, in this uncoordinated approach, the traffic is rerouted twice (after a failure to the backup link and again, when the first rerouting process ends, back to the primary link). If the optical layer is not able to repair the failure, the algorithm gives similar results to those presented in Sect. 6.1.1.

We conclude that the multi-layer architecture with the EHOT algorithm is a promising strategy in which the acceptable quality of transmission of all flows may be assured in case of a failure. WDM ensures that broken links are repaired quickly. 50 ms-long outages are acceptable by most currently used applications, including real-time ones.

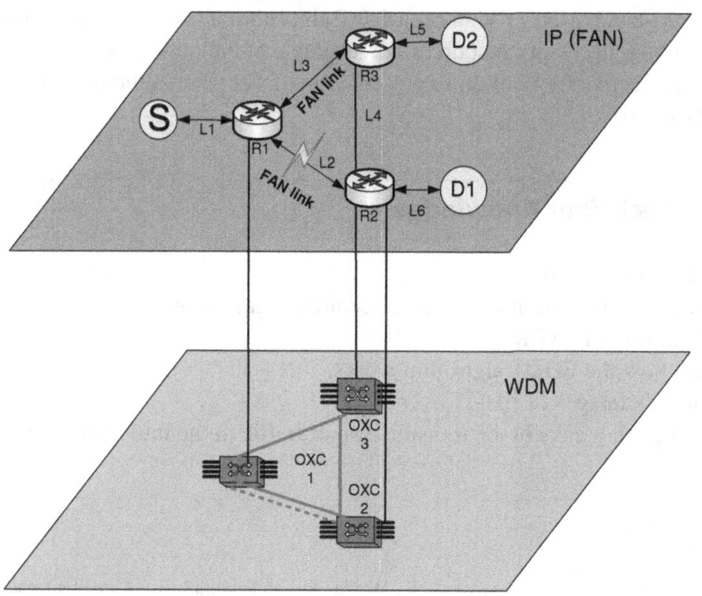

Fig. 6.11 The multi-layer topology

6.4 Conclusion

The RPAEF mechanism is one of the most promising solutions of all congestion control mechanisms proposed for FAN. It ensures fast acceptance times of streaming flows and good transmission performance for elastic flows. The RPAEF algorithm improved by implementing the limiting mechanism and GPFL creates a scalable system for reliable transmission in FAN. When it is implemented, streaming flows are prioritized. Such flows are accepted quickly and they send their traffic without breaks even after a network element failure. Outages in transmission of elastic flows are only observed following a failure. In normal conditions, once accepted, the flows are protected.

The new architecture—Flow-Aware Resilient Ring proposed for LAN and MAN networks—combines the advantages of Resilient Packet Ring and Flow-Aware Networks. In this solution, traffic is served as flows and implicitly classified to one of two traffic types: streaming or elastic. Streaming flows are served with a higher priority than elastic ones. The bandwidth not used by streaming flows is divided fairly among elastic flows. FARR networks ensure a good scalability and very good protection mechanisms which guarantee fast redirection of streaming traffic. Moreover, they conform to the net neutrality paradigm. The RPAEF congestion control mechanism and the limiting mechanism ensure fast acceptance of streaming flows without deteriorating network performance in FARR. Moreover, implementing GPFL in each router in the ring ensures continuous transmission (without outages) of streaming flows even when a network element fails.

The multi-layer strategy with the EHOT algorithm allows us to solve failures in FAN if only the necessary resources are available at the optical layer. This solution is the most effective from all those presented in this chapter, although it may also be the most expensive.

6.5 Check Your Knowledge

1. How does GPFL work?
2. FARR is a combination of two architectures. Name them.
3. Is GPFL used in FARR?
4. Explain how the EHOT algorithm works.
5. List the advantages of EHOT over MFAN.
6. How long are breaks in the transmission of traffic in the multi-layer approach?

References

1. P. Cholda, J. Domzal, A. Jajszczyk, K. Wajda, Reliability analysis of resilient packet rings, in *International Conference on Computer Safety, Reliability, and Security (Safecomp'06)*, Gdansk, Poland (2006)
2. P. Demeester, M. Gryseels, Resilience in multilayer networks. IEEE Commun. Mag. **37**, 70–76 (1999)
3. P. Demeester, M. Gryseels, Flow-aware resilient ring - new proposal for metropolitan area networks. Telecommun. Syst. **60**(3), (2015). https://doi.org/10.1007/s11235-015-0054-1
4. J. Domzal, K. Wajda, A. Jajszczyk, Flow-aware resilient ring, in *IEEE International Conference on Communications (ICC'10)*, Cape Town, South Africa (2010)
5. J. Domzal, K. Wajda, S. Spadaro, J. Sole-Pareta, D. Careglio, Recovery, fairness and congestion control mechanisms in RPR networks, in *12th Polish Teletraffic Symposium PSRT 2005*, Poznan (2005)
6. J. Domzal, R. Wojcik, A. Jajszczyk, The impact of congestion control mechanisms on network performance after failure in flow-aware networks, in *Proceedings of International Workshop on Traffic Management and Traffic Engineering for the Future Internet, FITraMEn 2008.* Book: Traffic Management and Traffic Engineering for the Future Internet, Lecture Notes on Computer Science 2009. Porto (2008)
7. J. Domzal, R. Wojcik, A. Jajszczyk, Reliable transmission in flow-aware networks, in *IEEE Globecom 2009*, Honolulu (2009)
8. J. Domzal, R. Wojcik, K. Wajda, A. Jajszczyk, V. Lopez, J. Hernandez, J. Aracil, C. Cardenas, M. Gagnaire, A multi-layer recovery strategy in FAN over WDM architectures, in *Proceedings of the 7th International Workshop on Design of Reliable Communication Networks, DRCN 2009*, Washington (2009), pp. 160 –167
9. Network grade of service parameters and target values for circuit-switched services in the evolving ISDN, ITU-T Recommendation E.721 (1999)
10. S. Ramamurthy, L. Sahasrabuddhe, B. Mukherjee, Survivable WDM mesh networks. J. Lightwave Technol. **21**, 870–883 (2003)

Service Differentiation in FAN

7

It is the quality rather than the quantity that matters.

—Lucius Annaeus Seneca

The differentiation of quality of service in FAN remains a major challenge. This is due to the fact that FAN does not use any signaling, which makes the process of informing nodes about incoming transmissions difficult. This chapter shows how service differentiation can be provided in FAN networks and the capabilities of this architecture.

In this chapter we present the following mechanisms:

- differentiation blocking approach,
- differentiated queuing approach,
  - bit rate differentiation,
  - fair rate ignoring scheme,
- Static Router Configuration approach,
- Class of Service on Demand approach

The chapter is organized as follows. Section 7.1 explains how implicit service differentiation works in FAN. Section 7.2 shows why new flows may wait a long time before they are admitted on a FAN link. These two sections are crucial to understanding the operation of the mechanisms introduced later. Section 7.3 presents the differentiated blocking approach. Although differentiated blocking offers extensive possibilities, it may have a negative impact on network performance. This issue is documented in Sects. 7.3.1 and 7.3.2. The following Sect. 7.4 shows the differentiated queuing scheme with its two variations: bit rate differentiation and fair rate ignoring. Section 7.5 presents the Static Router Configuration approach, which implements differentiated blocking in FAN. In Sect. 7.6, we present Class of

J. Domżał et al., *Guide to Flow-Aware Networking*, Computer Communications and Networks, https://doi.org/10.1007/978-3-030-57153-5_7

Service on Demand as an approach combining the options provided by differentiated blocking and differentiated queuing. Finally, Sect. 7.7 concludes the chapter.

7.1 Implicit Service Differentiation

To understand the importantance of the proposed service differentiation mechanisms, first let us look into the concept of implicit service differentiation in FAN. The general objective of FAN is to ensure low packet latency for streaming flows, while utilizing all residual bandwidth to provide maximum throughput to elastic flows. Figure 7.1 explains how this scheme works by showing a possible scenario on a 3 Mbit/s FAN link. Until the 4th second of the simulation, flows 1 and 2 realize their desired bit rates. It may be assumed that flow 1, emitting at approximately 50 kbit/s, comes from a streaming application, whereas flow 2 is likely to be elastic. Nevertheless, both flows emit at a lower rate than the current fair rate and, therefore, are treated with priority. However, in the 4th second, congestion occurs in the link as many new transmissions appear, resulting in a drop of the fair rate.

In such a situation, the rate of all existing flows would have been reduced in a classic IP link. However, due to FAN's implicit service differentiation scheme, flow 1 remains untouched and its service is preserved. The bitrate of flow 2 was reduced to the level of the fair rate, as this is effectively the maximum value that each flow could realize at the time.

This procedure is very useful, as it protects low rate flows from degradation should congestion occur. This is extremely important because even though they operate at low bit rates, the majority of streaming applications cannot function when

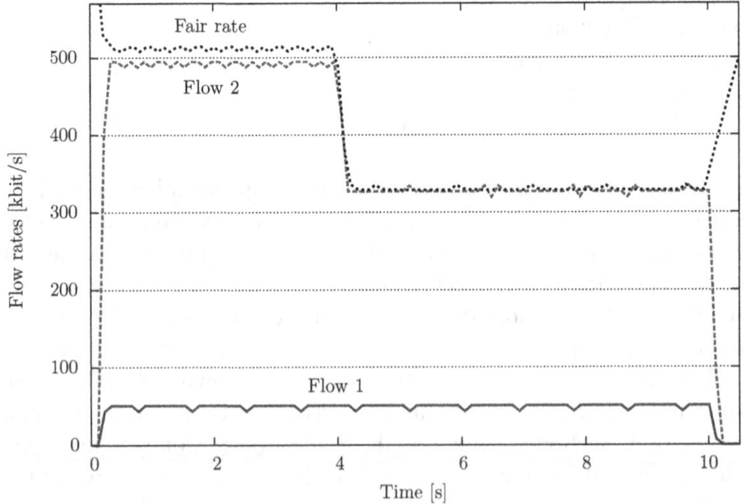

Fig. 7.1 Implicit service differentiation in FAN; flow rates and fair rate measurements

these bit rates are not provided. If flow 1 represents VoIP transmission, the carried voice may become unrecognizable in the existing IP network. As shown in Fig. 7.1, FAN is able to protect this service. The service associated with flow 2 must be degraded; however, the bit rate reduction in elastic applications has less significant consequences.

Under congestion, FAN performance may be considered superior to the behavior of classic IP networks. This is because only a limited number of flows may be simultaneously admitted on a link. This approach virtually guarantees that once a flow is admitted, it will perceive at least a minimum QoS. For VoIP technology, any accepted flow is bound to obtain a sufficient QoS level, which is not necessarily true in case of current, congested IP networks. To demonstrate the difference between the behavior of classic IP and FAN links, a simple simulation was performed. The scenario in which 300 TCP-based elastic flows and 25 UDP-based VoIP flows compete for resources of a 1 Mbit/s link was identical for both cases. Figure 7.2 compares the results by showing the measured fair rate values over time. As can be observed, these values fluctuate and the oscillations are caused by the high frequency of the measurements.

In the classic IP link (lower line), all flows are admitted, once they appear. Since their number is significant, the rate at which they can transmit quickly drops below 10 kbit/s. On the other hand, FAN (upper line) preserves the fair rate on a level of approximately 40–50 kbit/s. Unfortunately, in order to achieve this goal, some flows must be temporarily blocked. This process is documented in the next section.

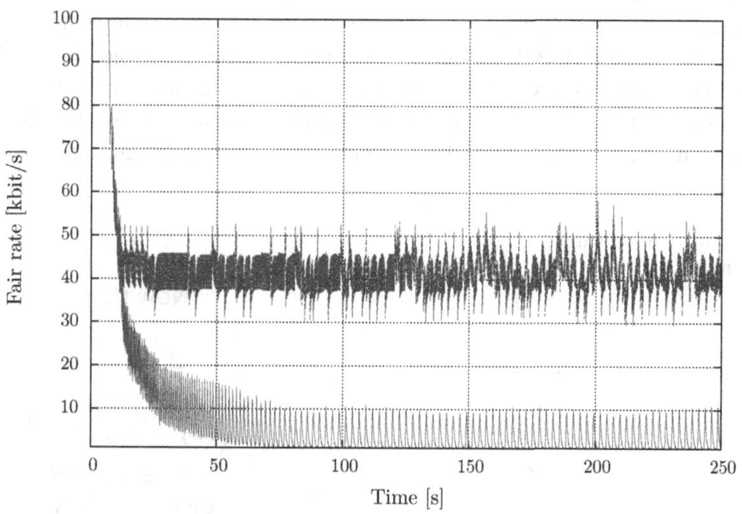

Fig. 7.2 Performance under congestion in a classic IP link (lower line) and a FAN link (upper line)

7.2 Waiting Times

Classic FAN thinking includes a general rule for limiting the number of active flows, so that the transmissions currently in progress can always reach a minimum acceptable QoS level. Although such behavior is considered beneficial for low-rate streaming applications (such as VoIP), in some cases it may be unsatisfactory, due to admission control flow blocking.

Two congestion indicators are calculated periodically in FAN routers. Fair rate is used to differentiate between streaming and elastic flows within the XP router. Additionally, along with the priority load, these indicators are used by admission control to block new incoming flows, provided a congestion state is detected. If the measured FR is currently below a certain pre-set minimum fair rate value (FR_{min}), or the PL exceeds its maximum threshold (PL_{max}), all new incoming flows are blocked. This routine is presented in Fig. 7.3. The values of FR_{min} and PL_{max} must be carefully chosen by network administrators, which should be done for each link individually.

Waiting times, which are not observed in current IP networks, must be taken into account while assessing the performance of any service, especially Internet telephony. The ability to make phone calls is essential for end users. Additionally, as the Internet has become a key part of everyday life, increasing number of customers use VoIP technology instead of the standard PSTN telephone service. This means that in an emergency, the ability to contact emergency services depends on the current congestion status in the network. For these customers, the ability to make a phone call is much more important than its quality.

Figure 7.4 presents waiting times for VoIP flows while they compete for network resources with other TCP flows during a scenario when the 1 Mbit/s link is FAN-aware . In this case, there were 300 background flows, with an average of 500 kbit/s to transmit. On top of that, 25 VoIP flows (20 kbit/s each) were waiting to begin transmission, starting from the 50th second of the simulation run, and continued

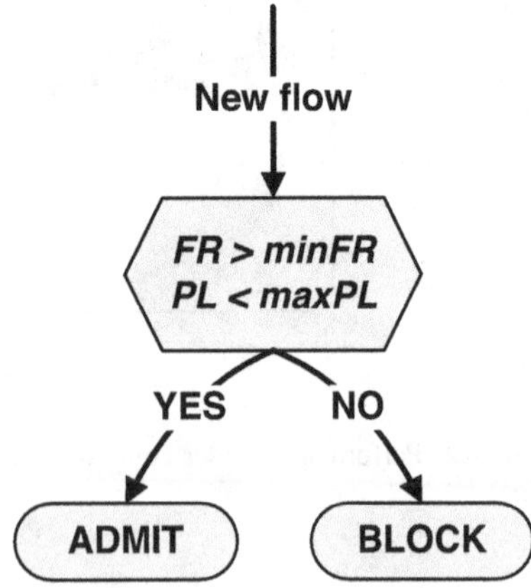

Fig. 7.3 Admission control routine in FAN

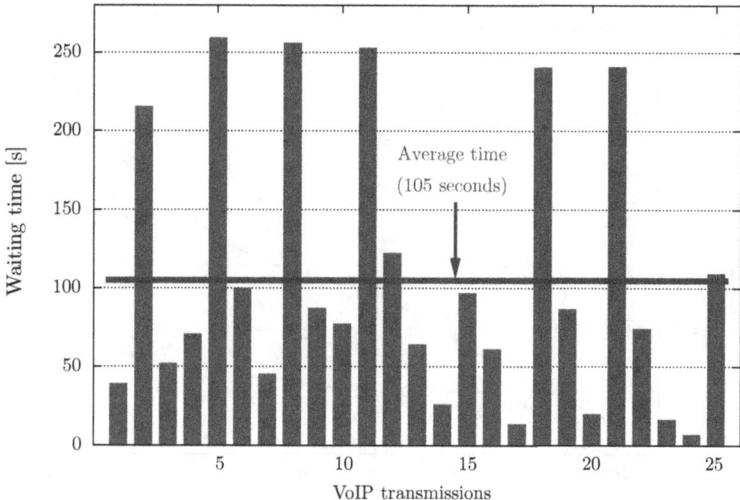

Fig. 7.4 Exemplary VoIP connection waiting times

their attempts until they were finally admitted. As can be observed, the FAN admission control block forced flows to wait until the congestion ended. For some flows, the waiting time was short and barely noticeable. Unfortunately, some flows had to wait for more than 200 s before their first packet could be transmitted. This situation is highly inconvenient for the realization of VoIP connections, especially for emergency calls. It should be noted that Fig. 7.4 is simply an example, although it illustrates the problem well. The most important lesson from this example is that, in FAN, it is possible for all new flows to be forced to wait for an unreasonable length of time should congestion occur.

To understand how certain volumes of traffic affect this waiting time, several simulations were performed, with a range of background traffic characteristics. Again, the absolute waiting time values are not as important as the general dependency and influence of background traffic on waiting times. Figure 7.5 presents mean VoIP flow waiting times with respect to the number of background flows and the mean background flow size. At least 10 simulations were performed; the averages and the 95% confidence intervals (using a Student's t distribution) were calculated.

In Fig. 7.5a, link congestion increases alongside the number of background flows, while in Fig. 7.5b the increased congestion is caused by varying the mean background flow size. As seen in both parts of the figure, the mean transmission waiting time increases alongside the offered load, which is expected. The greater the flow number, the lower the chance for that particular VoIP flow to be admitted, and therefore the longer the waiting time. On the other hand, when the flow number is constant but the mean size increases, flows end more rarely, therefore new ones may be admitted with a lower frequency, which also increases the average waiting time.

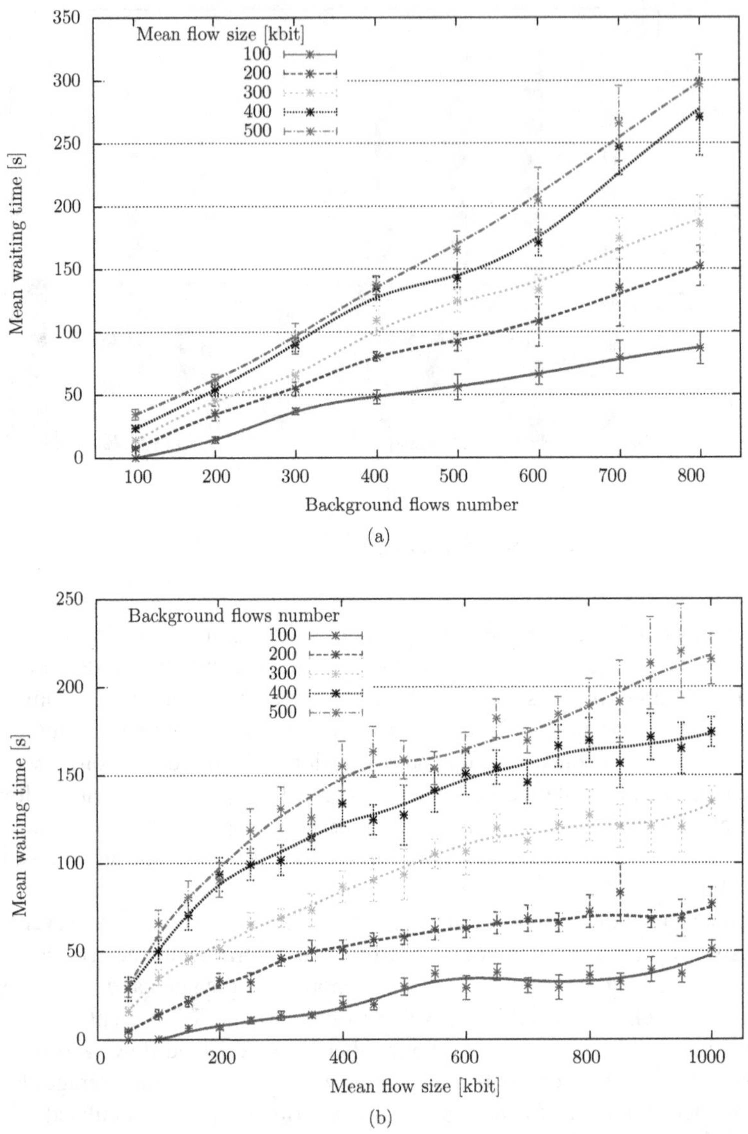

Fig. 7.5 Mean VoIP flow waiting time with respect to the number of background flows (BFN) (**a**) and the mean background flow size (MFS) (**b**)

The values presented in Fig. 7.5 are averaged. In fact, based on the example situation (shown in Fig. 7.4), a certain number of VoIP flows experienced short and acceptable waiting times. However, for the remaining flows this period was excessively long, in particular for emergency connections.

It should be noted that FAN does not degrade the performance of streaming flows in comparison to classic best-effort transmissions. In current IP networks, emergency connections do not observe excessive waiting times; however, they are endangered by congestion, as low transmission rates may render voice imperceptible. Although FAN networks provide superior transmission quality, they may force users to wait for network resources to become available. Fortunately, these disadvantages may be overcome by introducing differentiated blocking into FAN networks.

7.3 Differentiated Blocking

Differentiated (selective) blocking [1] aims to apply different blocking criteria to newly arriving flows. The standard FAN routine causes the admission control block to make the decision based on currently measured values of the fair rate and priority load (see Fig. 7.3). To eliminate long waiting times for certain flows, the differentiated blocking approach, which applies different blocking criteria to priority flows, may be used.

In the simplest example, the differentiated blocking scenario includes two classes of service: standard class and premium class. The admission control procedure in such a situation is presented in Fig. 7.6. The role of the class selector is to recognize which blocking criteria should be applied to the incoming flow. Flows belonging to the standard class are subject to admission control under the rules of the original classless FAN, whereas premium class flows are always admitted. It is also possible to introduce additional classes of service; however, for the purpose of prioritizing emergency calls, the premium class is sufficient.

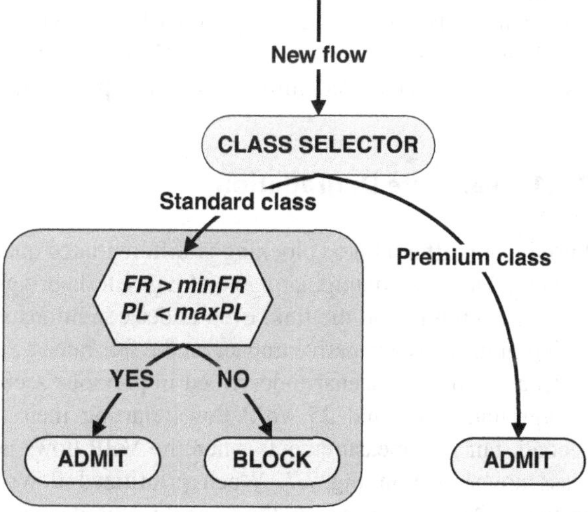

Fig. 7.6 Admission control routine of FAN with a premium class of flows. The grey area presents the original FAN routine

Differentiated blocking operates only when congestion occurs, since there is no need for blocking arriving flows otherwise. Additionally, this mechanism does not interfere with protected flows. Any flow that is already in the protected flow list is always forwarded. Furthermore, differentiated blocking does not prioritize flows that are in progress. In other words, the scheduling algorithm treats all flows the same way once they are admitted.

The procedure presented in Fig. 7.6 is well suited for emergency VoIP connections. All flows related to VoIP emergency calls would belong in the premium class, i.e., they would never be blocked by admission control in a FAN router, therefore connection waiting times would always be unnoticeable. This way, the quality of a voice call is kept high by the FAN's implicit service differentiation scheme, whereas the ability to make calls is protected by the differentiated blocking approach.

This scheme, however, has a drawback. As we interfere with the admission control mechanism, we may observe degradation of performance. This is due to the fact that prioritized flows are admitted on the link, even under circumstances when they would not be admitted.

Fortunately, in the case of VoIP connections, this behavior has limited impact on the overall link performance, for two reasons. First, the required bit rate of a single internet telephony connection is relatively low, especially compared to the core link capacities, and therefore admitting a few additional flows should not degrade the quality of the remaining transmissions significantly. Second, the fair rate degradation is a temporal process: this is because, while active flows terminate naturally, new ones are not admitted until the fair rate returns to its desired value.

Although introducing differentiation mechanisms to FAN routers is simple, the signaling issue remains. As the experiences of IntServ and DiffServ show, every method of introducing the understanding of the treatment of particular flows to the network is inevitably associated with a major increase of complexity or severe scalability reduction. Therefore, each explicit service differentiation mechanism should not rely on any signaling or packet marking procedures, as the original simplicity and scalability of the IP and FAN are to be preserved. To cope with this issue a Static Router Configuration approach presented in Sect. 7.5, may be used.

7.3.1 Fair Rate Degradation

Introducing differentiated blocking or differentiated queuing is beneficial for certain services. However, manipulating blocking criteria brings a new problem. Prioritized flows are admitted on the link, even under conditions in which they would not be, which in turn has a negative impact on the fair rate.

Considering the scenario described in previous sections, i.e.: 1 Mbit/s link, 300 background flows and 25 VoIP flows starting their transmission after the 50th second, fair rate measurements when the VoIP flows are assigned to the premium class are shown in Fig. 7.7. When prioritized flows appear, they are admitted instantly. As a consequence, the fair rate degrades, as the link has to concurrently serve more flows than it would normally. 25 VoIP flows start their transmission

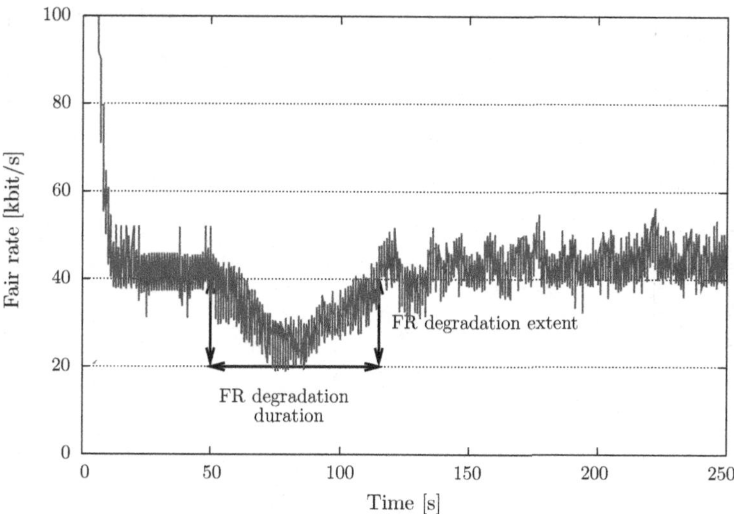

Fig. 7.7 Fair rate degradation with differentiated blocking

from the 50th second of the simulation at 1 s intervals. As may be observed, fair rate continuously drops until approximately the 75th second. From then on, each time a background flow ends, the FR raises until it reaches its nominal value (close to the minimum FR value).

It would be natural to try to mitigate this degradation by dropping some active flows from the protected flow list. However, this is not necessary when dealing with Internet telephony. Not introducing preemption seems to be more suitable for the following reasons. First, the required bit rate of a single Internet telephony connection is relatively low, especially compared to the core link capacities, and therefore admitting a few additional flows should not degrade the quality of the remaining transmissions significantly. Second, the fair rate degradation is a temporal process; this is because, while active flows terminate naturally, new ones are not admitted until the fair rate returns to its desired value. Finally, the FAN architecture does not become more complex, which is an obvious advantage.

To support these arguments and to evaluate the extent and length of FR degradation, several simulations were performed. Figure 7.8 shows the length of FR degradation with respect to the various mean background flow sizes, ranging from 500 kB to 5 MB. Apart from the mean background flow size, all the scenarios were the same as before. The minimum FR value was set to 5% of the link capacity, i.e., to 50 kbit/s and under normal circumstances this value does not drop below 45 kbit/s. Therefore, the period of FR degradation was defined as the length of time when the FR was below 45 kbit/s, due to the appearance of prioritized traffic. The length of the FR degradation process, as may be seen in this experiment, is strictly dependent on the mean background flow size. The longer the flows, the longer this FR degradation

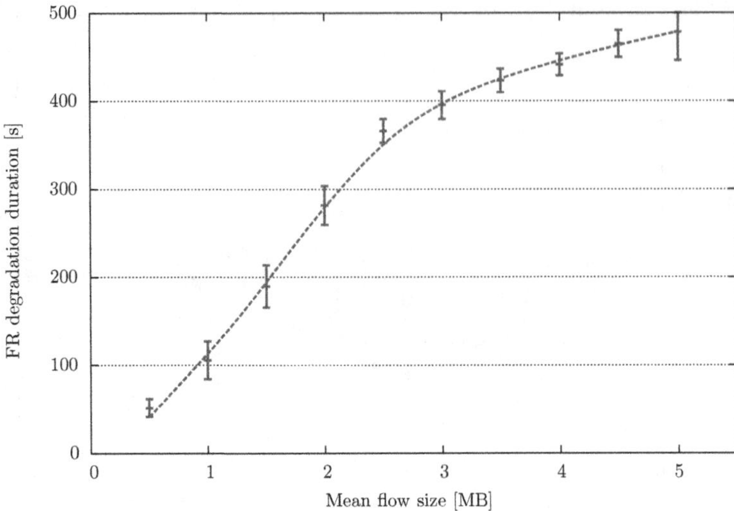

Fig. 7.8 Duration of the FR degradation with respect to mean flow size

process. This is because when flows are shorter, they end more frequently, therefore FR raises more rapidly.

Moreover, there is a second factor that contributes to the length of the FR degradation process: the number of active background flows.[1] The greater this number is, the more chances there are that an active flow ends naturally, and consequently the FR increases more rapidly. This number depends on the link capacity, the minimal FR value, and the traffic characteristics.

The temporality of the FR degradation process and the extent of this degradation should both be taken into account. Figures 7.9 and 7.10 show the impact of prioritized VoIP flows on the FR measurements on links with different capacities. Again, the setup was similar to the previous experiment, although here the average flow size was set to 1 MB and the link capacity was changing from 1 Mbit/s to 5 Mbit/s. In each case, the minimum FR value was set so that it would correspond to 50 kbit/s.

As can be observed, greater capacity links suffer less from prioritized traffic for two reasons. First, the same volume of prioritized traffic is less significant on a 5 Mbit/s link than on a 1 Mbit/s link. This is shown in Fig. 7.10 as the FR degradation extent is lower on higher capacity links. Second, higher capacity links may serve more flows simultaneously, and therefore the FR degradation process is shorter (Fig. 7.9).

The experiments presented in this section show that the FR degradation should not be considered a problem for emergency calls. The analysis was performed

[1]By 'active flow' we mean a flow whose *flow id* is on the PFL list.

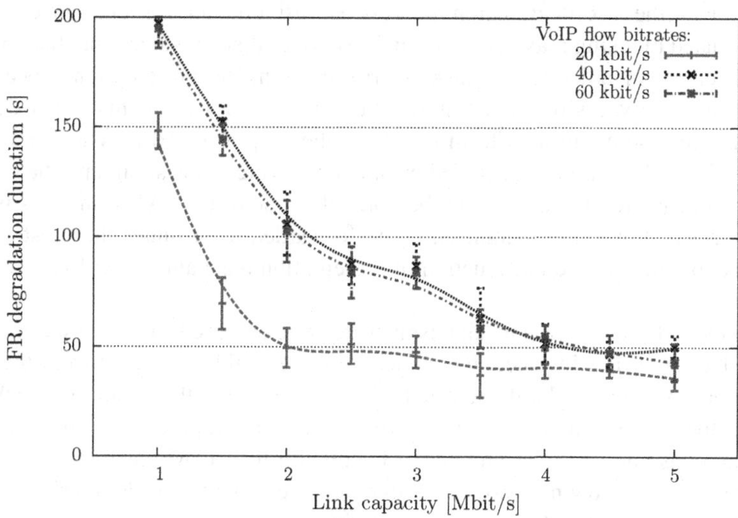

Fig. 7.9 FR degradation duration with respect to link capacity

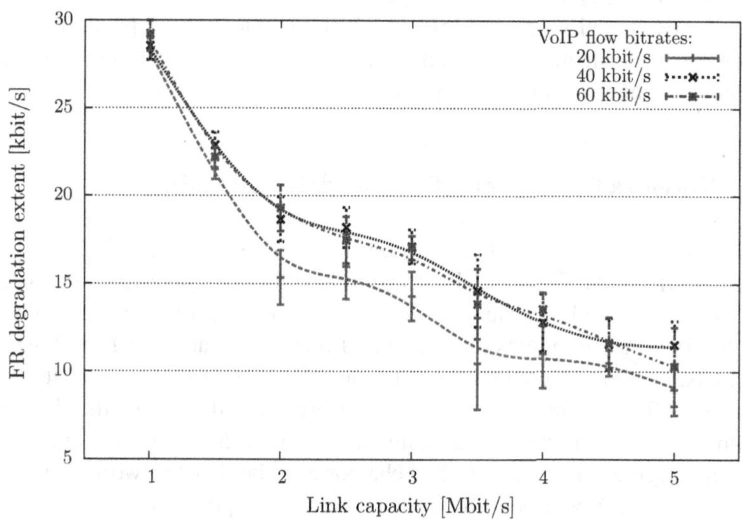

Fig. 7.10 FR degradation extent with respect to link capacity

on low capacity links. However, simulation results (especially those presented in Figs. 7.9 and 7.10) show a general trend that high capacity links to be less vulnerable to the negative effect of the differentiated blocking procedure. Therefore, we feel that disregarding the FR degradation for the purposes of Internet telephony (especially emergency calls) is appropriate.

Although the FR degradation process is insignificant for emergency calls, differentiated blocking may also be used for services that consume more bandwidth. In such cases, in order to obtain real prioritization, the pre-emption procedures may be necessary. As discussed above, pre-emption is a mechanism that deletes one (or some) active flow(s) from the PFL when a prioritized flow appears. This way, the FR values are not degraded even under severe congestion, and the overall performance is preserved. It should be noted that one of the FAN principles is that already active flows are guaranteed to be forwarded even under the most severe network conditions. The introduction of pre-emption mechanisms will violates this principle.

However, if pre-emption mechanisms were to be enforced, certain issues need to be resolved first. For instance, which active flow should be deleted from the PFL list? Should it be a randomly selected flow, or the one with the longest backlog? Answer these questions is vital when we consider that a potentially to-be-deleted flow can consume a similar amount of bandwidth than newly arriving prioritized one. Deleting one flow may not be enough, and we should consider erasing several small flows in order to admit one large prioritized flow.

These questions are not easy to answer, although a response is required for the pre-emption mechanism to operate correctly. Therefore, the pre-emption mechanism needs to be examined when possible prioritized services are defined. There is no need for this mechanism for emergency calls; however, as soon as other usages are identified, this concept should be reevaluated.

7.3.2 Network Failures and Differentiated Blocking

FAN operates well in terms of congestion. However, the introduction of premium class flows affects the fair rate, albeit insignificantly. As congestions in a network may also be related to link failures, this scenario should be investigated. Figure 7.11 shows fair rate measurements on a saturated link. There are 300 TCP flows, 10% of which belong to a premium class. In the 50th second of the simulation time, additional traffic of identical characteristics is transferred from another link due to a potential failure. Otherwise, the simulation setup is the same as in the previous experiment. Figure 7.11a presents the behavior of a classic IP network (bottom line) and the original FAN without differentiated blocking (upper line).

The results obtained on a classic IP link are extremely unsuccessful. After the 50th second, the fair rate[2] drops from very low to a completely unsatisfactory level. In contrast, the classic FAN link is indifferent to network failures. 50 kbit/s is the minimum fair rate threshold which is maintained when new flows appear in the 50th second. This approach is beneficial to the flows currently being realized, as they do not suffer from any service degradation.

[2] Although the method of estimating the fair rate in FAN cannot be applied to original IP networks, the fair rate in this case has the same meaning, i.e., the bitrate available to each flow.

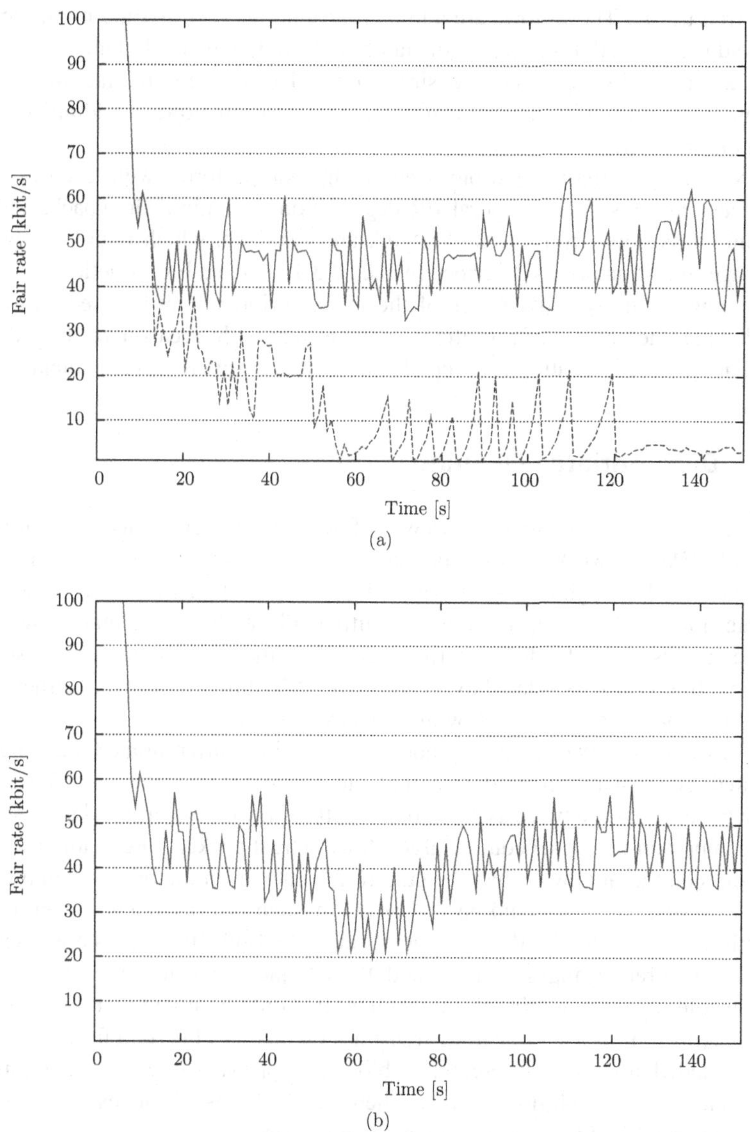

Fig. 7.11 Performance during network failures; (**a**) classic IP link (bottom line) and FAN link (upper line), (**b**) FAN with differentiated blocking

Figure 7.11b illustrates the behavior of a FAN link with the differentiated blocking scheme. Here, 10% of the total traffic is of premium class. Up until the network failure, the fair rate is similar to the case with the FAN link and to differentiated blocking, perhaps a little lower. In the 50th second, however, the FR drops by approximately 15 kbit/s, due to premium class flows that are present in the transferred traffic. These flows are admitted despite the fact that the minimum FR threshold is exceeded. Fortunately, the fair rate degradation is only temporary as FR grows, and it quickly achieves its desired values. This is due to the fact that certain flows naturally terminate their transmission, while no new flows are admitted to the link at the same time.

FAN with the differentiated blocking mechanism performs well, even in terms of network failures. The temporal FR degradation is a minor drawback, and the premium class flows from the broken link are sustained, which is the an obvious advantage. Additionally, as described in Sect. 7.3.1, to avoid FR reduction, the tactic of dropping currently active flows of the lowest priority may be used. However, provided that the volume of prioritized traffic is kept within reasonable boundaries, the extent of FR degradation is acceptable and FR recovers relatively quickly.

7.4 Differentiated Queuing

Applying differentiation blocking is a way of providing better service differentiation options to FAN networks. This approach originates from the need to reduce long waiting times. Although FAN provides basic service level guarantees by prioritizing low-rate flows and keeping the fair rate sufficiently high for the other flows, this scheme can also be extended. Altering scheduling mechanisms to provide service differentiation is strictly related to discarding FAN's ability to provide fairness, i.e., to establish that each admitted flow may achieve the same bit rate.

In this section, two main methods of applying differentiated queuing are presented. The first aims to assure a certain fair rate to different classes of flows, e.g., a priority flow may use twice as much bandwidth as any other normal class flow. The second approach forces scheduling algorithms to treat packets of certain flows as if they emitted at a rate lower than the current fair rate, even though they emit faster. In other words, packets would be forwarded through priority queues, even if they transmit with a rate greater than the current fair rate. Both approaches are described with the required changes to PFQ and PDRR queuing algorithms, as they are both capable of implementing these features. It should be noted that differentiated queuing aims to improve or degrade transmission quality of certain flows once they are admitted. Unless the differentiated blocking approach is used, the admission control block treats each flow equally. Therefore, in terms of congestion, flows are blocked regardless of their differentiated queuing class.

7.4.1 Bitrate Differentiation

Bitrate differentiation improves or degrades bitrates of certain flows under congestion. This method is not able to provide certain bandwidth assurances. Instead, better or worse QoS may be imposed only with respect to the normal class of flows. However, if we consider the minimum level of service assured by the minimum fair

```
11    (...)
12    flow_time_stamp(F) += L
13    (...)
```

(a)

```
11    (...)
12    get head of AFL, say flow i
13    DC_i += Q_i
14    (...)
```

(b)

Fig. 7.12 PFQ (**a**) and PDRR (**b**) pseudocode fragments to be changed to provide bit rate differentiation

rate value, we can easily provide twice the minimum fair rate, or half the minimum fair rate, to certain flows.

To realize bitrate differentiation, the parameter *differentiation factor* needs to be introduced. The differentiation factor represents the portion of the FR which is provided to a flow. For example, a differentiation factor of two means that twice the bitrate of the fair rate is provided to a flow.

Figure 7.12 presents the pseudocode fragments of the PFQ and PDRR queuing algorithms that are to be changed, so that these schedulers are able to realize the bit rate differentiation. For full pseudocode listings of the PFQ and PDRR operations, see Sect. 2.6 on page 61.

The PFQ algorithm organizes its queue by inserting new packets in the correct place. Each backlogged flow is described by certain variables, one of which is *flow time stamp*. This indicator describes the time in which the last packet of this flow will be transmitted. Normally, when a new packet is inserted into the queue, this variable is increased by the packet length (L) (Fig. 7.12a, line 12). This functionality provides fairness. In order to support bit rate differentiation, *flow time stamp* must be increased by values different than the incoming packet length, e.g., by its fraction. For instance, to achieve a bit rate twice as high as the fair rate, only $L/2$ should be added, while to achieve three times less than the fair rate, *flow time stamp* should be increased by as much as $3L$.

Modifying PDRR is more straightforward, as this algorithm was designed to provide the differentiation. In each cycle, the deficit counter of every flow (DC_i) is incremented by the correct value, referred to as quantum (Q_i) (Fig. 7.12b, line 13). PDRR in FAN aims to provide fairness, therefore the quantum variable is equal for every flow. However, the algorithm is capable of using different quanta. The more a certain flow receives, the more bandwidth it will be able to consume. For example, incrementing the deficit counter with two quanta instead of one results in achieving a bit rate twice as high as the current fair rate.

The idea of bit rate differentiating with respect to the currently realized fair rate is interesting due to the FAN admission control functionality. In classical IP networks the assurance of achieving twice the current fair rate would not be of a great value, as on a heavily congested link realizing 0.2 kbit/s instead of 0.1 kbit/s is still unsatisfactory. Fortunately, FAN preserves the minimum fair rate threshold, therefore ascertaining more than the current fair rate results in maintaining prioritized flows at a QoS level which is always reasonable.

7.4.2 Fair Rate Ignoring

While bit rate differentiation is likely to be sufficient for introducing differentiated queuing, the fair rate ignoring scheme aims to achieve the same goals in a different manner. As described in Sect. 2.6 on page 61, the SFQ and DRR algorithms were enhanced to be suited to FAN by implementing priority mechanisms, to support better treatment of streaming applications. These mechanisms are based on priority processing of flows which emit at a lower rate than the current fair rate. The fair rate ignoring scheme forces the queuing algorithms to treat certain flows with priority even if they transmit faster than the current fair rate. Figure 7.13 presents the pseudocode fragments of PFQ and PDRR queuing algorithms that must be changed so that the schedulers are able to realize the fair rate ignoring mechanism.

The fair rate ignoring procedure is based on not taking into account the FR measurements for certain flows. Fragments of codes presented in parts (a) and (b) of Fig. 7.13 concern PFQ and PDRR, respectively, although their functionality is the

```
(...)
if bytes ≥ MTU
        push {packet, flow_time_stamp} to PIFO
else begin
        push {packet, virtual_time} to PIFO behind P; update P
(...)
```

(a)

```
(...)
if ByteCount_i ≤ Q_i
        Enqueue( PQ, P)
        else
                Enqueue( Queue_i, P)
end
```

(b)

Fig. 7.13 PFQ (a) and PDRR (b) pseudocode fragments to be changed to provide fair rate ignoring

same. First, the correct condition is checked and based on this result the packet is either prioritized or not.

Both algorithms compare the number of bytes transmitted in an active cycle (*bytes* in PFQ and *ByteCount_i* in PDRR) with the maximum number of bytes that may be transmitted in a single cycle (*MTU* in PFQ, and *Q_i* in PDRR). If less than possible bytes were transmitted, the packet is prioritized, i.e., inserted at the head of the PIFO queue in PFQ (Fig. 7.13a, line 8), or in case of PDRR, it is forwarded through the priority queue (Fig. 7.13b, line 15). If the packet is not to be prioritized, PFQ inserts it to the queue according to its flow time stamp (Fig. 7.13a, line 6), while PDRR forwards it to its own queue (Fig. 7.13b, line 17).

In order to introduce the fair rate ignoring scheme, the comparisons between transmitted and maximum possible bytes need to be changed. As in the case of bit rate differentiation, the variables *MTU* in PFQ and *Q_i* in PDRR may be increased or decreased. Greater values mean that more bytes from a certain flow may be prioritized in an algorithm cycle, and therefore even high bit rate flows may experience the lowest possible packet latency and jitter.

Both methods of providing differentiated queuing are simple to implement, although they also carry some concerns. When the number of prioritized flows appears on a link and they consume more bandwidth than normal class flows, the measured fair rate degrades. This happens because FR is the estimate of the rates currently realized by backlogged flows; since some of them utilize more bandwidth than they should, other flows have fewer resources to share. Additionally, an excessive utilization of priority queues by the fair rate ignoring scheme may cause standard streaming flows to display a greater latency or jitter.

7.4.3 Feasibility Study

This section shows that by applying the differentiation factor to certain flows, the total number of active flows in the XP router changes. This is a natural consequence of the fact that we allow some flows to achieve higher or lower bit rates than the current fair rate. A flow with the differentiation factor of 2 is able to consume twice the fair rate at any time and can, therefore, take place of two regular flows.

Figure 7.14 illustrates this situation, as it shows the number of active flows with respect to the differentiation factor. In this scenario, 300 TCP flows with an average of 2.5 MB of data to send (Pareto distribution with the shape factor of 1.5) start the transmission following the exponential distribution with the mean value of 0.3 s. The link capacity is 5 Mbit/s and the minimum FR value is set to 5% of the link capacity, i.e., to 250 kbit/s. The differentiated factor of 1 means that all flows receive the same treatment. In other cases, approximately half the flows are differentiated with the corresponding differentiation factor.

As shown in Fig. 7.14, the number of active flows (both the mean number and the maximum number) rises when the differentiation factor is lower than 1, and decreases when it is higher than one. The operator must be aware that admitting traffic with various differentiation factors may change the number of active flows;

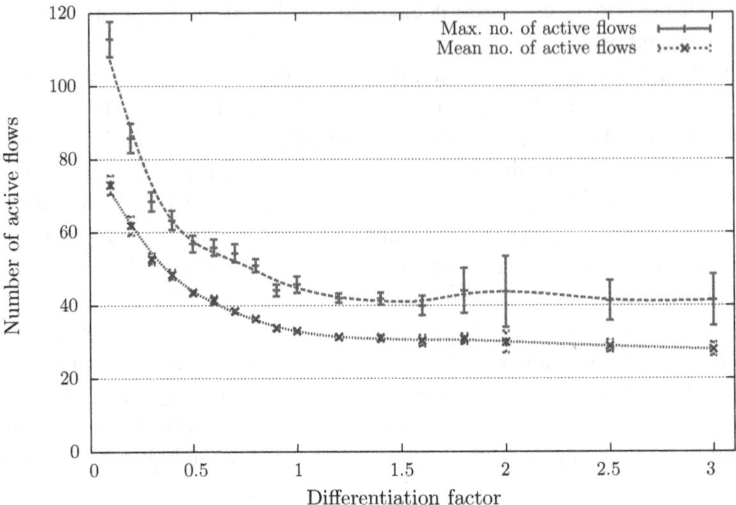

Fig. 7.14 The number of active flows with respect to the differentiation factor

however, the minimum FR value is still preserved by the admission control block and the computation process of the fair rate is unaffected by the differentiated queuing mechanism.

7.4.4 Usage Cases

Differentiated queuing has many possible implementations. The idea is that we can assure more or less than the current fair rate. Since FR changes dynamically, depending on the volume of traffic carried in the link, providing twice the FR for certain flows may not seem to be a major assurance. However, in FAN, FR is not allowed to drop below a certain threshold, and therefore the assurance of twice the FR is really an assurance of twice the minimum FR value in the worst case.

The differentiated queuing scheme may be offered to anyone who requires a better treatment of their traffic in the network, particularly for:

- video conferencing,
- Virtual Private Networks,
- premium customers, etc.

These examples show the instances in which flows would benefit from being provided with better performance. As presented in Sect. 7.1, VoIP flows do not need more bandwidth, as the bitrate associated with a single flow is, typically, far below the minimum FR value, and is therefore always assured. However, video conferences consume significantly higher bitrates, especially those with high video

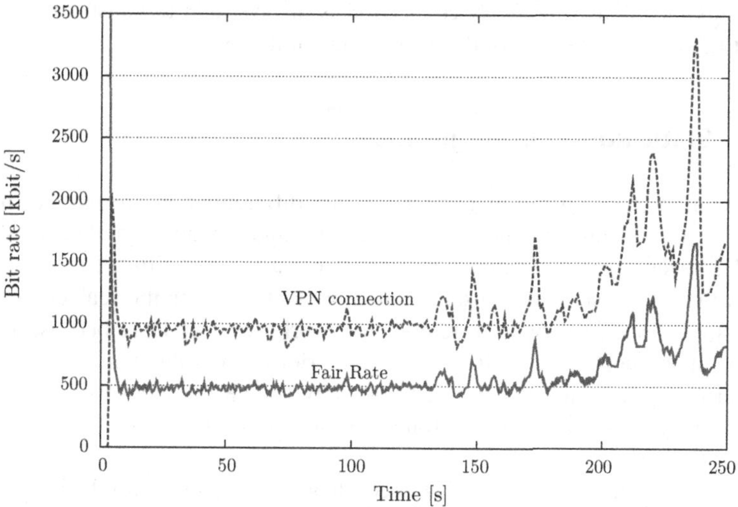

Fig. 7.15 Differentiated queuing in practice

quality. For these applications, the minimum FR threshold may not be sufficient. In such a case, a video conferencing application may be provided with a differentiation factor greater than 1, depending on the requirements and the network link capacities.

Similarly, a Virtual Private Network (VPN) may be established. A consumer may request that their VPN traffic utilizes as much bandwidth as is available at a given moment; however, during congestion periods, the bitrate is not allowed to fall below, say 5 Mbit/s. To achieve this, an operator can set the differentiation factor on each link in the VPN network such that the following formula is met:

$$differentiation\_factor \cdot minFR = 5\ \text{Mbit/s} \tag{7.1}$$

Figure 7.15 explains how this service differentiation scheme works in practice, as it shows the bitrate obtained by a flow exemplifying a VPN connection in which the differentiation factor was set to 2. There are 300 TCP flows with an average of 1 MB of data to send (Pareto distribution with the shape factor of 1.5), starting following exponential distribution with a mean value of 0.3 s. Also, there is one TCP flow with preferential treatment: its bitrate is doubled. The link capacity is 10 Mbit/s and the minimum FR value is set to 5% of the link capacity, i.e., to 500 kbit/s. This means, that when the current fair rate drops below 500 kbit/s, new elastic flows are not admitted on the link.

As seen in Fig. 7.15, the VPN connection obtains exactly twice the current fair rate. When the link is congested, FR oscillates around the minimum FR threshold (500 kbit/s), and therefore, the VPN connection is guaranteed at least twice the minimum fair rate bitrate. However, when the congestion ends and the current FR rises (after 150 s of the simulation) the bitrate obtained by the VPN connection also rises. This means that the VPN connection is always able to consume twice the current fair rate, irrespective of the actual value of this parameter.

7.5 Static Router Configuration

The proposed mechanisms of explicit service differentiation are easy to implement, do not require any new functionalities, and do not complicate existing ones. However, signaling remains an important issue. It is difficult to inform the nodes which flows should be discriminated without reducing the scalability of the architecture. Implicit service differentiation works well in FAN because it does not rely on any network signaling. Flows are prioritized or discriminated based on their performance which is measured internally by XP mechanisms. However, to implement differentiated blocking, routers must be informed which flows should be treated differently.

The IntServ and DiffServ experiences have shown that introducing explicit service differentiation is difficult, due to the signaling problems and the required inter-domain agreements. Therefore, it seems impossible to introduce differentiated blocking into FAN networks globally. However, for a limited scope, explicit service differentiation procedures may be used in FAN.

Static Router Configuration (SRC) [1] is a strategy of manually defining classes of flows and their treatment by network administrators. This approach cannot be used globally, although it is the easiest way of providing explicit service differentiation without any network complication or modification. SRC is an adequate and simple solution for introducing differentiated blocking to FAN networks.

It is especially well suited to emergency calls. Because emergency calling is a local matter (always to the nearest emergency center), the SRC approach may be used. An emergency center is responsible for a certain geographical region (Fig. 7.16). For the differentiated blocking scheme to be used, all nodes in the region must recognize and prioritize flows with the source or destination IP address equal to the address of the appropriate emergency center. Provided that the emergency center's IP address is static (does not change over time), all routers in the region need to be configured only once.

The SRC strategy is the only solution that does not interfere with FAN's superior scalability. This approach is clearly not sufficient for many services, although it is perfectly suited for VoIP emergency connections. Moreover, with SRC, the differentiated blocking scheme may be used for any other local scope service.

When global services are required, and the SRC scheme cannot be used, there is also the option of using the external signaling protocol. Although IntServ's experience with the RSVP protocol shows that such an approach is highly unscalable, the configuration signaling protocol for FAN could be quite different. It is different mainly because its operation is not associated with each single flow. Once a node is configured to treat certain groups of flows with priority, the signaling protocol is not needed, unless a change is required. Considering the limited required functionality of a signaling protocol, this may be a real alternative to SRC for global services.

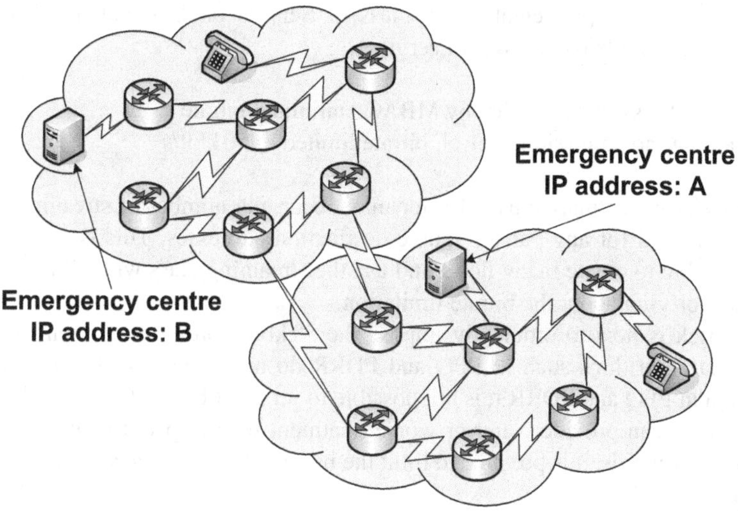

Fig. 7.16 Emergency connections scope

7.6 Class of Service on Demand

Arming FAN with differentiated blocking and differentiated queuing greatly increases the service differentiation capabilities of this QoS architecture. Unfortunately, as explained above, the issue related to signaling still remains. We can either stick to the local nature of the traffic and use the SRC approach, or we can apply a simple signaling protocol to inform the nodes of the preferential treatment for certain flows.

However, there is a third option, namely Class of Service of Demand. This method combines differentiated blocking and differentiated queuing. Here, a user decides to which class of service their packets belong. There are many options on how to transmit and realize the end-user class selection. The simplest would be to set a certain value in the IP packet headers, e.g., to use the ToS field in IPv4 (also known as the DSCP field) or flow label in IPv6.

The most important issue in this approach is the correct design of the classes. Classes should be designed in such a way that one class is generally not better than the others. For example, if two classes were proposed as in Fig. 7.6 and each user is able to choose freely between them, everyone is bound to use the premium class simply because it is better. To make the scheme reasonable, the *quid pro quo*[3] approach must be applied. Classes should be designed for certain applications, but no class should be objectively better than the other.

[3]from the Latin meaning "this for that".

One possible implementation of Class of Service on Demand in FAN is as follows. We provide two classes of service:

1. elastic: admission controlled by MBAC, unlimited bitrate
2. streaming: no admission control, bitrate limited to 50 kbit/s

Additionally, since malicious behavior may occur, the number of streaming flows must be limited for any pair of source-destination addresses. This is so that end-users are able to create many flows and use the streaming class with all its benefits without worrying about the bitrate limitation.

The trick is how to efficiently impose the 50 kbit/s bitrate limitation to flows, given that algorithms such as PFQ and PDRR do not provide such functionality. Although in PFQ and PDRR it is not possible to set strict bitrate limits, as shown in Sect. 7.4, we can provide better or worse treatment with respect to the current fair rate. In other words, it is possible to limit the bitrate of a flow to a certain amount of the current fair rate.

Figure 7.17 presents the feasibility of the presented scenario. There are 300 TCP flows with an average of 2.5 MB to send (Pareto distribution with the shape factor of 1.5), and starting following the exponential distribution with a mean value of 0.3 s. Also, there is one streaming flow, UDP transmission, with a constant bitrate of 200 kbit/s which starts the connection in the 55th second of the simulation. The link capacity is 10 Mbit/s and the minimum FR value is set to 5% of the link capacity, i.e., to 500 kbit/s. This means that when the current fair rate drops below 500 kbit/s, new elastic flows are not admitted. Streaming flows, however, are never blocked. To achieve the limit of 50 kbit/s for streaming flows, the differentiated queuing

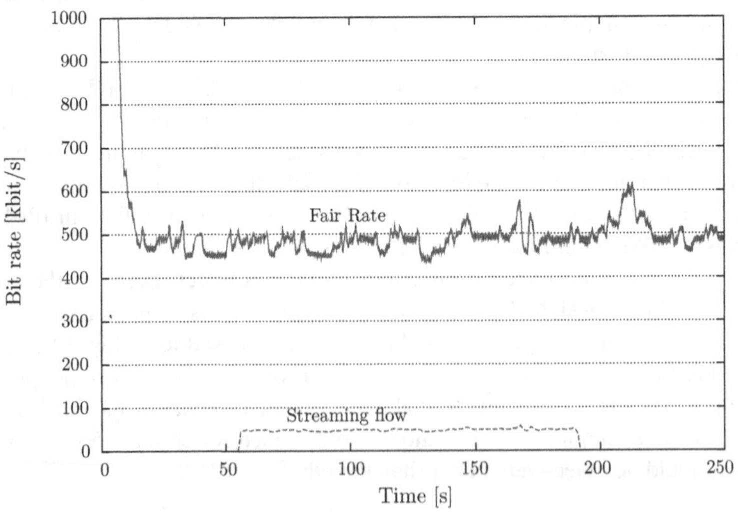

Fig. 7.17 Streaming flow achieved bitrate

mechanism is set so that they can realize up to 10% of the current FR. When the link is congested, this effectively restricts the bitrate of streaming flows to roughly 50 kbit/s. When the link is not congested the limit also applies; however, since FR is greater than its minimum threshold, the streaming flows can also obtain a greater bitrate. In Fig. 7.17, we can see that the streaming flow is admitted on the link instantaneously, and it transmits with roughly 50 kbit/s bitrate even though its desired speed is set to 200 kbit/s.

There are many potential configurations of the Class of Service on Demand in FAN. In this section we presented only one possible implementation. The most important advantage of this approach is that it does not need any kind of signaling to operate. This method can also be combined with SRC to provide an even greater service differentiation. For example, the scenario presented here may be augmented with the option to protect emergency connections and prioritize traffic related to virtual private networks. This way, FAN service differentiation is significantly enriched.

7.7 Conclusion

Admission control and scheduling blocks of a FAN's XP router are the key components responsible for improving network performance in case of overload. Active flows may perceive a sufficiently high QoS, if only a certain number of flows is simultaneously admitted on a link. Unfortunately, this mechanism may be risky for Internet telephony, especially for emergency connections.

To overcome this negative behavior, the differentiated blocking scheme makes all flows related to realizing emergency connections unblockable by admission control blocks. To achieve this goal, the Static Router Configuration can be used to inform all nodes which flows should be prioritized. Considering its significant benefits, along with reasonably low cost, the differentiated blocking and the SRC approach greatly improve the end-user perception of the FAN architecture. Lastly, it has been evaluated that for the purpose of Internet telephony, the solutions do not interfere with the overall performance of the architecture.

Differentiated queuing is also possible in FAN. Bitrate differentiation enables FAN networks to provide guarantees on a different level than the minimum fair rate threshold. Moreover, to implement differentiated queueing, only slight alterations to the FAN queuing disciplines are required.

The mechanisms interfere with the admission control and scheduling blocks of the XP router, potentially resulting in temporal performance degradation of the carried traffic. This issue has been extensively documented and shown to be insignificant to the overall performance of the FAN architecture, provided that the volume of prioritized traffic remains within reasonable boundaries. Otherwise, the pre-emption-based methods need to be applied.

Finally, the Class of Service on Demand approach was presented. This scheme uses the options provided by differentiated blocking and differentiated queuing. This way, the service differentiation options offered by the FAN architecture are greatly enhanced.

7.8 Check Your Knowledge

1. Explain the connection waiting time problem in FAN.
2. What is the main challenge in providing the differentiated blocking scheme?
3. Is it possible to provide Bit Rate Differentiation in both PDRR and PFQ algorithms?
4. Why is fair rate degradation due to the differentiated blocking mechanism temporal?

Reference

1. A. Jajszczyk, R. Wojcik, Emergency calls in flow-aware networks. IEEE Commun. Lett. **11**(9), 753–755 (2007)

Service Degradation in FAN

8

Stop thinking in terms of limitations and start thinking in terms of possibilities.

—Terry Josephson

To assure a certain level of guaranteed bandwidth, some admission control procedures must be applied. In FAN, admission control is measurement-based. Moreover, as FAN does not use any kind of signaling, network routers are not aware of the incoming flow characteristics. This fact makes admission decisions more challenging than, for example, in IntServ supported IP or ATM, where transmission parameters are more or less known before the transmission starts.

FAN aims to provide a minimum level of resources for each active flow. It does so by blocking new flows when congestion indicators exceed their fixed thresholds. It is assumed that these thresholds define the minimum level of assured service on each FAN link. However, it is shown in this chapter that this assumption does not stand in FAN. In fact, this is the downside of all measurement-based admission controls. The problem is that when many new flows arrive at the same instant, a router does not have enough time to react and too many flows are accepted.

This chapter starts by showing the problem and its effects on transmission performance in detail. Next, several ways of solving it are presented. Since admitting too many flows is the problem, all the solutions revolve around limiting the number of flows that a router can admit in a certain amount of time. These solutions improve QoS assurance capabilities of FAN, and enhance its scalability.

The chapter is organized as follows. Section 8.1 describes the fair rate degradation problem of FAN networks, i.e., the inability to ensure a certain level of QoS when the number of incoming flows is high. Subsequent sections provide solutions to the problem. Section 8.2 shows a simple yet efficient approach, i.e., the static limitation mechanism, where the number of allowable flows per a certain amount of time is fixed. Section 8.3 shows enhancements to the static limitations

J. Domżał et al., *Guide to Flow-Aware Networking*, Computer Communications and Networks, https://doi.org/10.1007/978-3-030-57153-5_8

in which the number of allowable flows is dynamically adjusted to the current situation. Section 8.4 shows a different approach to the implementation of the admission control block in FAN networks, namely the predictive approach. In the predictive approach, FAN routers are able to react to imminent congestion faster, which results in better performance. The automatic mechanism which facilitates the limit selection process is presented in Sect. 8.5.

8.1 Fair Rate Degradation

The occurrence of fair rate degradation was presented in Chap. 7 as a consequence of admitting priority flows under conditions in which a regular flow would not have been accepted. Here, we show that fair rate degradations also happen as a natural effect of the admission control routine designed for FAN [3]. The XP mechanism in FAN is supposed to provide at least a minimum fair transmission rate to all the active flows. To achieve this, each time the measured fair rate drops below the minimum threshold, the admission control starts blocking all new connections. Therefore, this procedure does not guarantee the maintenance of the threshold value under congestion since appropriate action is undertaken only after the threshold is crossed. A similar situation concerns the second congestion parameter, i.e., the priority load.

In theory, fair rate should be allowed to drop below the threshold only slightly before the admission control block starts functioning. Unfortunately, in practice, these drops may be significant [3].

Figure 8.1 demonstrates the problem as it shows the measured fair rate values over time on severely congested FAN links with 1000 flows arriving with the frequency of 5 flows per second on average. In this scenario, a 100 Mbit/s FAN link was analyzed. The *minFR* parameter was set to 5% of the link capacity (5 Mbit/s) and was measured every 0.4 s in (a) and every 2 s in (b). The volume of traffic to be sent by each flow was generated following the Pareto distribution (15 MB on average, shape factor: 1.5). Exponential distribution for generating the time intervals between the beginnings of the transmissions of the flows was used. The duration of each simulation run was set to 400 s.

As can be seen, in both cases presented in Fig. 8.1, FR drops well below the *minFR* threshold (5% of the link capacity, marked with solid flat lines). In (a), the degradations are shorter and reach up to 2 Mbit/s, whereas in (b), the degradations are much longer and more intense (up to 4 Mbit/s). Such situations occur when many new flows arrive between two consecutive FR measurements and are admitted before the router realizes that the admission control should be in the blocking state. The repeating routine shown in Fig. 8.1 comprises the following four steps:

1. FR drops below *minFR* threshold and no new flows are admitted,
2. existing flows naturally end their transmission and FR increases slowly,
3. FR increases above *minFR*,
4. the admission control block starts accepting all new flows until FR drops below *minFR*.

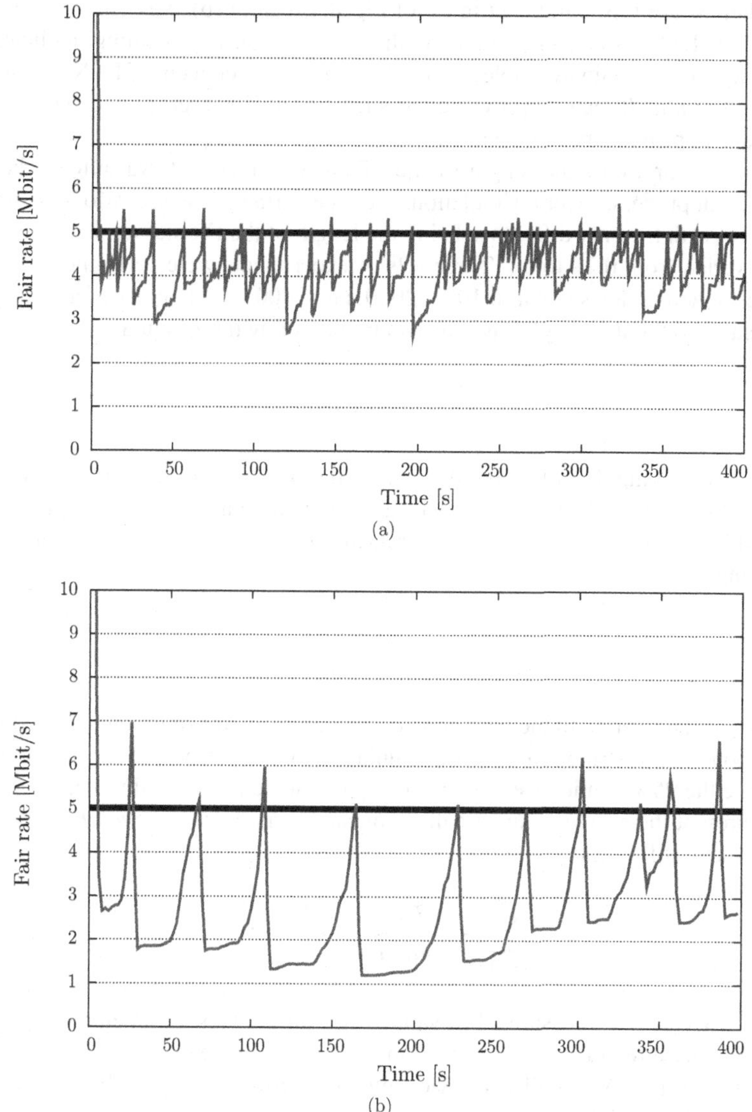

Fig. 8.1 Measured FR values over time on a congested FAN link: FR measured once every (**a**) 0.4 s, (**b**) 2 s

This behavior is a consequence of step 4. As the admission control block relies on data delivered by the scheduling blocks, and the fact that the scheduler performs measurements periodically, the admission control block can only start to block new flows after the next measurement. Since the frequency of measurements directly contributes to the extent and the duration of degradations, it explains why FR degradations are less significant in (a) of Fig. 8.1 than in (b). Nevertheless, in both cases the FR drops are undesirable as they pose a risk to streaming applications which require a certain available bandwidth. The whole concept of FAN is that this bandwidth (*minFR*) can be provided for such flows. However, Fig. 8.1 shows that FAN fails to provide this key quality.

To understand how the length of the FR measurement interval affects the FR degradation process, several simulations were performed. The scenario was similar to before, with the only difference being the length of the FR measurement interval, which varied from 0.2 s to 3 s. Three sets of experiments were performed with the number of active flows equal to 1000, 2000, and 3000. The number of active flows was related to the intensity of their arrival by the following formula:

$$\frac{N}{\lambda} = T = const \tag{8.1}$$

where N is the number of active flows, λ is the intensity of their arrival and T is the simulation time. The intensity was set in the simulator by changing the mean interval between the start points of the transmissions of new flows, according to the following formula:

$$\lambda = \frac{1}{t_e} \tag{8.2}$$

where t_e is the interval to the beginning of the next flow transmission obtained from the exponential distribution. Several simulations were performed for each case to calculate the 95% confidence intervals using the Student's t-distribution.

To present the problem numerically, a mean deviation from the *minFR* threshold was defined as follows:

$$\frac{1}{n}\sum_{i=1}^{n}\frac{|minFR - FR_i|}{minFR} \cdot 100\% \tag{8.3}$$

where FR_i are the measured FR values over time. This parameter shows how much the measured FR values differ from *minFR* during the total measurement time (simulation time). As, in all cases, we simulate overloaded links only, the ideal FR values should oscillate around the threshold, and the deviation should be very low.

Figure 8.2 shows how the length of the FR measurement interval affects the mean deviation from *minFR*, as defined by formula 8.3. Two trends can be seen: the deviation from *minFR* increases with the increased FR measurement interval, and with the number of active flows. The reason behind the first trend was explained earlier. When the duration between two consecutive measurement is longer, statistically more flows will appear and be admitted, which results in significant over-admission. The second trend affects the degradations in a similar manner, i.e., when there are more active flows, more of them will appear during a certain period which increases the over-admission.

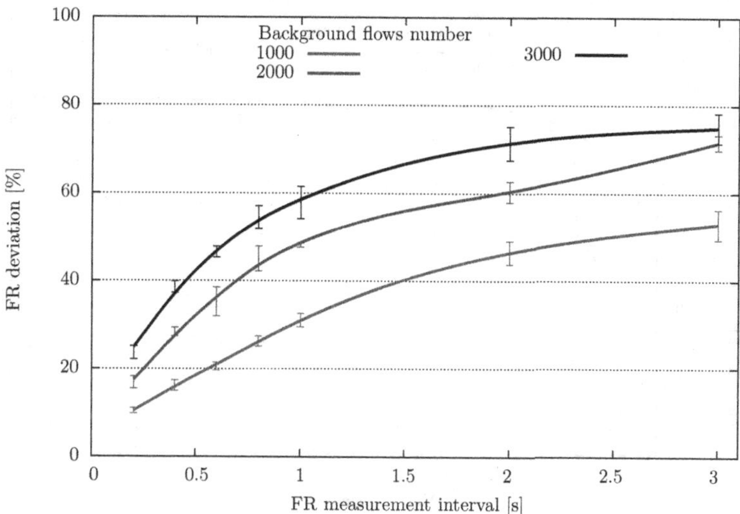

Fig. 8.2 FR deviation from minimum FR with respect to FR measurement interval

The mean deviation from *minFR* is the indicator which compares the performance of the system under different setups. For individual flows, the length of time during which certain bitrates are not assured is more important. Figure 8.3 shows the length of time in which FR drops below (a) 90% and (b) 80% of the minimum FR from the previous experiment. This characteristic is very important for streaming applications which require a certain amount of bandwidth. Being aware of the fact that FR boundaries can be and are constantly crossed, network administrator may wish to set the threshold a bit higher, e.g., in order to provide a guaranteed level of 5% of the link's bandwidth, a *minFR* value could be set to 7%. However, as shown in Fig. 8.3, this approach may be deceptive, as FR degradations are uncontrollable and unforeseeable.

It can be seen that the length of time in which FR drops below a certain value is strictly correlated with the mean deviation from *minFR* described previously. The longer the interval between the measurements, the more substantial the time during which FR drops significantly. The values in Fig. 8.3 should be read as follows: if the time when FR drops below 80% of *minFR* is equal to 50%, it means that half of the time the actual FR is below 80% of *minFR*. As an example, consider a 10 Mbit/s FAN link with the minimum FR value set to 5% of the link capacity, i.e., 500 kbit/s. FAN should be able to provide this bitrate to all the flows. However, in this case, for 50% of the time, the actual FR is going to be lower than $80\% \cdot 500$ kbit/s = 400 kbit/s. From the absolute values presented in Fig. 8.3 it can be seen that minimum FR guarantees have little meaning in plain FAN networks, as under heavy congestion, in some cases more than 90% of the time the actual FR is significantly below the guaranteed threshold.

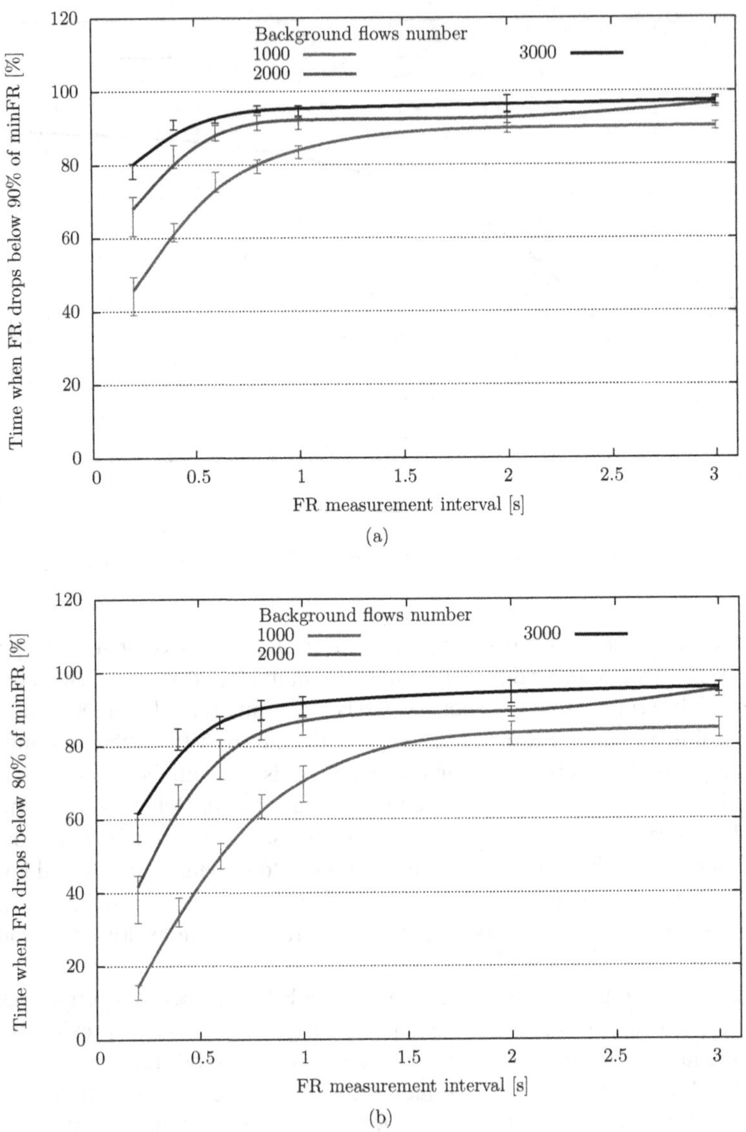

Fig. 8.3 FR drops below (**a**) 90% and (**b**) 80% of *minFR* with respect to the FR measurement interval

There are two approaches to mitigating the problem. One is to reduce the interval between two consecutive measurements of the fair rate. If the FR is estimated more frequently, statistically fewer flows are admitted between the measurements and the system reacts more quickly. The downside of this method is that frequent estimations require more computational power from the router's CPU. This issue becomes even more significant in core networks, as these devices deal with numerous flows and must react almost instantly.

The FR measurement interval values chosen for this section's experiments aimed to illustrate the problem. In real devices these intervals are bound to be much shorter. It is easy to imagine that routers should be able to provide measurements once every 0.1 s, or even more frequently. However, as seen in Figs. 8.2 and 8.3, FR degradations increase with the increased number of active flows. Therefore, for the core devices which deal with numerous flows the problem becomes more significant, up to the point where further reduction of the measurement interval is no longer an option. At that point the only solution is to limit the number of flows that can be admitted between two measurements. We discuss this solution in the following sections.

8.2 The Limitation Mechanism

In literature, numerous admission control mechanisms have been proposed over the years, mainly for Integrated Services, Differentiated Services, and call admission control procedures in ATM. The PhD dissertation of A. W. Moore [2] contains a detailed comparison of the mechanisms. However, most of the proposals rely on the fact that at least some information about the incoming flow is available through signaling. As FAN does not use any kind of signaling, these methods are not applicable.

Some of the admission control mechanisms also notice the problem of over-admitting. In [1], it is stated that the system needs to wait for a period of time after any change to the number of connections in progress happens, before the link congestion status can be re-estimated. The author proposes a timescale solution, which regards a time interval as a function of the number of active flows. As the number increases considerably, the interval is decreased to reduce the probability that a situation in a link changes significantly within that interval. Unfortunately, increasing the frequency of measurements imposes more strict demands on the router CPUs. Therefore, it is argued that by providing even the simplest limitation mechanisms, we can resolve the over-admitting problem while not increasing the computational power requirements of the router.

The limitation mechanism [3] in FAN enhances the functionality of the admission control block. The idea is that between any two consecutive measurements, only a limited, fixed number of new flows may be admitted. This approach protects the admission control block from over-admitting, i.e., from allowing too many new flows to acquire access to the link, which consequently degrades the FR.

To provide limitations, we need to introduce a simple counter, incremented on arrival of each new flow, and reset on each measurement. When it reaches a certain number, all new flows are rejected. This way, the extra CPU power required is hardly noticeable, while the benefits are considerable.

Figure 8.4 shows the mean deviation of the measured FR with respect to the number of active flows and different measurement intervals. All the simulation

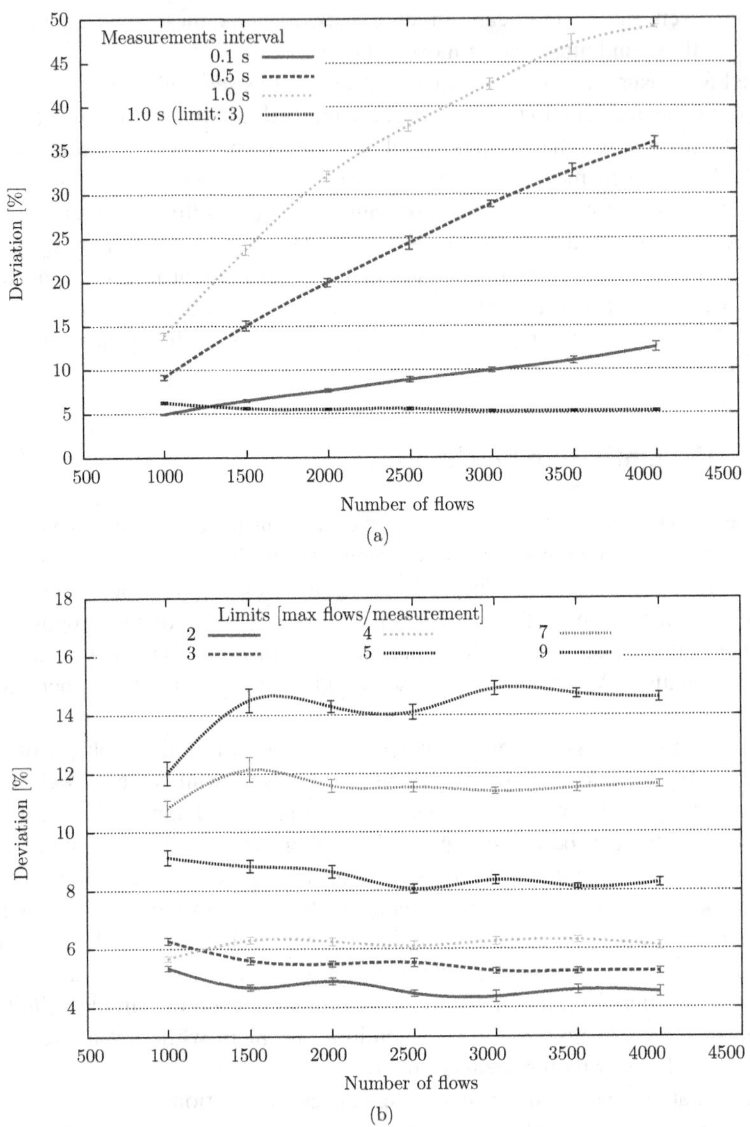

Fig. 8.4 Mean deviation of the measured FR from the *minFR* threshold with respect to: (**a**) the measurement interval length, (**b**) the maximum number of flows accepted in one interval

scenario parameters were presented in the previous section. As shown in Fig. 8.4a, when limiting is not applied (three rising curves), the deviation rises along with the number of active flows, and is greater when larger measurement intervals are set. Both dependencies are natural and were explained in detail in Sect. 8.1. The number of active flows, associated with the statistical intensity of their arrival, affects the number of flows which request the resources every second, while the measurement interval affects the duration of that arrival. Both factors contribute to the fact that more or fewer flows may be over-admitted. However, when the limitation is used (the flat line, 3 flows per measurement in this case) we observe almost constant deviation, which is significantly lower than that when the limits are not applied. The fact that the deviation does not increase with the number of active flows helps to administer the network, as the operators can keep the links in good condition regardless of the current network overload.

The limit of 3 flows per measurement was chosen experimentally. Figure 8.4(b) shows how various limits affect the FR deviation under the same conditions. Choosing a limit which is too strict (low) results in under-feeding the link, as the link serves flows faster than they can be admitted. This happened when the limit of 1 flow per measurement was applied (not shown in the figure, as the deviation was way over the presented scale). On the other hand, choosing a high limit does not solve the problem, as the deviations start to increase. Figure 8.4(b) shows that limiting the admission of new flows to 2–4 per measurement is sufficient under these network conditions. The deviation is around 5–6% and is wholly acceptable.

Currently, it is only a matter of conducting experiments to find the right limit. In our simulation scenario, picking the limit of 2–4 flows per measurement is adequate; however, in will be different in other situations, especially on links with a different capacity.

Table 8.1 shows the mean percentage of time in which FR drops below 90% (a) and 80% (b) of *minFR*. As shown in Table 8.1, by introducing limitations (marked rows), we can drastically reduce the FR degradation. When limitations are present, the FR drops below 90% of its minimum threshold 5–10 times less than in the comparable situation (measurements once every second). The outcome is even more convincing in the second case, as the FR value hardly ever drops below 80% of the *minFR* threshold, which is a good result. Similarly, as for deviation, this characteristic is almost independent of the number of flows when limitations are applied.

For comparison, Table 8.1 also shows the times when we increase the frequency of measurements. They show that reducing the inter-measurement time even 10 times does not provide better performance than introducing a simple limitation mechanism. This demonstrates that increasing the frequency of measurements is a less effective way of mitigating the FR degradation problem than limitations. Finally, even if were possible to provide a proper frequency of measurements, the dependency on the number of active flows remains and cannot be neglected, whereas the limitation mechanism solves the problem.

8.3 Dynamic Limitations

There are numerous possibilities concerning the actual process of limiting the number of flows in the limitation mechanism. The method presented in Sect. 8.2 is the simplest, yet it remains efficient. Dynamic limitations [5] differ from static

Table 8.1 The percentage of time in which FR drops below 90% (a) and 80% (b) of the *minFR* threshold

	Number of flows						
Measurement interval	1000	1500	2000	2500	3000	3500	4000
90% (a)							
0.1	10.96 ± 0.92	25.18 ± 1.39	34.01 ± 1.26	41.60 ± 1.02	47.32 ± 1.33	52.59 ± 1.55	58.06 ± 1.85
0.5	34.82 ± 1.26	60.28 ± 1.81	73.49 ± 0.85	80.12 ± 1.08	83.22 ± 0.44	86.73 ± 0.55	87.26 ± 0.32
1.0	53.61 ± 1.74	76.69 ± 0.65	85.00 ± 0.48	87.49 ± 0.33	89.01 ± 0.51	91.69 ± 0.96	92.29 ± 0.19
1.0 (limit: 3)	**13.90 ± 1.11**	**10.49 ± 0.85**	**8.89 ± 0.97**	**9.16 ± 0.84**	**7.97 ± 0.75**	**8.21 ± 0.76**	**7.58 ± 0.94**
80% (b)							
0.1	0.03 ± 0.06	1.18 ± 0.28	3.50 ± 0.71	7.21 ± 0.71	11.56 ± 0.99	15.64 ± 1.98	21.62 ± 2.59
0.5	9.07 ± 1.52	30.32 ± 2.12	47.53 ± 1.78	59.04 ± 2.09	68.40 ± 0.82	74.00 ± 1.50	76.11 ± 0.56
1.0	24.62 ± 1.30	56.46 ± 2.11	72.73 ± 1.19	77.79 ± 0.54	82.42 ± 0.57	85.83 ± 0.93	84.84 ± 0.32
1.0 (limit: 3)	**0.10 ± 0.06**	**0.01 ± 0.03**	**0.01 ± 0.03**	**0.00 ± 0**	**0.00 ± 0**	**0.00 ± 0**	**0.00 ± 0**

ones in that the limit is calculated dynamically and changes over time. The idea is that we gain more flexibility and it is easier to adjust to dynamic changes of the link traffic.

For implementing the dynamic limit, a graded system is evaluated. There is a base admission limit, just as in the static limitation mechanism, but this limit is increased by 1 for each $step$ the FR is further from the *minFR* threshold. The admission limit (AL) in this mechanism is calculated with the following formula:

$$AL = BaseAL + \left\lfloor \frac{FR - minFR}{step} \right\rfloor \tag{8.4}$$

where: AL is the calculated admission limit, $BaseAL$ is the preset base admission limit, FR is the currently measured FR, $minFR$ is the minimum FR threshold, $step$ is a predefined value which affects the frequency of changes and $\lfloor x \rfloor$ is the highest integer lower than x. The formula has the following meaning: when $minFR < FR \leq minFR + step$, the admission limit $AL = baseAL$, when $minFR + step < FR \leq minFR + 2 \cdot step$, the admission limit $AL = baseAL + 1$, etc.

This method allows us to use a low base admission limit when the current FR is close to the threshold, thereby better assuring the guaranteed bitrate, and to increase the admission limit when there is more room to do so. The other advantage of this approach is that the system is less prone to the under-admission problem. This issue derives from the fact that, in a lightly loaded link, under the static limitation mechanism, we are not able to admit all new incoming flows immediately, even though the system is far from being congested. The dynamic limitation mechanism solves this problem.

Dynamic limitation is a natural way of approaching the static limitations as $step$ approaches the link capacity. Figure 8.5 illustrates this tendency as it shows the FR deviation and FR drop duration with respect to the $step$ parameter. The simulation experiment was identical to that presented in Sect. 8.2. The solid horizontal lines represent the results obtained with the static limitation mechanism under the same network conditions, in which the static limit was equal to $baseAL$. The plots can be annotated as follows: (1) with both the FR deviation and FR drop duration, a clear tendency approaching the static limits can be observed, (2) the performance of the dynamic limitations is inferior with respect to the static limitation mechanism.

In this example, the inferior performance of the dynamic limitation mechanism results from the fact that the static limitation of 1 flow per measurement was perfectly sufficient. Therefore, when the option of admitting more flows appears, the performance degrades. However, the dynamic limitations are seen most clearly when the static limitation mechanism needs more than 1 flow per measurement to perform adequately. Table 8.2 compares the performance of both the static and the dynamic limitation mechanisms under the same network conditions, and only the mean flow size (the volume of data to be sent) is reduced 4 times. The effect of such an action is that significantly more flows end during a certain time interval, therefore, more new flows may be admitted on the link. Exactly the same effect

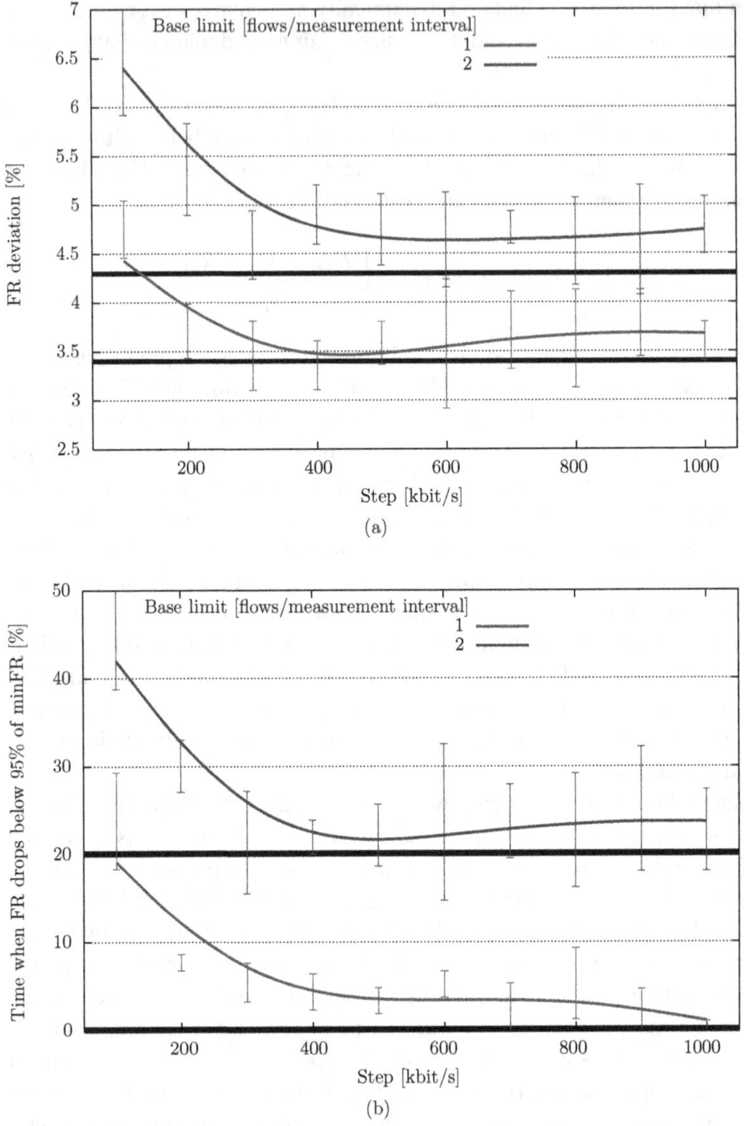

Fig. 8.5 FR deviation (**a**) and FR drops duration (**b**) with respect to the step parameter

would appear if, instead of changing the traffic characteristics, the link capacity was increased four times.

Applying static limitation of 1 flow per measurement results in severe under-admitting. In this case FR never reaches the *minFR* threshold, therefore the assumed warm-up time (until FR reaches the *minFR* threshold for the first time) does not end. Out of the remaining static possibilities, the limit of 3 flows per measurement seems

Table 8.2 Performance of static and dynamic limitation mechanisms: comparison

Static limitation mechanism (a)						
	Limit [flows/measurement]					
Performance factor	1	2	**3**	4	5	6
Deviation	–	16.69 ± 11.07	**7.49 ± 1.52**	7.49 ± 1.05	7.77 ± 0.42	8.97 ± 0.32
95% drop duration	–	3.00 ± 2.07	**14.67 ± 4.14**	28.25 ± 5.50	42.18 ± 3.79	49.17 ± 3.27
Dynamic limitation mechanism (b)						
	Step [kbit/s]					
Performance factor	100	**200**	**300**	400	500	600
Deviation	6.88 ± 0.77	**7.76 ± 1.38**	**9.39 ± 1.80**	11.13 ± 2.08	13.12 ± 1.70	15.19 ± 1.96
95% drop duration	12.14 ± 0.17	**4.22 ± 3.21**	**1.16 ± 1.18**	0.33 ± 0.61	0	0

to be the best solution: the deviation is relatively low which indicates that there is no problem with under-admitting, although the FR drop duration is significant. The only better static solution is when the static limit is set to two, although deviation becomes a problem.

The dynamic limitation mechanism has more flexibility. Table 8.2 (b) presents the case with the base admission limit of 1 flow per measurement. By adjusting the step factor we can observe much better performance. For example, cases with the step set to 200 and 300 kbit/s seem to be the best solution. The deviation is kept within reasonable boundaries, whereas the FR drop duration is almost irrelevant. This example shows that using the dynamic limitation mechanism may be beneficial with respect to the static procedure. The key quality provided by this scheme is that we can use the lowest possible limit of 1 flow per measurement under the network conditions in which such a limit leads to severe under-admitting. Although this limit is not used all the time, its benefits are clearly visible.

The presented method of providing dynamic limitations gives more flexibility to the static limitation mechanism; however, there are many other possibilities. One would be to define a certain formula to calculate the current limit based on the network conditions. The problem with this approach is that there is not much information available in FAN. For the sake of simplicity, the volume of provided information was reduced to minimum. As there is no signaling, flows transmission characteristics or requirements are unknown, and the router does not keep stateful information about single flows. Furthermore, there is no indication when a flow ends its transmission. A FAN router erases this flow from the protected flow list only when a certain time from the last forwarded packet elapses. If the flow termination information were available instantly, the limitation mechanism may be altered to intelligently compensate for the no longer active flows.

8.4 Predictive Approach

The root of FR degradations in FAN lies in the very design of the admission control block. The key issue is the fact that admission criteria rely on the information delivered by the scheduling block, which implies passive control. Only after the congestion is noticed, can admission control start to block new flows. Therefore, the minimum level of FR in FAN is not a guaranteed value, as appropriate actions are taken after this boundary is crossed. The active approach would be to undertake measures even before the congestion occurs.

FR prediction [4] is an active approach to implementing the admission control routine in FAN. In this mechanism, the admission control block tries to estimate the value of the next FR measurement and take appropriate action based on the predicted FR, rather than on the current real measurements. Two actions can happen:

1. $FR \geq minFR$ and $expectedFR < minFR \implies$ the MBAC block will block new flows despite FR being over the threshold,

2. $FR < minFR$ and $expectedFR \geq minFR \Longrightarrow$ the MBAC block will allow new flows despite FR being below the threshold.

From the perspective of service assurance, the first action is more important, as it tries to preserve the minimum guaranteed FR. Therefore, two predictive mechanisms can be defined: *half prediction* which uses the first action, and *double prediction* which uses both. The following formula presents the method of estimating the nearest value of FR:

$$expectedFR = FR_t + p \cdot (FR_t - FR_{t-1}) \tag{8.5}$$

where: $expectedFR$ represents the predicted next value of FR, FR_t is the measured FR in time t and p is the predictor. As FAN is a simple architecture, new mechanisms should not overcomplicate it. To implement this scheme, the XP router needs to additionally remember the previously measured value of FR and the admission control routine needs to be altered with no new functionalities.

Predictor p is a number which tries to emulate the dynamics of the changes in the FAN link. When $p = 1$, the difference between the current FR and the previous FR is calculated and this difference is added to the current FR. In this way, the system assumes that the current FR tendency is constant. When the changes are more dynamic, especially on high-capacity links, the use of higher predictors may be more adequate.

To show the efficiency of the proposed mechanism a number of simulations were performed. The overall scenario setup is presented in Sect. 8.1. The flow admission limit was set to 3 flows per measurement, and the predictor p was set to 1. Figure 8.6

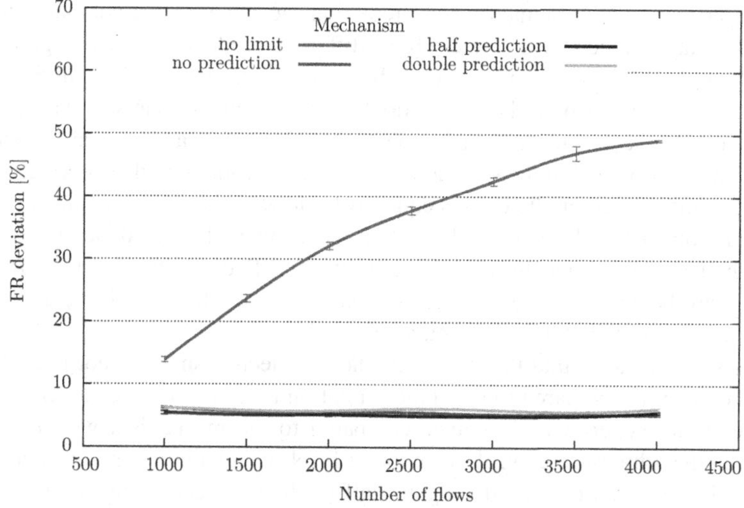

Fig. 8.6 FR deviation from minimum FR with respect to the number of active flows

shows the FR deviation from the minimum FR with respect to the number of active flows when different mechanism are used. As can be seen, the prediction mechanism does not provide significantly lower deviations than the standard static limiting mechanism (case: no prediction). It should be noted, however, that the deviations observed after the static limitation mechanism is applied are reduced to a completely acceptable level, making it difficult to make further improvements. The deviations are greatly reduced when compared to the case in which no limiting mechanism is used. Additionally, the deviations are independent of the volume of the carried traffic, represented by the number of active flows.

The deviations remained on the same level as when only static limitations were proposed; however, the length of time in which FR drops below a certain level can be improved substantially. Table 8.3 shows how often the measured FR drops below 95%, 90%, and 80% of the minimum FR threshold. To compare the efficiency of the proposed mechanisms, the case with no limitations and the case when static limitation is performed are presented as well. From the numbers in Table 8.3 we can see that the half prediction mechanism outperforms all the other approaches. The time in which FR drops below a certain threshold is shortened by 30–80% compared to the best case with static limitations. Given that static limitations offer a drastic reduction of this time compared to the standard FAN routine, the result obtained by the half-prediction mechanism should be considered as outstanding.

It may be somewhat surprising that the double prediction mechanism does not provide an improvement over static limitations. There are two reasons for such behavior. First, as the FR deviation is around a few percent, there is hardly any room for predicting the next values, since the FR trend and the over and under the threshold situation change rapidly. Second, the fact that admission control may admit new flows even when the current FR is below the threshold does not contribute to the reduction of the duration of FR drops.

Similar results are obtained when prediction mechanisms are compared to the static limitation mechanism under three different predictor values. Figures 8.7 and 8.8 show the mean deviation and FR drops duration, as defined in Sect. 8.1, respectively. The top plot shows the double prediction mechanism, whereas the bottom one presents the half-prediction mechanism. As can be seen, under the traffic pattern provided in the simulated scenario, the double prediction mechanism performs better when predictor p is equal to 1. However, the performance is worse than that obtained with the static limitation mechanism. This tendency is not seen in the half-prediction mechanism. Here, both the FR deviation and the FR drop duration are better than when no predictions are made, although the relationships between various predictors are unnoticeable.

This section shows that the double prediction mechanism does not provide the expected benefits compared to the static limitation mechanism. The half prediction scheme shows superior performance compared to the mechanism which already improves the admission control behavior in FAN. Compared to the original FAN routine, the benefits from introducing the half-prediction mechanism are substantial.

Table 8.3 The percentage of time in which FR drops below 95% (a), 90% (b), and 80% (c) of the *minFR* threshold

	Number of flows						
Mechanism	1000	1500	2000	2500	3000	3500	4000
95% (a)							
No limitation	68.73 ± 1.61	84.79 ± 0.72	89.30 ± 0.32	93.09 ± 1.54	92.17 ± 0.36	94.35 ± 0.33	94.79 ± 0.12
No prediction	35.92 ± 1.18	35.64 ± 1.29	31.43 ± 1.25	33.46 ± 1.78	33.18 ± 0.97	31.83 ± 1.12	30.91 ± 1.38
Half prediction	**23.94 ± 3.08**	**23.00 ± 2.64**	**23.43 ± 4.52**	**25.55 ± 1.34**	**24.52 ± 2.01**	**22.99 ± 2.34**	**24.89 ± 2.03**
Double prediction	37.37 ± 3.17	38.00 ± 1.51	36.60 ± 1.79	43.92 ± 1.72	41.05 ± 1.56	40.05 ± 2.38	43.68 ± 2.70
90% (b)							
No limitation	53.61 ± 1.74	76.69 ± 0.65	85.00 ± 0.48	87.49 ± 0.33	89.01 ± 0.51	91.69 ± 0.96	92.29 ± 0.19
No prediction	13.90 ± 1.11	10.49 ± 0.85	8.89 ± 0.97	9.16 ± 0.84	7.97 ± 0.75	8.21 ± 0.76	7.58 ± 0.94
Half prediction	**3.97 ± 1.60**	**4.80 ± 0.60**	**5.04 ± 1.67**	**3.36 ± 0.63**	**3.12 ± 1.05**	**4.78 ± 1.25**	**6.11 ± 0.65**
Double prediction	13.14 ± 3.31	9.87 ± 1.23	11.88 ± 0.72	13.81 ± 1.35	11.52 ± 1.87	13.58 ± 1.47	17.53 ± 2.29
80% (c)							
No limitation	24.62 ± 1.30	56.46 ± 2.11	72.73 ± 1.19	77.79 ± 0.54	82.42 ± 0.57	85.83 ± 0.93	84.84 ± 0.32
No prediction	0.10 ± 0.06	0.01 ± 0.03	0.01 ± 0.03	0.00 ± 0	0.00 ± 0	0.00 ± 0	0.00 ± 0
Half prediction	**0**	**0**	**0**	**0**	**0**	**0**	**0**
Double prediction	0	0	0	0	0	0	0

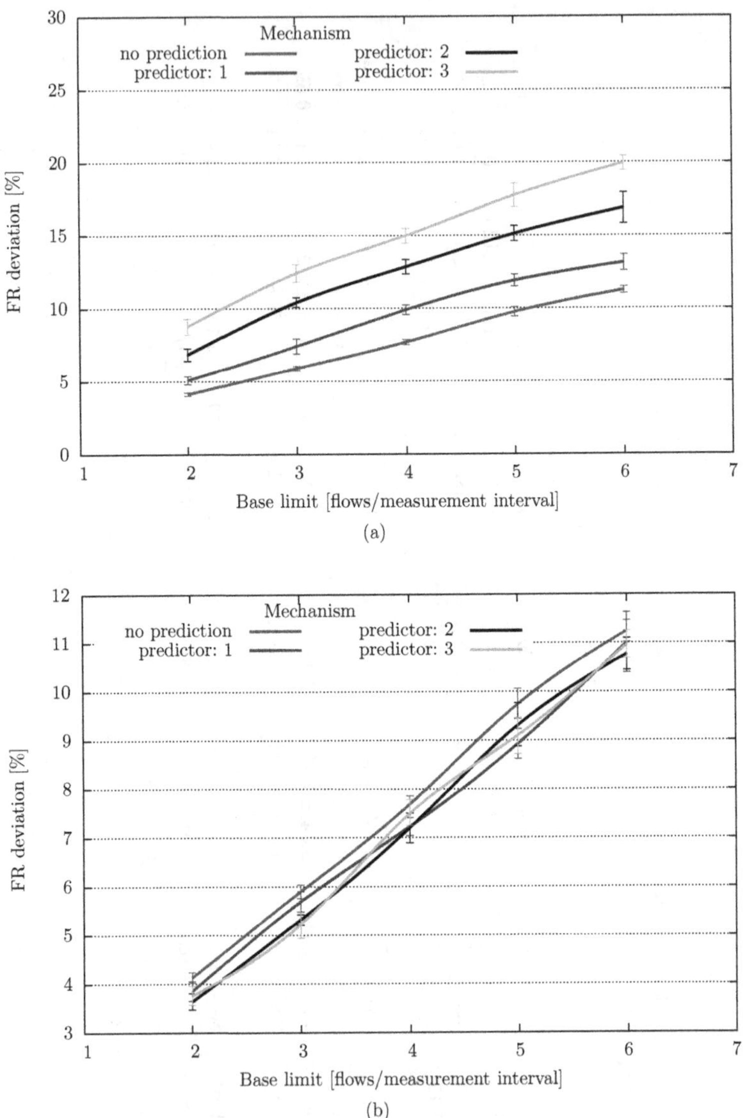

Fig. 8.7 FR deviation from minimum FR with respect to the admission limit and (**a**) double prediction, (**b**) half-prediction mechanisms

The predictor is a factor which does not seem to have a significant impact on the performance of the half prediction mechanism, although under different traffic characteristics, especially related to high-capacity links, the choice of an appropriate predictor may play an important role.

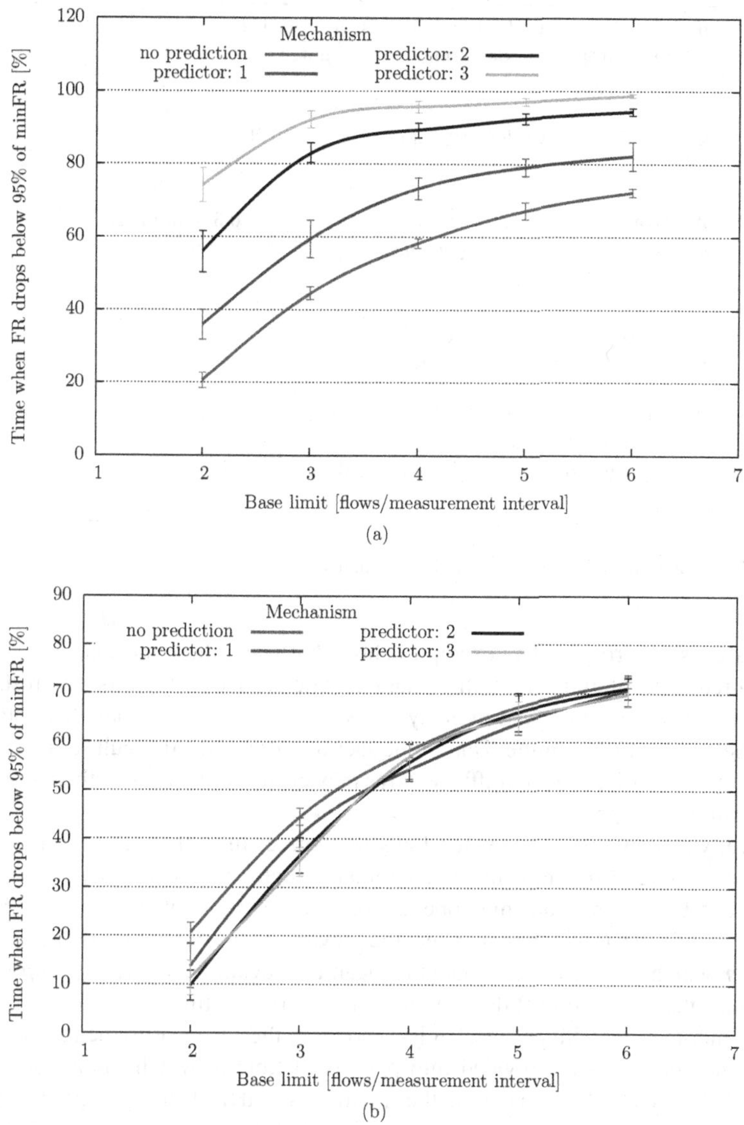

Fig. 8.8 FR deviation from minimum FR with respect to the admission limit and (**a**) double prediction, (**b**) half-prediction mechanisms

8.5 Automatic Intelligent Limitations

The performance benefits obtained by using any of the proposed limitation mechanisms are substantial. However, this only applies provided that static or dynamic

```
1   if ((prevFR > minFR) and (FR < minFR)) {
2       max_drop = 0;  deviation = 0;  counter = 0;
3   }
4
5   if (counter >= 0) deviation += FR - minFR;
6   counter++;
7
8   if ((counter > 0) and (deviation / counter > 0.3 * minFR)) {
9       AdmissionLimitFR++; counter = -5; deviation = 0;
10  }
11
12  drop = (minFR - FR) / (minFR);
13  if (drop > max_drop) max_drop = drop;
14
15  if ((prevFR < minFR) and (FR > minFR)) {
16      #FR drop period has ended
17      if (max_drop > 0.15) AdmissionLimitFR --;
18  }
```

Fig. 8.9 The automatic intelligent limitation mechanism

limit is chosen correctly. The examples show that when these mechanisms are not configured adequately to the traffic characteristic carried in the link, the resulting performance is not better, and in many cases it is actually worse than that obtained with the regular FAN routine. Due to the fact that it is often difficult to predict the traffic characteristic, and the traffic features may change dynamically, there is a need for an automatic approach.

Here, we show a scheme which finds the correct limit through trial and error. The pseudocode of the implemented automatic intelligent mechanism is presented in Fig. 8.9. For the mechanism to operate, only four new variables need to be maintained, i.e., $prevFR$ which remembers the previous value of the FR, $deviation$ and $counter$ which are used to calculate the mean FR deviation, and max_drop which represents the maximum FR drop in the current period of time.

The automatic intelligent mechanism monitors the FR measurements on a link. These measurements are divided into periods of time in which FR is above and below the threshold. In each period, the situation is analyzed and appropriate actions are undertaken if necessary. If the system entered the phase below the threshold (line 1) the variables must be reset (line 2). When FR is below the threshold the system counts the minimum value of FR which is achieved during the period (lines 12 and 13). If this value is lower than the predefined limit (or the FR drop is greater than the predefined limit), it means that due to over-admitting, too many flows were active during this period. Therefore, the admission limit is reduced (line 17). Similarly, in the periods in which the FR is above the threshold, the system calculates the deviation as defined in Eq. 8.3 (line 5). When this deviation is greater than a predefined limit, it means that too few flows are active at the moment, and the admission limit must be increased (lines 8 and 9). After the admission limit is

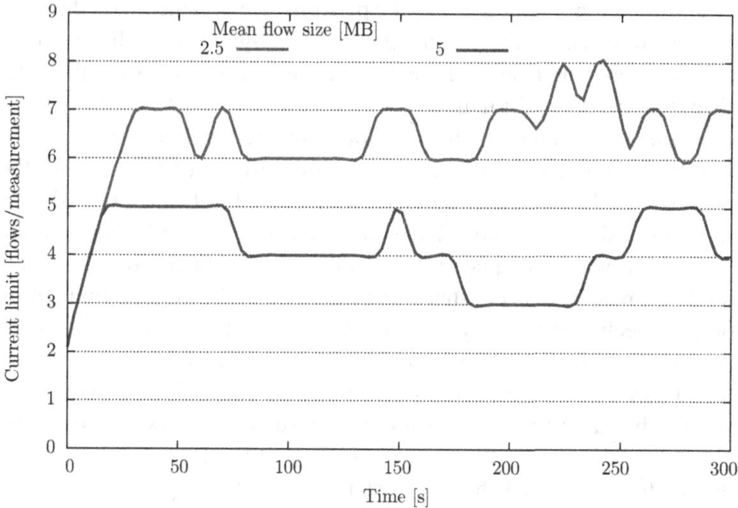

Fig. 8.10 Limit applied by the automatic intelligent mechanism over time

increased, the deviation is reset and the counter is set to −5 which gives the system the time of 5 full measurement periods to adjust to the new limit before another actions are undertaken.

Experimentally, the thresholds were determined as follows: the admission limit is reduced when the maximum drop exceeds 15% of *minFR*, and the admission limit is increased when the deviation exceeds 30% of *minFR*. For these values, the system provides sufficient performance while not changing the limit too frequently. To show the performance of the mechanism, several simulations were performed. The scenario parameters were similar to those presented in previous sections of this chapter. The number of active flows was set to 2000 and the mean flow size varied from 2.5 MB to 15 MB. The effect of such a flow size differentiation is that when flows are shorter, they end more frequently and, therefore, more flows need to be admitted on a link in the same period. Exactly the same effect is achieved by changing the link capacity while not altering traffic characteristics. This set of experiments shows that the automatic intelligent mechanism performs well under various traffic characteristics and on links with different capacity.

Figure 8.10 shows the limit which was applied by the automatic mechanism in two example scenarios, with the mean flow size of 2.5 (upper line) and 5 MB (lower line). Initially, the admission limit was set to 2 flows per measurement. Since for this traffic characteristic the limit was far too low, we can see the limit rising from the start of the simulation. When the mean flow size is set to 2.5 MB, the automatic limit varies from 6 to 8, whereas for 5 MB flows, the limit sets itself at 3–5 flows per measurement. Such a relationship is natural, since when flows are shorter, more of them need to be admitted in the same period of time because more end in the same period. The simulations also show that the performance obtained with the automatic mechanism is no worse than that of the properly configured static limitations.

Table 8.4 presents the results of the entire experiment, comparing the automatic mechanism with the static limitations. The last row in both parts of the table shows the average admission limit which was applied by the automatic mechanism. This is to show that automation produces great results by accurately finding the best possible static limit. The marked values show the static limit which provides the best results in terms of deviation and FR drop duration. Unfilled cells represent the case in which the limit was inadequately low, which resulted in severe under-admitting (the link did not reach its steady state). We can see that the average limit applied by the automatic mechanism is very close to the static limit yielding the best results, which demonstrates the efficiency of the automatic mechanism.

For the cases with the mean flow size equal to 12.5 and 15 MB, the best results are obtained with the static limit of 2 flows per measurement; however, the automatic mechanism sets the limit to 3 flows per measurement for the most of the simulation time. This is due to the fact that the system does not change the limit when the currently measured performance is sufficient. Even though choosing 3 flows per measurement is suboptimal, the achieved performance is still good enough. It is possible to configure the mechanism to more actively seek the optimal solution by changing the performance indicator thresholds, although such a modification inflicts more frequent admission limit changes.

The most important benefit of the automatic intelligent mechanism is not the performance achieved, but rather the fact that the performance is close to optimal regardless of the current network condition and the traffic characteristics. By implementing this mechanism, the network operator does not need to analyze the link and set the proper limit, which is a clear advantage of this solution.

8.6 Conclusion

Flow-Aware Networking is a simple and efficient architecture which provides QoS differentiation in IP networks. This chapter showns that frequent degradations of the FR may occur on FAN links when there are too many flows attempting to acquire access to the link's bandwidth. To prevent these degradations, either FR needs to be measured more often, or we need to introduce some kind of limitation. The first option, as explained, consumes significantly more of the router's CPU power, which is undesirable. Limitations, on the other hand, are viable, easy to implement and the benefits from introducing them are remarkable.

There are two variants of the limiting mechanism, i.e., the static hard-coded limit pre-set by the administrator, and the dynamic limit which changes according to the link's current traffic characteristics. Despite the simplicity of the proposed mechanisms, the performance improvement is significant. Our simulations show that it is much better to introduce these mechanisms than to increase the frequency of measurement even 10 times.

Table 8.4 Mean deviation and FR drops duration under various limiting configurations and mean flow sizes

	Mean flow size [MB]					
Limit [flows/measurement]	2.5	5	7.5	10	12.5	15
FR deviation from *minFR* [%]						
1	–	–	–	–	–	–
2	–	–	28.26 ± 30.10	7.57 ± 1.13	**5.38 ± 0.81**	**4.45 ± 0.64**
3	–	30.82 ± 35.67	**7.61 ± 1.36**	**5.74 ± 0.70**	5.31 ± 0.15	5.21 ± 0.23
4	–	**12.55 ± 4.57**	7.43 ± 0.20	6.32 ± 0.41	6.72 ± 0.36	6.57 ± 0.37
5	–	10.06 ± 0.45	8.02 ± 0.67	7.90 ± 0.41	7.73 ± 0.63	7.96 ± 0.35
6	67.88 ± 57.86	11.52 ± 1.64	9.05 ± 1.00	9.12 ± 0.98	9.13 ± 0.64	9.36 ± 0.26
7	**28.76 ± 7.70**	12.02 ± 0.79	10.65 ± 0.28	11.10 ± 1.04	11.03 ± 0.80	11.64 ± 0.25
8	29.42 ± 6.86	14.34 ± 1.23	11.89 ± 0.74	12.02 ± 1.25	12.50 ± 0.56	13.32 ± 0.78
Intelligent	26.77 ± 2.20	11.39 ± 1.15	7.22 ± 0.48	6.03 ± 0.47	5.79 ± 0.27	5.20 ± 0.22
Average limit	7.26 ± 0.38	4.10 ± 0.30	3.33 ± 0.21	2.97 ± 0.20	3.17 ± 0.31	2.78 ± 0.36
FR drop duration (below 90% of *minFR*) [%]						
1	–	–	–	–	–	–
2	–	–	0.00 ± 0.00	0.00 ± 0.00	**0.44 ± 0.59**	**0.07 ± 0.20**
3	–	0.82 ± 0.77	**3.34 ± 1.59**	**4.48 ± 2.28**	6.59 ± 2.59	6.37 ± 2.53
4	–	**5.13 ± 2.39**	10.91 ± 2.73	14.47 ± 3.41	19.19 ± 5.40	18.22 ± 3.49
5	–	13.20 ± 4.63	21.40 ± 3.40	27.03 ± 4.58	27.22 ± 4.41	31.49 ± 2.77
6	2.63 ± 2.30	24.09 ± 4.96	28.90 ± 4.48	34.38 ± 4.85	40.63 ± 6.07	43.08 ± 2.71
7	**8.11 ± 2.11**	32.63 ± 4.06	40.14 ± 1.68	47.82 ± 6.05	51.37 ± 4.19	52.82 ± 3.05
8	17.89 ± 5.70	40.99 ± 0.40	47.24 ± 1.31	51.17 ± 5.45	56.11 ± 2.96	60.11 ± 3.42
Intelligent	12.02 ± 1.33	6.38 ± 1.11	6.00 ± 1.50	6.28 ± 1.26	9.53 ± 2.85	6.25 ± 1.48
Average limit	7.26 ± 0.38	4.10 ± 0.30	3.33 ± 0.21	2.97 ± 0.20	3.17 ± 0.31	2.78 ± 0.36

Additionally, the prediction mechanism which enhances the admission control routine in the FAN routers is presented. Once again the results show that we can observe improvement over results obtained by the plain limitation mechanism. In comparison with standard FAN performance, the performance improvement is even more impressive. Finally, a mechanism which automatically selects the most suitable limit is shown. In this way, the system becomes more robust and invulnerable to faulty set-ups. The simulations show that the average admission limit applied by the automatic mechanism is very close to the static limit which provides the best performance, which demonstrates the great efficiency of the automatic mechanism.

8.7 Check Your Knowledge

1. What is fair rate degradation in FAN?
2. What causes fair rate degradation?
3. How does the static limitation mechanism work?
4. What is the main disadvantage of the static limitation mechanism?
5. How does the predictive approach work?

References

1. N.G. Bean, Robust connection acceptance control for ATM networks with incomplete source information. Ann. Oper. Res. **48**(4), 357–379 (1994)
2. A.W. Moore, *Measurement-Based Management of Network Resources*, Ph.D. dissertation (University of Cambridge, Cambridge, 2002)
3. R. Wojcik, J. Domzal, A. Jajszczyk, Fair rate degradation in flow-aware networks, in *Proceedings of the IEEE International Conference on Communications (ICC 2010)* (2010), pp. 1–5
4. R. Wojcik, J. Domzal, A. Jajszczyk, Predictive flow-aware networks, in *Proceedings of the 2011 IEEE Global Telecommunications Conference (GLOBECOM 2011)* (2011), pp. 1–5
5. R. Wojcik, D. Garbacz, A. Jajszczyk, A dynamic limitation mechanism for flow-aware networks, in *Proceedings of the 2013 IEEE International Conference on Communications (ICC)* (2013), pp. 2529–2533

Implementation of Cross-Protect Router

9

Being busy does not always mean real work. The object of all work is production or accomplishment and to either of these ends there must be forethought, system, planning, intelligence, and honest purpose, as well as perspiration. Seeming to do is not doing.

—Thomas A. Edison

In this chapter we describe the first implementation of the cross-protect router. Moreover, we present the results of tests of our prototype conducted in a laboratory. They were first published in [2] and show the advantages of the XP router over the IP router. It is shown that traffic in FAN is served fairly and the packets of streaming flows are transmitted with high priority. Moreover, test results confirm that streaming flows are served with acceptable quality even in highly loaded links, which is not observed for the classic IP network. The tests also show several problems which were not caught by the simulation studies presented before. First of all, to increase efficiency, a flow list had to be implemented in a different way than was originally proposed. Also, a queuing algorithm had to be altered to eliminate too frequent changes of flow states which resulted in a lack of stability. The tests ultimately show that FAN works as a concept, and that, by reaching maturity, it is ready for large-scale deployment. As a software framework for our implementation we chose the Click Modular Router environment which is widely used for building experimental software routers and switches.

9.1 Click Modular Router

Click Modular Router (hereafter Click) is a suite for building flexible and configurable software packet processors. It is a Linux-based environment proposed at MIT with further enhancements by Mazu Networks, ICIR, UCLA, and Meraki

J. Domżał et al., *Guide to Flow-Aware Networking*, Computer Communications and Networks, https://doi.org/10.1007/978-3-030-57153-5_9

[1]. Click is usually used for building experimental software routers and switches. It is a perfect platform for researchers experimenting with new protocols and novel solutions for networks. Therefore, we chose to use this software as an implementation environment for an XP router. Its many advantages include great flexibility, ease of adding new features, clear and scalable architecture and relatively high performance.

Flexibility in Click is achieved due to its modularity. Click is an object-oriented software, assembled from fine-grained packet processing modules called *elements*, which are technically C++ classes. Each particular element performs a simple operation on packets, such as queuing, dequeuing or decrementing packet TTL fields. Each element is equipped with input and output ports, which serve as the endpoints of connections between them.

Click users build router configurations from a combination of elements, by connecting them into a directed graph. Packets are sent between elements, along the graph's edges. The behavior of a router is determined by choosing the elements and connections among them. Several elements are delivered by default with the Click distribution. The user can simply compose them in many different ways, but they can also create new ones, tailored to their needs. In addition, creating new elements is relatively quick and easy.

Click can be run in one of two available modes: kernel mode or user-level mode. In kernel mode, Click runs as a module in the Linux kernel. The Click module replaces the operating system (OS) networking stack, so the OS does not handle the packets. Packet processing is done solely by the Click code running inside the kernel. Therefore, this mode ensures better performance.

It should be noted that Click does not implement dynamic routing protocols but only a simple static routing. However, dynamic routing can be used in Click. One way is to integrate Click with an external routing daemon, e.g., XORP, which is an open source IP routing software suite. XORP can fill up Click routing tables automatically. Another option is to redirect packets to the OS to perform routing decisions.

A configuration which provides basic IP router functionality has already been developed by the Click authors, and is included in the Click environment. This configuration was used as a starting point for implementing FAN functionality. The implementation steps are described in the following section.

9.2 Implementation of the XP Router

To implement the Cross-Protect router in Click it was necessary to develop several new Click elements and prepare a new router configuration file. This file combines new elements with the originally available IP router configuration. New elements realize various functions. They were added to the standard router configuration file. We present them written in italic type with grey background in Fig. 9.1. First, in order to effectively identify different flows in a router, an element calculating the flow identifier was created (SetFlowAnno). A hash function value for input

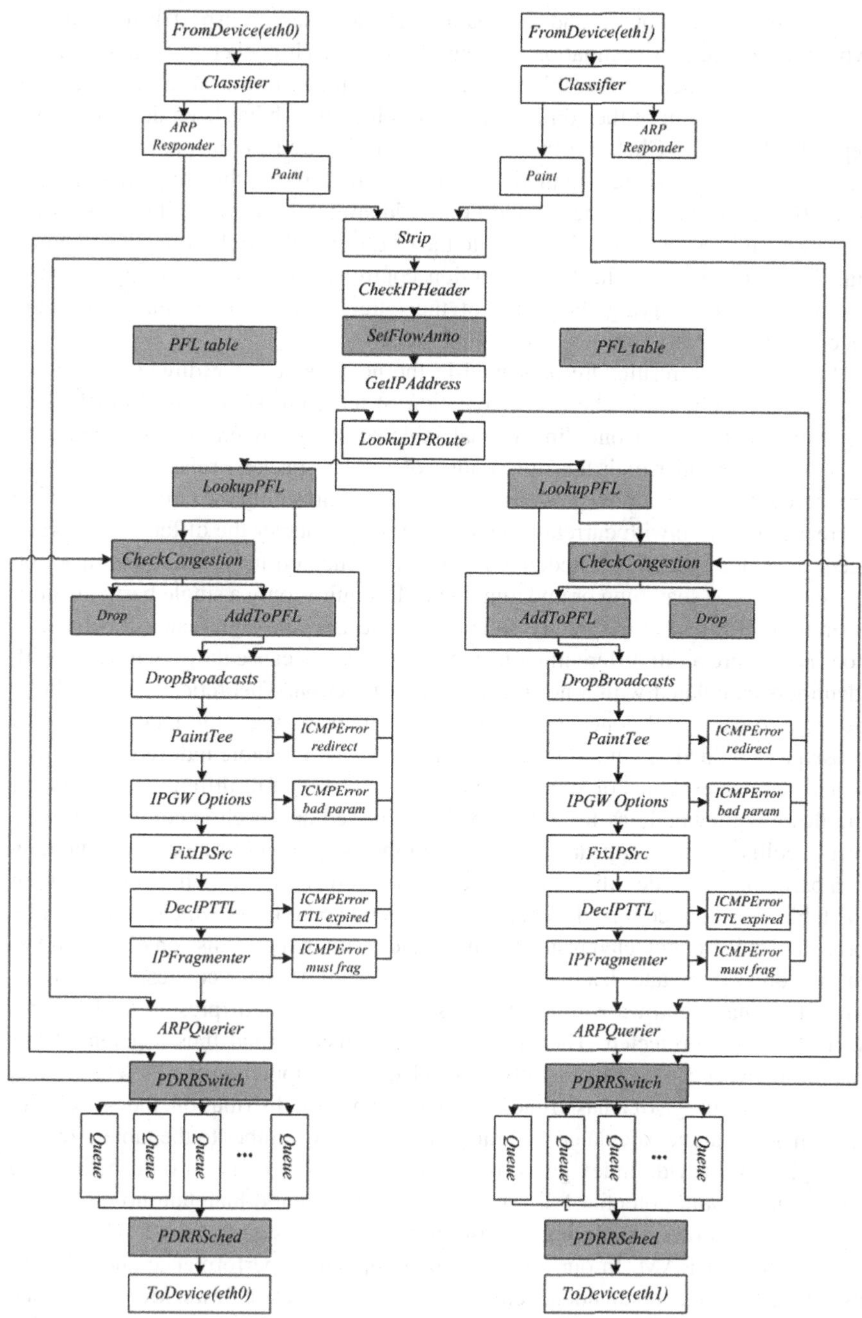

Fig. 9.1 Router elements in the click configuration file (marked blocks are FAN related)

arguments such as source and destination IP addresses, transport layer protocol type, and source and destination port numbers for each packet was implemented. The identifiers calculated in this way are used to index flows on the PFL. PFL is the main component of the admission control block which has been developed as a separate element in Click. Further two new elements are responsible for operations on the PFL: one for searching the PFL content and verifying the presence of proper flows (LookupPFL), and one for adding new identifiers of flows to it (AddToPFL). However, adding a new flow identifier to the PFL is possible only when the outgoing link is not congested. The last admission control element (CheckCongestion) is responsible for verifying the status of the outgoing link, based on information received periodically from the scheduling block.

In tests whose results are presented in the next section, the directly addressed approach was chosen in the implementation of the admission control block. This solution implements a one-dimensional table of a predefined size, indexed with flow identifiers, in which the timestamps of the last packets related to the flows are stored. Verifying a flow presence in the PFL requires only the comparison of the correct time stamp with current time and checking whether the difference between them does not exceed the predefined timer. This method has a positive impact on performance, as searching or updating the PFL requires only a single basic memory operation. However, the directly addressed table has one significant drawback: it does not ensure a full differentiation among the flows because they are indexed with identifiers calculated with a not-injective hash function. Theoretically, it would be possible to use a full concatenation of header fields as the table index, without a subsequent reduction with a hash function. However, the table indexed in this way would require exabytes of storage. Therefore, a lack of full differentiation among the flows is inevitable as far as a directly addressed approach is considered. As a result, collisions may appear which result in the assignment of more than one flow to a particular flow identifier (table index). Therefore, a flow which is not present in the table may be recognized as being present, and some flows which should not be protected may be protected instead. This would result in the admission of more flows in the congestion state, leading to a fair rate drop and longer congestion recovery time. Fortunately, flows which actually should be protected (present in the table) will always be protected. The probability of collisions (and thus a potential fair rate drop level) can be successfully controlled by manipulating the PFL table size. Assuming the usage of a hash function giving a uniform distribution, the probability of collisions can be calculated as a ratio of active flow number to the table size. For example, 24 bit-wide index gives us a table with $\sim$16M slots. In order to achieve the 1% maximum potential fair rate drop level, we should maintain no more than $\sim$167k active flows. Assuming the use of a 32 bit timestamp, such a table would need 67 MB of RAM. In our approach, table operation performance and memory usage are constant and do not depend on the number of active flows. Moreover, since the router will be used in laboratory networks, the number of simultaneous active flows will be low, so the collisions will not be a problem.

The PDRR algorithm was selected for implementation in the scheduler block. The algorithm is less complex than others, and the implementation process was the simplest of all the three algorithms available. During the development process, two new Click elements were created. The first (PDRRSwitch) is responsible for the classification of flows (elastic or streaming) based on measured flow traffic characteristics, and for switching packets to the correct outgoing queues. The goal of the second, more complex scheduling element (PDRRSched) is to serve outgoing queues according to the PDRR algorithm, i.e., whenever the priority queue is not empty, it is served first and undergoes bufferless multiplexing while packets stored in other queues share the remaining bandwidth in a fair manner. In addition, this second element is also responsible for performing outgoing link measurements. The values of the two parameters, FR and PL, are estimated while packets exit queues, and are then sent to the admission control block.

Other issues related to practical implementation were observed during the scheduling block implementation. As a consequence of the PDRR assumption that each new flow (i.e., one that has no packets in its queue) arriving at the scheduling block should be treated with priority as a streaming one, some flows of evidently elastic nature were served so quickly that their next packets arrived when the flow queue had already been emptied. Hence, they were treated as streaming flows and competed with actual streaming ones in the priority queue. Therefore, we implemented an additional mechanism to prevent such behavior. A simple change was introduced which meant that flows which were classified as elastic could be classified back as streaming, after the expiration of a predefined timer, instead of classifying flows as streaming immediately after their queues become empty. Introducing this mechanism improves the performance of streaming flows as they do not have to compete with flows which are generally classified as elastic but are assigned to the priority queue from time to time (during one transmission). As later tests showed, it significantly improved streaming traffic performance in some specific scenarios. Timing values were adjusted based on empirical observations during the tests. The timer is fixed but configurable in the Click router configuration file.

9.3 Tests of the XP Router

After the implementation of new Click elements and preparation of the router configuration file, it was possible to conduct the first tests of the developed prototype in a network laboratory. The results obtained for the XP router are compared with those obtained for a standard IP router provided by the Click environment.

9.3.1 Testing Methodology

The main goal of the tests was to show a working XP router and to confirm the usefulness of its functions. So far, only simulation results or numerical analyses presenting how the XP router works have been published. However, the implementation and tests in a real network, even if it is simple, allow us to note certain problems and effects which are usually overlooked in simulation experiments. The best testing environment is a real network where traffic is generated by real users. If a device passes such tests, we can be almost certain that the device works well and is scalable. However, it is difficult and risky to test a prototype of a new device in a real network. On the other hand, numerical and simulation experiments usually show basic functionality. They are of course very useful; however, the results may be obtained based on too general assumptions. As a result, some features of the proposed solution may not be noticed.

During the tests, our goal was to confirm the usefulness of the device in a small network with traffic generated by source nodes. Such tests allowed us to observe problems not noticed in simulation experiments performed before. First of all, the PFL was implemented in a different way than it was originally proposed. Moreover, the PDRR algorithm was modified to eliminate too frequent changes of flow states. The tests should be treated as a step between simulation experiments and performance analysis in real networks. They also set an option for further analysis of new mechanisms and algorithms proposed for the XP router in a laboratory environment.

The router prototype was implemented on relatively slow PCs. Therefore, it was impossible to analyze router scalability. Dedicated platforms should be used in order to verify it. The hardware on which both routers (IP and XP) were tested was based on a single-core processor platform with two external network cards. The results discussed below confirm the expectations that hardware resources influence the performance of the router. The most important factor is the CPU speed which is directly related to the router's throughput. One Gbit/s network cards were used while the Click router maximum throughput varied between 100 and 300 Mbit/s depending on the CPU used. Some additional equipment was also used, including network switches, VoIP PBX, IP Phones, computers serving as traffic sources/sinks, etc.

9.3.2 Test Results

The first experiment was designed to analyze the functionality of the XP router, and especially the PDRR scheduling block. One of the main aims of the PDDR is to assign bandwidth to the elastic flows equally in a highly loaded link. In the laboratory environment a simple topology consisting of hosts and a server on opposite sides of the router was setup. Tests were carried out in two configurations (with the standard IP router and the XP router) and in several scenarios, each of which assumed a different number of hosts sending data to the server (from one to six). The UDP traffic generated by hosts (one flow per host) and carrying bandwidth on the server side were measured. Table 9.1 shows the results from the selected scenario (with six hosts). All experiments were repeated at least 10 times. Ninety Five percentage confidence intervals were calculated using the Student's t-distribution.

In this scenario, complete fairness of each flow is observed for the XP router. Independently of the volume of the offered traffic, which varied from almost 100

Table 9.1 Tests results of PDRR scheduling

Flow no.	Offered bitrate [Mbit/s]	Carried bandwidth [Mbit/s]		Carried bandwidth [%]	
		IP router	XP router	IP router	XP router
1	99.82 ± 0.14	21.78 ± 0.63	47.23 ± 1.57	21.82	47.32
2	158.07 ± 4.00	40.97 ± 6.87	47.95 ± 2.13	25.92	30.33
3	367.78 ± 24.66	64.43 ± 2.33	48.63 ± 0.91	17.52	13.22
4	365.59 ± 21.30	63.76 ± 2.52	49.05 ± 0.98	17.44	13.42
5	340.76 ± 8.27	62.91 ± 2.15	48.34 ± 1.02	18.46	14.19
6	403.76 ± 26.23	60.84 ± 3.76	47.25 ± 1.33	15.07	11.70

Mbit/s to over 400 Mbit/s, the assigned bandwidth is almost the same for each flow. On the other hand, in the IP router, flows are not balanced—they transmit at different rates. The IP router offers higher bandwidth to larger flows since it does not ensure fairness and usually tries to serve flows proportionally to incoming packets. The total traffic transmitted in a network with the XP router is lower than that observed for the IP router. The implementation of the XP router is more complex than that of a traditional IP router, and the device was not able to serve the same amount of traffic in both cases. More operations had to be performed in the XP router, consuming more processor power. As a result, a lower number of packets could be served in the same time period. The difference in the total transmitted traffic is around 10%. It may be treated as a first approximation of additional complexity added to the XP router in relation to the standard IP router. We suppose that at least 10% of additional resources will be needed in the XP router to serve the same volume of traffic as in the standard IP router.

In the second experiment, the operation of the admission control block and the method of estimating the values of the FR parameter were verified. The network environment was the same as in the previous experiment. Four scenarios, with 3, 4, 5 and 6 hosts transmitting traffic, were analyzed. The FR measurement was carried out for each scenario. Results of this test are shown in Fig. 9.2.

The obtained results fully agree with the FAN concept. With increasing occupancy of router resources (more traffic was generated), the value of FR decreases. This behavior fits the FR definition—the maximum rate that is or may be realized by a flow. It is worth noting that small confidence intervals indicate a stability of the FR values. The obtained values of FR are comparable with bandwidth carried by a flow in a congested FAN link (in a case with six hosts, each source received around 47–49 Mbit/s).

Finally, the XP router was also tested as a network device for use in a home or in a small company. An example network was prepared for test purposes (Fig. 9.3). A few new elements were added to the previous environment to make it possible to set up VoIP connections.

Some Internet traffic, such as file downloads, and VoIP transmission between the hosts, was transmitted in the analyzed network. An important component of this network was the VoIP PBX server, located on the Internet side. This element was

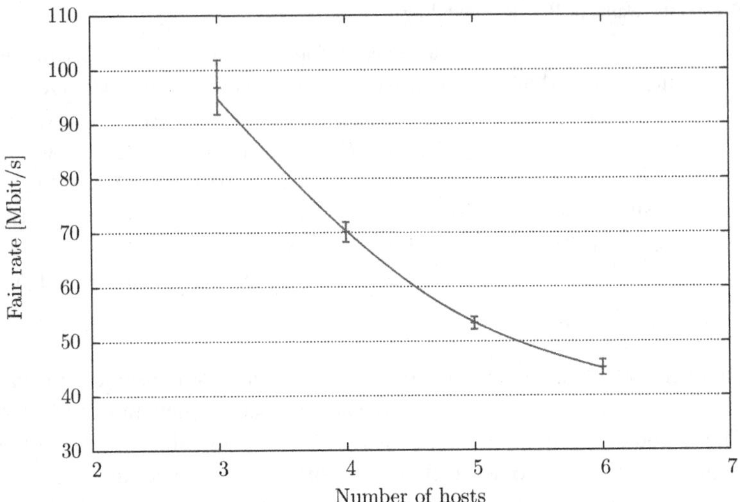

Fig. 9.2 Fair rate measurements

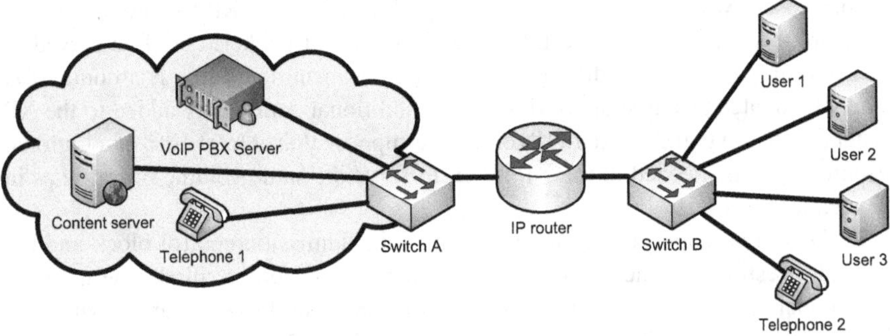

Fig. 9.3 Network topology used for testing the XP router in home/small corporate network environments

responsible for serving calls and for measuring the values of the quality parameters. The aim of the tests was to check how the XP router handles the provision of call quality (VoIP calls were served as streaming flows) while other network users use the Internet intensively. One phone call was ongoing while the volume of elastic traffic was increasing. Voice traffic bitrate was lower than 100 kbit/s, while other traffic varied between 0 and 400 Mbit/s. Analysis of router behavior was performed based on the following four criteria: Packet Loss [%], Jitter [ms], Round-trip delay [ms] and Mean Opinion Score (MOS) subjective rating. The values of the three first parameters were read directly from the PBX management interface. The MOS scale serves as a metric of Quality of Experience (QoE) [3]. The MOS scores were granted subjectively by several telephone users. Figure 9.4 shows a comparison of

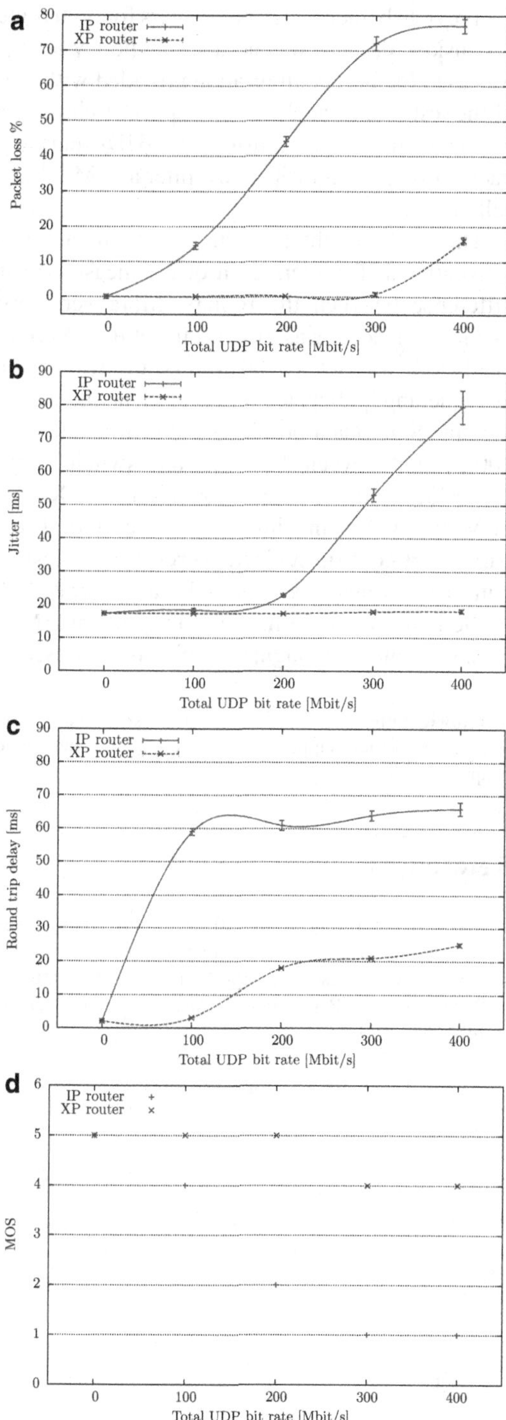

Fig. 9.4 Variation of packet loss (**a**), jitter (**b**), round-trip dela y(**c**) and MOS (**d**) in relation to UDP stream

the previously mentioned parameters for both routers. As far as a conventional router is considered, there was no queuing policy at all, as a single outgoing FIFO queue was used (default configuration provided with the Click environment). The purpose of the test was to analyze the impact of elastic traffic on the VoIP call parameters. Traffic volume was measured for UDP elastic flows, while parameters such as Packet Loss, Round-trip delay, jitter and MOS were measured for the ongoing VoIP call only.

The results of the tests show a significant advantage of the XP router over the conventional IP router. Each of the measured parameters indicates a considerable difference between the routers. Moreover, during tests of the IP router under maximum load, it was difficult to set up a VoIP connection. Because outgoing link bandwidth was set to 100 Mbit/s, the results for the conventional router without any queuing policy are poor even at the level of 100 Mbit/s of elastic traffic volume. Significant problems with call quality occurred during the transmission of 200 Mbit/s between the router and switch B, and call setup was impossible over this value. Under the same conditions, the XP router provided good call quality (4 in MOS) even if maximum load occurred. The values of the measured objective parameters confirm subjective user rates. In tests, only one priority (streaming) flow with a low transmission speed was generated. As a result its influence on other traffic in an observed link was insignificant. Moreover, in FAN even elastic flows have guaranteed throughput, which is not observed for standard IP networks.

Acknowledgments The authors would like to thank Piotr Jurkiewicz, Jakub Dudek and Łukasz Romański for their support, valuable comments and suggestions on improving the quality of this chapter.

References

1. Retrieved on 30 June 2015. (2015). http://read.cs.ucla.edu/click/click
2. J. Domzal, J. Dudek, P. Jurkiewicz, L. Romanski, R. Wojcik, The cross-protect router: implementation tests and opportunities. IEEE Commun. Mag. **52**(9), 115–123 (2014)
3. R. Stankiewicz, P. Cholda, A. Jajszczyk, Qox: what is it really? IEEE Commun. Mag. **49**(4), 148–158 (2011)

Implementation of Advanced Mechanisms for Cross-Protect Router 10

There is only one thing that makes a dream impossible to achieve: the fear of failure

—Paulo Coelho

In this chapter we demonstrate implementation tests of a Cross-Protect router enhanced with the following additional mechanisms: Emergency Connections, Efficient Congestion Control, Global Protected Flow List and Per-User Fairness. These mechanisms allow for immediate acceptance of high priority traffic, protection of streaming flows in congestion, and ensure high reliability and fairness. We show that these mechanisms work successfully in a real network. Moreover, they all work at the same time providing ultimate coordinated performance. Test results show significant advantages of the cross-protect architecture over standard IP routers in several areas. The results have been presented in [6], which was accepted for publication to the IEEE GLOBECOM 2020 conference.

In the previous chapter, we have shown several advantages of FAN, proving that the main concept works. However, the original FAN can be enhanced with new mechanisms. Here, we present tests of additional mechanisms for the XP router. We discuss our experiences in building a prototype and implementing new mechanisms. The aim was to test the efficiency in real network conditions and validate the results obtained earlier through network simulations. Based on post-implementation tests, we were able to show real pros and cons of FAN.

In the literature, several concepts were proposed to enhance FAN. However, all of them were validated through simulations only. The simulation analysis is usually provided with limitations and not all factors from real networks can be taken into account. For example, it is assumed that flow identifiers are written in a table, but it is not explained and analyzed how to do this in detail and whether it would be efficient. Moreover, it is usually hard to observe times of flows switching or implement real

J. Domżał et al., *Guide to Flow-Aware Networking*, Computer Communications and Networks, https://doi.org/10.1007/978-3-030-57153-5_10

mechanisms to observe congestions in a simulator. Here, we analyze test results obtained during laboratory tests in which we used the prototype of an XP router.

The prototype was built in a Click modular router environment [8] based on the original implementation presented in the previous chapter. Figure 10.1 shows a block diagram of Click in which several new blocks were added. These blocks (presented written in italic type with grey background) implement FAN-related functions and new mechanisms which were tested. In comparison to the basic router configuration presented in the previous section, we added new flow lists, which allow us to implement new mechanisms (GPFL table, PUFL table). We also added the *CheckCongestionECCM* block, which is responsible for analyzing the congestion status of the link. All the lists in the router are analyzed depending on the status of the outgoing link. The blocks in the scheduler decide whether to add flows to or remove them from the global router list depending on flow classification. The code of our implementation is available at [1].

We selected four mechanisms to evaluate: Emergency Connections, Efficient Congestion Control, Global Protected Flow List and Per-User Fairness. These mechanisms were chosen because they assure fair and reliable transmission and priority treatment for streaming traffic.

The main contribution of this chapter can be summarized as:

- first implementation of Cross-Protect router with the Emergency Connections, Efficient Congestion Control, Global Protected Flow List and Per-User Fairness mechanisms,
- functionality and performance tests results of Cross-Protect router implementation,
- description of problems observed during implementation of some selected mechanisms.

10.1 Emergency Connections Mechanism

Although providing superior transmission quality, FAN may force flows to wait for the network resources. Such a situation is inconvenient for the realization of emergency VoIP connections. To overcome the presented problem, an Emergency Connections Mechanism (ECM) based on a differentiated (selective) blocking algorithm can be implemented in FAN. It is simple, adequate, and above all, a feasible solution.

Differentiated blocking aims to apply different blocking criteria to newly arriving flows. The standard FAN routine causes the admission control block to make the decision based on currently measured values of the fair rate and priority load. To eliminate long acceptance delays for certain flows, the differentiated blocking approach, which applies different blocking criteria to priority flows, may be used. This method does not need to use additional resources. The available resources are assigned according to the new rules. However, the only new operation is to check the headers of flows and to analyze the values of priorities.

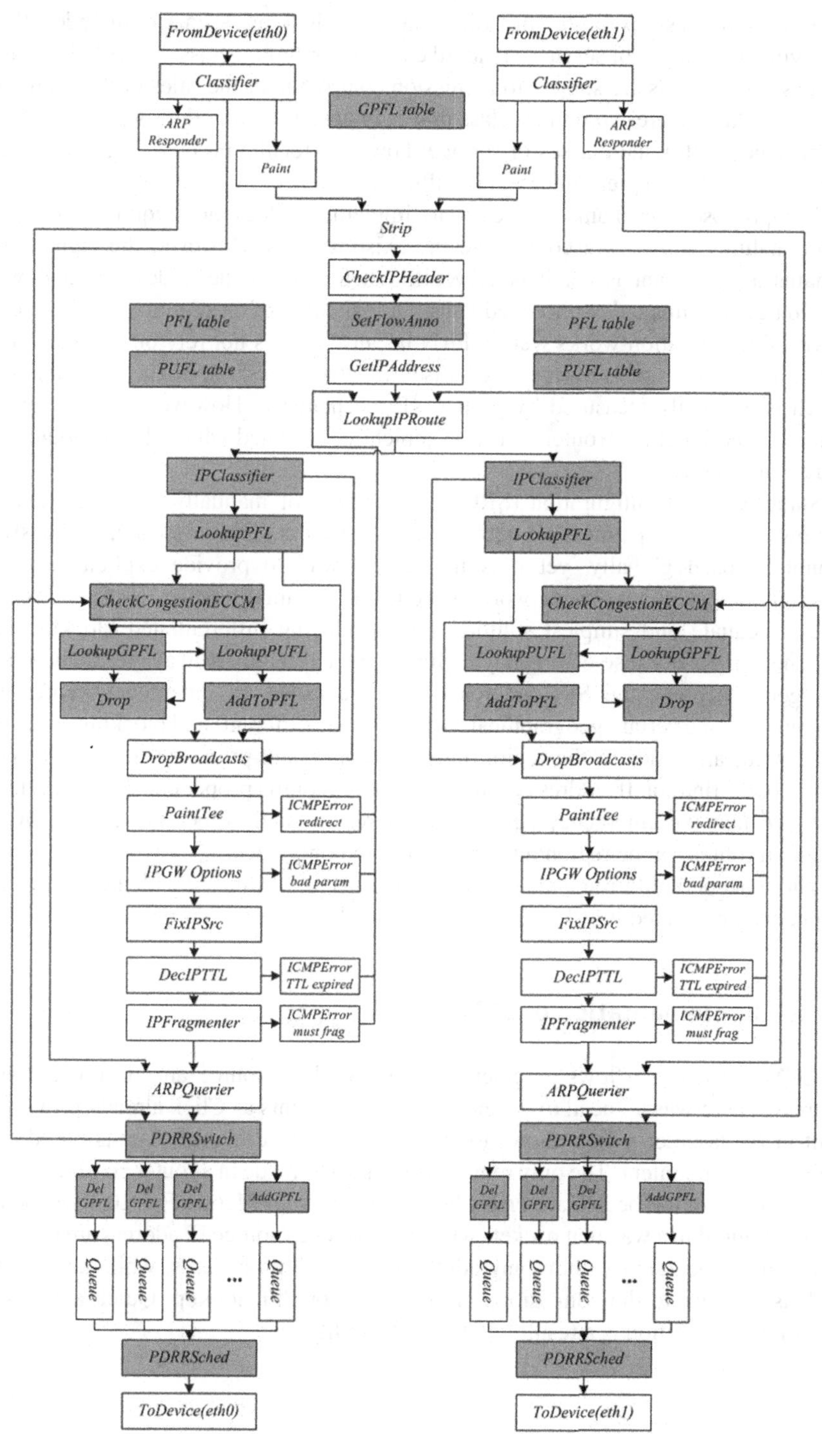

Fig. 10.1 XP router with advanced mechanisms—block scheme

In the simplest example, the differentiated blocking scenario includes the following two classes of service: standard class and premium class. Flows belonging to the standard class are subject to admission control under the rules of the original classless FAN, whereas premium class flows are always admitted. It is also possible to introduce additional classes of service; however, for the purpose of prioritizing emergency calls, the premium class is sufficient.

The proposed mechanism is easy to implement, does not require any new functionalities and hardly complicate the existing ones. However, the signalling remains a significant issue. It is very difficult to inform the nodes which flows should be discriminated, without reducing the scalability of the architecture. Implicit service differentiation works well in FAN because it does not rely on any network signalling. Flows are prioritized or discriminated based on their performance which is internally measured by proper XP mechanisms. However, to implement differentiated blocking, routers must be somehow informed which flows should be treated differently.

Static Router Configuration (SRC) is a strategy of manually defining classes of flows and their treatment by network administrators. This approach, obviously, cannot be used globally, yet it is the easiest way to provide explicit service differentiation without any network complication or modification. SRC seems to be an adequate and simplest solution for introducing differentiated blocking to FAN networks. Because emergency calling is a local matter (always to the nearest emergency center), the SRC approach may be used. An emergency center is responsible for a certain geographical region. For the differentiated blocking scheme to be used, all nodes in the region must recognize and prioritize flows with the source or destination IP address equal to the address of the proper emergency center. Provided that the emergency center's IP address is static (does not change over time), all routers in the region must be configured only once.

The concept of differentiated blocking can also be coordinated with the limitation mechanism presented in [9] which allows to block selected types of traffic.

10.1.1 Implementation of ECM in Click

In ECM, classifying flows as emergency is based on source and destination IP address. There was no need to develop any new elements as Click already provides built-in IPClassifier which allows to switch packets to different outputs based on their IP header content. The only required change was made in a router configuration file. IPClassifier has been placed right before the LookupPFL (see Fig. 10.1) element and configured in a way that packets with an emergency source IP address are passed for further processing without any admission control procedures, while any other packets are sent to the admission control block for PFL lookup. Quick and easy ECM implementation is a result of Click's flexibility.

10.2 Efficient Congestion Control Mechanism

The Efficient Congestion Control Mechanism (ECCM) was first proposed in [4]. ECCM is the newest and the most promising congestion control mechanism proposed for FAN. It is a modification of the SCCM mechanism. The only difference is that when the mechanism starts, the FR is set to $minFR$ (not to zero as it is in SCCM). It allows for more stabel transmission in FAN.

The pseudo-code for realizing the ECCM functionality in FAN is presented in Fig. 10.2. The mechanism starts when the outgoing link is congested for at least max_accept_delay time and a new flow wants to begin its transmission. In such a case FR is set to $minFR$ (lines 4–8 in Fig. 10.2). Moreover, new values of FR are not estimated for a period of $0.5 \times FR\_interval$ (half of time interval between two estimations of the fair rate values; lines 6, 12 and 15). It ensures that the link becomes uncongested (when FR is lower than $minFR$ the link is considered as congested). $0.5 \times FR\_interval$ is sufficient to accept all flows waiting for acceptance. The value of the max_accept_delay parameter should be set statically, e.g., to 6 s. Finally, after time equal to the interval between two estimations of the fair rate values from the starting point of the ECCM, it is necessary to remove, from PFL, all identifiers of elastic flows added when the fair rate was equal to min_FR (lines 19–30). According to the FAN assumptions, a flow is considered as elastic when it has more than MTU bytes in the queue.

ECCM is more efficient than its predecessors, which is confirmed by simulation results presented in [4]. It ensures short acceptance delays for streaming flows and minimum impact on other flows. Moreover, this mechanism can be relatively easily implemented in Click. However, as can be seen in Fig. 10.2, some new operations are necessary to be completed to serve packets of flows. The routers do not need new extra resources to work properly. However, the usage of memory and processors will be higher than in the original routers. This usage depends on the number of flows. Nevertheless, even if this number is large, currently available hardware is definitely able to operate efficiently.

10.2.1 Implementation of ECCM in Click

For the purpose of ECCM implementation, previously developed *CheckCongestion* element has been replaced with a new *CheckCongestionECCM* element implementing all the ECCM rules with the configurable max_accept_delay parameter (see Fig. 10.1). We had to incorporate a slight modification of the ECCM algorithm because of the structure of PFL we were using (directly addressed table storing only a timestamp of flow's last packet). ECCM assumes removal of elastic flows admitted during congestion. However, with the directly addressed table approach, it is impossible to differentiate which flows have been admitted when a link was congested. Hence, a new ECCM table has been created to store all the flows admitted

```
###### on a new flow packet p arrival in congestion ######
curr_time = Scheduler :: instance().clock()
if curr_time − cong_time > max_accept_delay
    && cont_param = 0 then
begin
    stop procedure of estimation of FR
    cont_param = 1
    FR = min_FR
    ECCM_time = curr_time
end
if cont_param = 1
    && curr_time > ECCM_time + 0.5 × FR_int then
begin
    cong_time = curr_time
    start procedure of estimation of FR
    cont_param = 2
end
if cont_param = 2
    && curr_time > ECCM_time + FR_int then
begin
    for (i = 1; i <= pfl_size; i++) do
    begin
        active_time(i) = curr_time − first_time(i)
        if flow_bytes(i)eqMTU then
        begin
            if active_time(i) > 0.5 × FR_int
                && active_time(i) < FR_int then
                remove ID( i) from PFL
        end
    end
    cont_param = 0
end
#######################################
######### in procedure of estimation of FR #########
if FR > min_FR then
    cong_time = Scheduler :: instance().clock()
```

Fig. 10.2 Pseudo-code of the ECCM

by ECCM during congestion. This way, we are able to identify which elastic flows admitted by ECCM should be removed from PFL when required.

10.3 Global Protected Flow List

In a standard XP router, for each outgoing link a separate PFL is implemented. The concept of Global Protected Flow List (GPFL) assumes that one additional list is implemented in each router with at least two outgoing links. This list contains

```
1   ##### on a packet p of flow F arrival #####
2   if ID(F) is in the PFL then
3   begin
4       if F is streaming then
5           set F_prior = 1 in the GPFL
6       else set F_prior = 0 in the GPFL
7       send p for queuing
8   end
9   else (not in the PFL)
10  begin
11      If link is congested then
12      begin
13          if ID(F) is in GPFL and F_prior = 1 then
14          begin
15              add ID (F) to PFL
16              send p for queuing
17          end
18          else drop p
19      end
20      else (link not congested)
21      begin
22          if ID(F) is not in GPFL then
23          begin
24              add ID (F) to GPFL
25              add ID (F) to PFL
26              send P for queuing
27          end
28      end
29  end
```

Fig. 10.3 Pseudo-code for implementing the GPFL in XP router [2]

identifiers of all flows active in all outgoing links, while streaming flows are marked with high priority. When a link fails, all streaming flows from this link can continue transmission in the backup link without breaks (if only the outgoing link is not saturated). When a routing protocol calculates a new path, identifiers of streaming flows are accepted immediately on this path.

The pseudo-code for implementing the GPFL in an XP router is presented in Fig. 10.3. If a packet p of a flow F arrives at the XP router and its ID is in the PFL of the correct outgoing link it means that its ID has already been added to the GPFL. Then, the status of the flow is analyzed (lines 1–4 in Fig. 10.3). The proper parameter F_prior is then set and the packet is sent for queuing (lines 5–7). In other case, when ID of F is not in PFL and the link is congested, the flow ID can be added to the PFL only if this flow was previously added to the GPFL and its priority is set to 1 (lines 9–19). In a congestion-less state, the ID of a new flow is added to GPFL and PFL (lines 20–29).

The positive influence of the GPFL operations on network transmission when failures occur has also been presented in [5]. The implementation of the GPFL needs to use additional flow table. However, this table is analyzed only for new flows (not accepted yet). As a result, the memory and processors usage is in most cases negligible.

10.3.1 Implementation of GPFL in Click

A few simplifications, as compared to the original GPFL concept, were introduced to optimize its implementation. We have dropped the concept of putting both elastic and streaming flows to GPFL with different priorities. In our implementation only streaming flows can be added to GPFL as these are the only type of flows that can benefit from it. Such an approach implies that the type of flow has to be known when the decision about adding to GPFL is being made. Therefore, elements *AddGPFL* and *DelGPFL* are responsible for adding and deleting flows from GPFL respectively. They have been moved to the scheduling block of XP router. *AddGPFL* is connected to the input of the priority queue while *DelGPFL* is connected to the input of standard queues for elastic flows. As a result, when an initially streaming flow becomes elastic over time, it is no longer kept on GPFL.

Besides these two elements, the *GlobalFlowTable* element containing the table itself has been added. Most of the implementation has been reused from an already developed PFL table. The last element required for the GPFL mechanism is *LookupGPFL* which verifies the presence of a flow on the list. It is used when the flow is not on a PFL and congestion is detected. If the flow is not on GPFL as well, it is discarded. Otherwise, it is admitted for further processing. The location of the new GPFL elements in the router block scheme is shown in Fig. 10.1.

10.4 Per-User Fairness

In standard FAN, all elastic flows are treated equally. This means that an XP router tends to provide each elastic flow with the same rate, not lower than $minFR$. For example, in a 100 Mbit/s FAN link, each of 10 TCP flows will be served with rate equal to around 10 Mbit/s. When $minFR$ is 5 Mbit/s, up to 20 flows should be served at the same time in the link. $minFR$ is a value of flows speed that is set by a network operation. It is assumed that each flow should have guarantee to send traffic with at least this speed value.

Such an assumption may result in an unfair bandwidth share among users. For example, users may divide their traffic into several flows, receiving more bandwidth in contrast to other users. The per-user fairness concept resolves this problem guaranteeing that each user is treated equally.

The concept of per-user fairness (PUF) in FAN was introduced in [3]. The PUF works in a relatively simple way. When a packet of the new flow arrives at the router, it is checked how many flows have been accepted in current measurement interval of

FR. It is assumed that maximum N flows can be accepted for a user. Therefore, the incoming packet is dropped if the number of accepted flows for its source is higher than N. In the other case, the counter of admitted flows is increased, an identifier of flow related to the incoming flow is added to PFL and the packet is sent to the correct queue in the scheduler. Each time a new value of FR is estimated, counters for all sources are set to zero. The value of N is assumed by the operator. This value should be estimated based, e.g. on simulation experiments and should ensure fair access to the resources.

10.4.1 Implementation of PUF in Click

The following two new elements have been added to implement PUF in Click: the PUFL table and *LookupPUFL* (see Fig. 10.1). The PUFL table implements the table itself. The *HashTable* data type available already in Click has been used to build the table. It is indexed by source IP addresses and stores the number of active flows for each source. The *LookupPUFL* element serves packets of flows not present on PFL right before the addition to PFL. It has configurable parameter N (which means the maximum number of flows allowed for a user). It discards a new flow when the number of flows for a particular source exceeds N. Otherwise, a flow is added to PFL and further processed. In addition to these two elements, a new function has been added to the *PDRRSched* element responsible for cleaning the PUFL table at the end of the fair rate measurement interval (garbage collection mechanism). The implementation of this mechanism needs to add one table. The content of this table is analyzed for each new flow. As a result, the resource usage is negligible.

10.5 Tests of the XP Router with Advanced Mechanisms

The results of tests conducted in the laboratory are presented in this section. The main aim was to present advantages of mechanisms described in previous sections implemented in the XP router.

10.5.1 Testing Methodology

So far, the mechanisms analyzed in this paper have been tested only based on simulation experiments conducted in the ns-2 simulator. The simulation results confirm their advantages comparing to a standard FAN router. However, tests performed in a real network are more credible. The most valuable analysis is conducted when the router is tested in a network in which real users generate traffic. We tested our prototype router in a laboratory network with real traffic generated in network nodes. The basic network topology used in our tests is presented in Fig. 10.4.

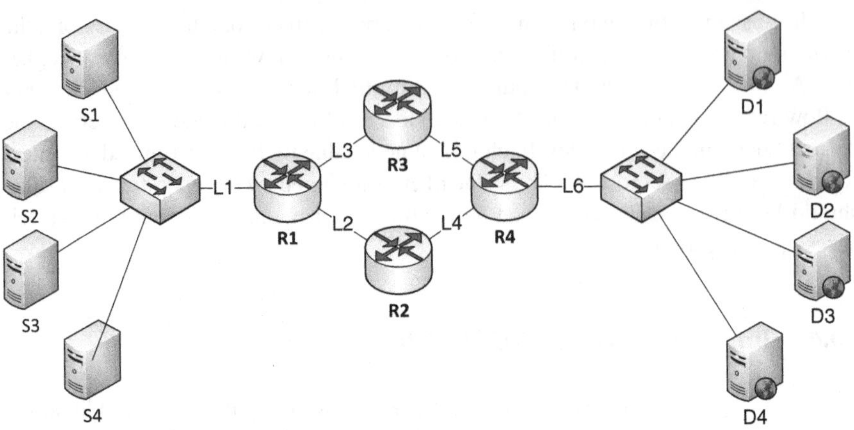

Fig. 10.4 Testing topology

For each implemented mechanism, some basic functional tests as well as more advanced numerical evaluation were performed. Finally, all mechanisms were connected together in a single configuration file and tested.

Traffic was generated in source nodes S1–S4. These were PC computers generating traffic. We used the D-ITG generator to generate traffic and to collect statistical data. The capacity of all core links was 10 Mbit/s, while the capacity of access links was 100 Mbit/s. Each testing experiment was repeated several times (at least five times) which allowed us to collect statistically credible results.

In tests conducted by us, the used XP router prototypes were implemented on relatively slow PCs with a single-core processor platform and with two external network cards. Therefore, we were not able to analyze the mechanisms' scalability. In a router with a 1 Gbit/s network card we were able to serve traffic with the maximum speed of 300 Mbit/s.

10.5.2 Tests in Laboratory

To validate the ECM mechanism, the outgoing link L2 of R1 was put into permanent congestion state and then two hosts (S1 and S2) transmitted streaming flows to the destination nodes D1 and D2, respectively. The one with emergency source IP address (originated from S1) was admitted despite congestion while the second one (originated from S2) was rejected according to expectations.

The main emergency connection mechanism evaluation consisted of measuring acceptance delays of flows in the network. The background traffic consisting of a different number of concurrent elastic flows was generated in all sources and was sent to all destination nodes. Background flows sizes were generated from the Pareto distribution with 2 MB as the mean value to send and shape factor equal to 1.5. Intervals between flows were generated from an exponential distribution but

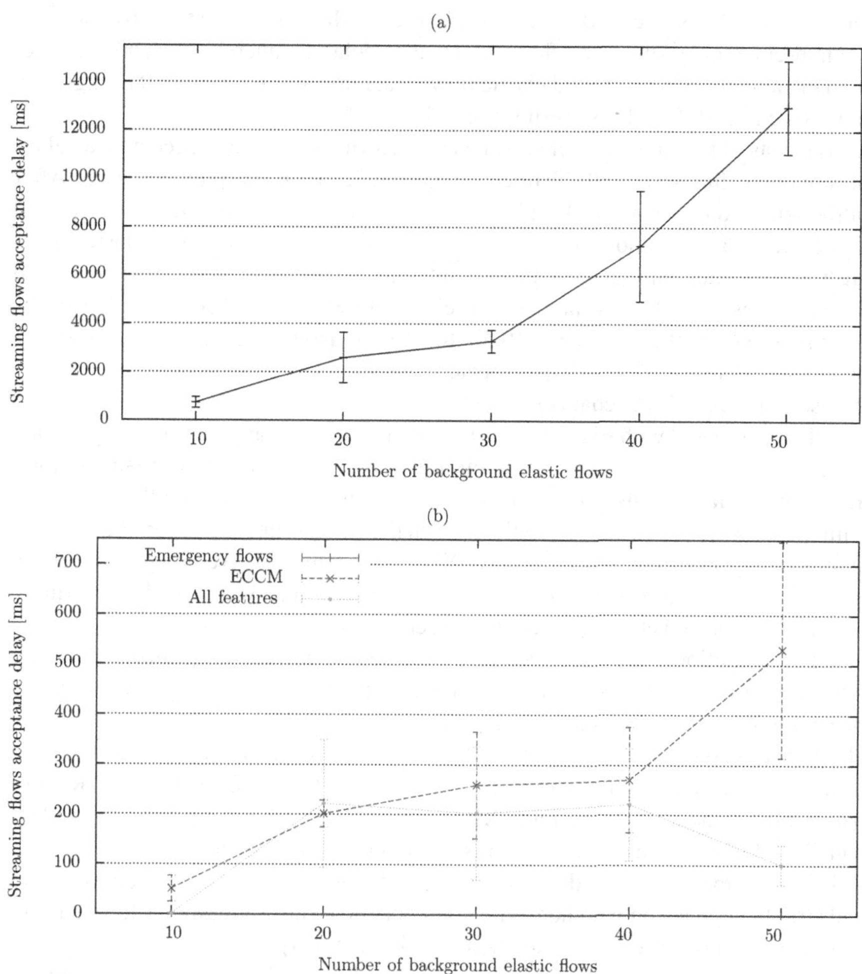

Fig. 10.5 Streaming flows acceptance delay for different number of background elastic flows: (**a**) standard XP router (**b**) standard XP router with advanced mechanisms

the mean interval value varied between the scenarios which resulted in different number of elastic background flows. Tests were performed in five scenarios with different number of elastic flows as the background traffic. Ninety five percentage confidence intervals were calculated using the Student's t-distribution. The results of this test are shown in Fig. 10.5b. Similar results but for the standard non-emergency streaming flows may be observed in Fig. 10.5a.

The obtained results agree with the emergency connection mechanism assumption. Acceptance delays of emergency flows are lower than 1 ms, i.e., they are negligible irrespectively of the number of elastic flows transmitted in the background. We, therefore, conclude that emergency connection feature fulfills its role and works fully as intended accepting emergency flows immediately. To compare, the non-emergency streaming flows acceptance delay is much higher and increases with the number of background elastic flows reaching almost 13 s for 50 background flows (see Fig. 10.5a). These results are in line with [7].

The tests of the ECCM mechanism were performed to observe acceptance delays of streaming flows as well. Traffic was generated as in the previous case. After introducing congestion and keeping it for max_accept_delay, we have verified that both streaming and elastic flows are temporarily accepted but elastic flows are rejected after fair rate calculation interval. Acceptance delay was measured for scenarios of different number of elastic flows in the background. Results are presented in the same Fig. 10.5b for comparison. The max_accept_delay parameter was set to 2 s and, as expected, the acceptance delay never exceeded it in case of the ECCM mechanism.

When compared with Fig. 10.5a and results for the standard XP router, significant advantage of the ECCM mechanism introduction is visible as far as streaming flows acceptance delay is considered. The acceptance delays for streaming flows increase with the increasing number of elastic flows in the background, however, they are still significantly lower than those for basic XP router in the observed range. Moreover, transmission of the elastic flows active in a background was not affected (more packet drops or higher delays were not observed).

GPFL functional test scenario was to execute failure of primary outgoing interface for a set of flows while the secondary interface is congested. As expected, streaming flows have been accepted without significant delay on a new path, while elastic ones had to wait for congestion to end. For numerical evaluation, comparison of the flow switchover times from primary (R1-R2-R4) to secondary (R1-R3-R4) path for the standard XP router and XP router with GPFL has been done. Secondary path was loaded with traffic that was, periodically, introducing congestion. The switchover time for standard XP router is the same for elastic and streaming flows and strictly depends on whether switchover occurs during congestion (flows have to wait until it ends) or not (flows are admitted immediately).

On average, the switchover time was equal to 2105.96±209.45 ms. For a router with GPFL implemented, the average switchover time for elastic flows was very similar and equal to 2176.67±6.97 ms. However, as expected, a significant difference was observed for streaming flows, for which the switchover time was very low for a router with GPFL, namely 3.89±0.35 ms. Introduction of GPFL significantly improves FAN network reliability for streaming flows.

Per-user fairness functional tests were performed in scenario with sources which generated different number and types of flows and had N set to a fixed value. When the number of generated flows exceeded this value within FR measurement interval, new flows from a particular source were rejected by the router according to the expectations.

As far as numerical assessment is considered, the per-user fairness mechanism was tested in the environment which consisted of three sources (users) generating flows with different mean intervals (exponential distribution was used). User 1 (S1) was transmitting with the highest interval while User 3 (S3) with the lowest. Tests

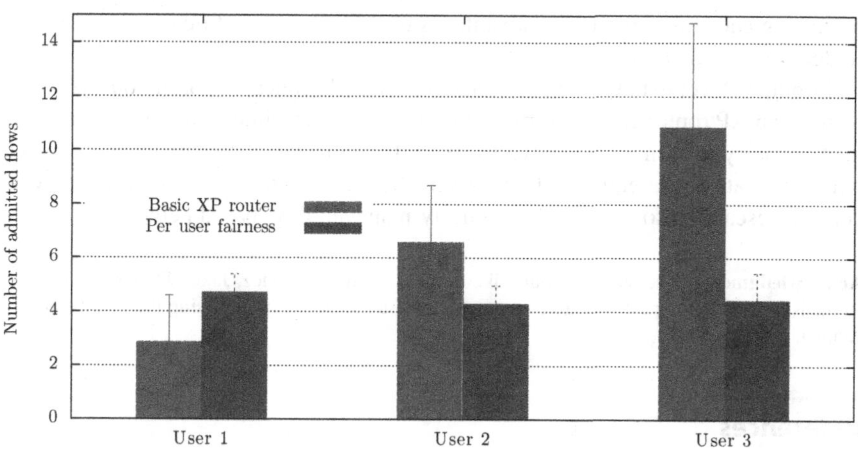

Fig. 10.6 Number of admitted flows within measurement interval for users transmitting with different frequencies

were performed in two scenarios: for an XP router with and without the per-user fairness feature. In case of the XP router with per-user fairness, router R1 was configured to accept maximum 2 flows per user in one fair rate computing cycle (4 s was set for this test). The measurement time was 40 s in both cases. Figure 10.6 shows a comparison of the number of accepted flows for each host in both scenarios during the measurement period.

The XP router without the per-user mechanism accepts flows according to FAN concept, so the largest number of flows has been accepted from the host which had the shortest mean interval. The router with the PUF mechanism worked fully fair and accepted similar number of flows for each user. It is worth to note that the total number of accepted flows is higher in the basic XP router scenario as PUF rejects some flows from aggressively transmitting sources besides standard congestion based rejection as in the XP router.

Finally, all implemented mechanisms have been tested together in a single configuration file. As part of functional testing we have repeated validation for each of the mechanisms to show that it is possible to implement them in one network. As part of more advanced testing, streaming flows acceptance delay has been measured in the same scenarios as for ECCM, PUF and the basic XP router. As can be observed in Fig. 10.5b, results are even better than for ECCM alone. This is due to the fact that when PUF and ECCM are working together, PUF by rejecting too extensive traffic from a particular source creates a better environment for streaming flows acceptance improved by ECCM, ensuring at the same time acceptable transmission performance for accepted elastic flows.

We showed that the proposed respective mechanisms to enhance FAN operation implemented alone as well as in a coordinated approach. These mechanisms all working at the same time provide the ultimate performance. Test results are very promising and show significant advantages of the XP architecture over standard IP routers in several areas.

Conducted work shows the advantages of the FAN concept. Continuous development of an XP router enables further FAN tests and experiments to be performed in the laboratory or even in real networks. We believe that tests presented in this chapter will accelerate the research on Flow-Aware Networks and will open the window to conduct research also on partially centrally-managed flow-based networks.

Acknowledgments The authors would like to thank Piotr Jurkiewicz, Jakub Dudek and Łukasz Romański for their support, valuable comments and suggestions on improving the quality of this chapter.

References

1. Cross-Protect router in Click. http://kt.agh.edu.pl/~jdomzal/fan-click-router.zip
2. J. Domzal, R. Wojcik, E. Biernacka, Reliable transmission in flow-aware networks, in *Proceedings of the IEEE Global Communications Conference GLOBECOM 2009*, Honolulu (2009), pp. 1–6
3. J. Domzal, R. Wojcik, E. Biernacka, Per user fairness in flow-aware networks, in *Proceedings of IEEE Intenational Conference on Communications, ICC 2012*, Ottawa (2012)
4. J. Domzal, R. Wojcik, P. Cholda, R. Stankiewicz, A. Jajszczyk, Efficient congestion control mechanism for Flow-aware Networks. Int. J. Commun. Syst. **29**(4), 787–800 (2016)
5. J. Domzal, R. Wojcik, E. Biernacka, Efficient and reliable transmission in Flow-Aware Networks - an integrated approach based on SDN concept, in *2017 International Conference on Computing, Networking and Communications (ICNC)* (2017), pp. 837–842
6. J. Domzal, et al., Click-based tests of QoS mechanisms for flow-based router, in *Proceedings of the IEEE GLOBECOM* 2020 (accepted for publication)
7. A. Jajszczyk, R. Wojcik, Emergency calls in flow-aware networks. IEEE Commun. Lett. **11**(9), 753–755 (2007)
8. E. Kohler, R. Morris, B. Chen, J. Jannotti, M.F. Kaashoek, The click modular router. ACM Trans. Comput. Syst. **18**, 263–297 (2000)
9. R. Wojcik, J. Domzal, Intelligent configuration of the limitation mechanism in Flow-Aware Networks, in *2016 17th International Telecommunications Network Strategy and Planning Symposium (Networks)* (2016), pp. 195–199

Summary 11

Flow-Aware Networking is a promising concept for Future Internet. It is a simple, scalable solution which conforms to the net neutrality paradigm. In this book, we presented detailed descriptions of FAN alongside new algorithms and mechanisms which may improve transmission in this environment.

The new architecture proposal, AFAN, simplifies the scheduling process and is less complex than PFQ or PDRR. Congestions may be eliminated by implementing one of the congestion control mechanisms proposed in this book. Moreover, transmission performance may be improved by using TCP NewJersey, MFAN, or a new routing algorithm proposed for FAN.

FAN ensures fairness among flows accepted in the routers. However, the per-user fairness looks to be a more desirable solution, especially in networks where some users generate more flows than others. There are several proposals to solve the problem of failures in FAN. The GPFL or multi-layer strategy with the EHOT algorithm ensures stable transmission of streaming flows without breaks, even if they need to be redirected.

The implementation of the XP router in the Click environment allowed us to show that the Flow-Aware Networking architecture does work and can be implemented in real networks. We presented the implementational process, problems and solutions. Tests of FAN with advanced mechanisms in a real network confirm that this a promising architecture for Future Internet.

We hope that the solutions and concepts presented in this book will be helpful and stimulating for a wide range of readers.

J. Domżał et al., *Guide to Flow-Aware Networking*, Computer Communications and Networks, https://doi.org/10.1007/978-3-030-57153-5_11

Answers

Chapter 1: Flow-Oriented Approaches

1. IETF's Integrated Services
2. The 5-tuple is the combination of 5 header fields: source and destination IPv4 addresses, source and destination port numbers and the transport protocol used for transmission.
3. Although IETF developed the RSVP protocol for signaling purposes in IntServ, any signaling protocol can be used.
4. ARS (Available Rate Service), GRS (Guaranteed Rate Service), MRS (Maximum Rate Service), VRS (Variable Rate Service)
5. By assigning weights in the scheduler according to the number of active flows in each queue.
6. Connectionless Approach and Flow-Aware Networking
7. Flows are classified into classes based on measurements.
8. In FAN, flows are classified as streaming or elastic. The decision is based on whether the current flow rate is above or below the current fair rate.
9. The biggest problem of IntServ is its low scalability. This is the result of the need to keep and monitor all flow states by each router.
10. Signaling in DPS uses the following IP packet header fields: Type of Service and Fragment Offset.

Chapter 2: Flow-Aware Networking

1. No. It will receive the first chance in 3.5 s and will be accepted if the FR is equal to at least 5 Mbit/s.
2. No. AFAN was also proposed.
3. No.
4. Scheduler.
5. No. It was accepted when its packet arrived at the XP router in the congestionless state.
6. $FR = 1.5$ Mbit/s, $PL = 33\%$.

J. Domżał et al., *Guide to Flow-Aware Networking*, Computer Communications and Networks, https://doi.org/10.1007/978-3-030-57153-5

7. $FR = 2.5$ Mbit/s, $PL = 60\%$.
8. $FR = 1$ Mbit/s, $PL = 66\%$.
9. When it is not congested, i.e., when $FR > minFR$ and $PL < maxPL$.
10. All packets of this flow are accepted.
11. PFQ uses one PIFO queue, PDRR uses one FIFO queue for each elastic flow and one FIFO queue for streaming flows, AFAN uses two FIFO queues.
12. ID is computed based on source and destination IDs, source and destination ports and transmission protocol identifier.
13. Streaming and elastic.
14. In depends on the number of bytes in the queue.
15. No.
16. Yes.
17. Streaming packets are served first.
18. Yes.
19. Yes.
20. Yes.
21. Yes.
22. When the flow timeout is exceeded.

Chapter 3: Flow-Aware Networking for Net Neutrality

1. It is extremely difficult if not impossible to create a fair law regarding network neutrality.
2. For: users, ISPs; against: network operators
3. No. Quality of service techniques can work but they need to remain neutral, which means that operators cannot favor certain traffic over other.
4. Network operators do not want to be lawfully regulated. Also, restricted service differentiation might decrease revenue streams.
5. Network operators say that market rules protect against any unfair treatment.

Chapter 4: Congestion Control Mechanisms

1. 7 — EFM, EFMP, RAEF, RBAEF, RPAEF, RAMAF, SCCM
2. To minimize the acceptance delay of streaming flows.
3. (2) FR.
4. TCP NewJersey.
5. As many as optical paths there are set up.
6. EFM.
7. 99.
8. Newest-flow, Oldest-flow, Most-active-flow.
9. 6 s.
10. Because they are slowed down due to the removing process or acceptance of new flows after a congestion mechanism run.

11. New flows are accepted on new paths when congestion occurs on basic paths.
12. ID of the outgoing interface.

Chapter 5: Fairness in Flow-Aware Networks

1. Fairness per flow.
2. Users are able to transmit the same number of flows.
3. Users have fair access to resources

Chapter 6: FAN in Case of Failure

1. It collects IDs of all streaming flows in a router which accepts them on a new path when a failure occurs.
2. FAN and RPR.
3. Yes.
4. See Sect. 6.3.
5. EHOT ensures coordination between layers and makes impossible to repair a failure at the optical layer.
6. Less than 50 ms if optical resources are available.

Chapter 7: Service Differentiation in FAN

1. When the outgoing link is congested, FAN's admission control does not allow any new flows. Therefore, new flows must wait until the congestion on the link terminates. If active flows have high volume of data to send, the connection waiting time becomes excessively long.
2. FAN does not use any kind of signaling. Therefore, the challenge is to inform the nodes which flows should be treated with priority.
3. Yes.
4. It is temporal because active flows end naturally while new flows are not accepted. This causes the fair rate to grow.

Chapter 8: Service Degradation in FAN

1. Fair rate degradations are drops of the fair rate deep below the minimum threshold value which should be protected by FAN.
2. Fair rate degradation happens when there are too many flows waiting for transmission. Congestion indicators are measured periodically. When the link becomes available, it is available to each new flow until the next measurement. If too many flows appear between the measurements, all are accepted which results in a fair rate drop.

3. The static limitation mechanism applies a limit on the number of flows that may be admitted between any two consecutive measurements.
4. The static limitation mechanism provides great results, albeit only when the mechanism is tuned properly. It is difficult to predict the proper setup of the mechanism as it depends on traffic characteristics.
5. The predictive approach analyzes the fair rate trend and anticipates the next measurement value. Appropriate actions can be taken before the actual measurements mark the link as congested or available.

Index

J. Domżał et al., *Guide to Flow-Aware Networking*, Computer Communications and Networks, https://doi.org/10.1007/978-3-030-57153-5

Printed in the United States
By Baker & Taylor Publisher Services

Printed in the United States
by Baker & Taylor Publisher Services